A Kind
of Wild Justice

A Kind
of Wild Justice

Revenge in Shakespeare's Comedies

Linda Anderson

DELAWARE

NEWARK: University of Delaware Press
LONDON AND TORONTO: Associated University Presses

Associated University Presses
440 Forsgate Drive
Cranbury, NJ 08512

Associated University Presses
25 Sicilian Avenue
London WC1A 2QH, England

Associated University Presses
2133 Royal Windsor Drive
Unit 1
Mississauga, Ontario
Canada L5J 1K5

The paper used in this publication meets the requirements
of the American National Standard for Permanence of Paper
for Printed Library Materials Z39.48-1984.

Library of Congress Cataloging-in-Publication Data

Anderson, Linda, 1949 May 24–
    A kind of wild justice.

    Bibliography: p.
    Includes index.
    1. Shakespeare, William, 1564–1616—Comedies.
2. Revenge in literature.   I. Title.
PR2981.A63   1987   822.3'3   86-40586
ISBN 0-87413-319-X (alk. paper)

PRINTED IN THE UNITED STATES OF AMERICA

For
Raymond and Lucille Uelmen Anderson
my parents

Revenge is a kind of wild justice.

—Francis Bacon, "Of Revenge"

Contents

Acknowledgments

My most important scholarly debt is owed to Thomas Clayton, for whose advice and encouragement I am profoundly grateful and without whom this book would never have been completed. I am also grateful to Shirley Garner, Jackson Hershbell, Gordon O'Brien, Robert Sonkowsky, and Ellen Stekert for their advice on various aspects of this study. I owe Kerry Cork a debt of thanks for generously taking the time to edit portions of the manuscript. Karen Callahan and Janis Lull made valuable suggestions regarding both substance and style. Karen Schaffer and Steve Glennon provided valuable technical advice.

Thanks are also due to Deborah Anderson, June Powers, and Mary and Carl Trone for reading and commenting on this book, and to Jon Anderson, Scott Anderson, Kate Cannon, Barb Ego, Lance Morrow, Diane O'Brien, Elena Pierce, Regene Radniecki, and Peter Robinson for their help and encouragement.

I would also like to thank the University of Minnesota Graduate School and the Bush Foundation, which provided a fellowship that relieved me of financial pressures for a year.

Finally, I would like to thank Jay Halio of the University of Delaware Press, who offered numerous suggestions that improved the manuscript; Beth Gianfagna of Associated University Presses, who guided the book through production; and copy editor Ronald Roth, who corrected a number of errors and infelicities.

1

Introduction

Life being what it is, one dreams of revenge.
—Paul Gauguin, *Avant et Après*

Revenge is a word with such negative connotations for most people that it is difficult to consider objectively the concept it represents. Even the denotations of the word are negative: "The act of doing hurt or harm to another in return for wrong or injury suffered; satisfaction obtained by repayment of injuries. . . . A desire to repay injuries by inflicting hurt in return. . . . One's desire to be revenged, or the gratification of this. . . . Repayment *of* some wrong, injury, etc., by the infliction of hurt or harm."[1]

Religious teaching, specifically—for the purposes of this study—Christianity, has long condemned revenge. More important, perhaps, to our present attitude toward this concept and the actions that arise from it is our recognition that "taking the law into one's own hands" undermines our legal system, coupled with the fact that this system has expanded to the point where a person can attempt to redress almost any injury (real or imagined) through the courts. Whereas in an earlier period the injured party might go after an enemy with a sword or gun, a lawsuit is now the weapon of choice for most people. But revenge is not—officially, at least—recognized as a legal principle.[2] A crime is considered an offense against the state; the victim has no special standing or claim on the offender.[3] Accordingly, in sentencing a convicted criminal, the state professes such motives as protection of the populace, rehabilitation, and punishment, but not vengeance.

Not only religion and the law but "high" art (as opposed to "popular" art) has largely renounced revenge. It is not a theme that modern artists seem anxious to deal with, although from the time of Homer it has been one of the great themes of Western literature.[4] Heirs of a tradition involving centuries of legal and millennia of religious condemnation of revenge, we are ashamed of our vengeful impulses, find them difficult to justify (except when persons under great provocation act in the heat of

13

the moment), and generally desire to see ourselves, if not as forgiving, at least as understanding persons whose principal concern is for justice tempered with mercy.

And yet we cannot easily escape our vengeful impulses. Although revenge is largely absent from our "high" art, our "popular" art—novels, movies, comic books, rock and roll, country-and-western music, and especially television—positively abounds with it. Much of this popular art expresses the feeling that our legal system is inadequate to redress many wrongs and that revenge often serves the purposes of justice better than the law. Our wealth of phrases for revenge—get back at, get even with, get satisfaction, give her a dose of her own medicine, give him what's coming to him, pay back in kind, return the compliment, settle the score, square accounts, and so on—indicates a continuing concern with the concept. Despite hundreds of years of religious, legal, and ethical condemnation, popular concern with revenge seems as lively as ever.

The Elizabethans faced much the same dichotomy between official and popular opinions of revenge, but there were some distinct differences between their situation and ours. For one thing, the word *revenge* had not only the negative meanings that have survived down to our day, but could also be used neutrally to mean "punishment" or "chastisement" or even "(in good sense) in recompense for." *Revenge* meant not only personal retaliation for an injury, but legal justice and God's judgments (Broude 1975, 39–40). Although Elizabethan legal authorities were as firm in their condemnation as modern ones are, they were upholding not a long-established tradition but a relatively innovative doctrine. The monarchy had long been attempting to establish itself as the sole source of justice by substituting law for the Anglo-Saxon tradition of the feud (which in its time was legally recognized), but the Elizabethans were not far removed from the several generations of vendetta that constituted the Wars of the Roses. Interestingly, as Bowers points out, the substitution of law for revenge did not come about because of a concern for justice: "The feud was finally broken up not so much by Christianity as by the growth of a central power which made attempts to concern itself in what had always been considered private wrongs" ([1940] 1959, 5). Furthermore, large numbers of men habitually went about armed, and the code duello dictated the use of weapons in response to particular injuries. Finally, religious authorities might stress such passages as Rom. 12:19: "Dearly beloved, avenge not your selves, but give place unto wrath: for it is written, Vengeance is mine: I wil repaye, saith the Lord"[5] (see also Ps. 8:2 and Ps. 94:1); but the Elizabethans, who were more familiar with the Bible than most of us are, would also have been aware of such justified revengers as Samson (Judg.

16:28) and Deborah (Judg. 5:2), and of references to apparently acceptable acts of revenge: "The revenger of the blood him selfe shal slay the
murtherer: when he meteth him, he shal slay him" (Num. 35:19; see
also Num. 35:12, 21; Deut. 19:6; and Prov. 6:34).

Some critics believe that the condemnation of revenge by the Elizabethan legal and clerical establishments was so overwhelming that
however much an audience might sympathize with a revenger, it could
not approve of him (Prosser 1973, chaps. 1 and 2; Lily B. Campbell 1931,
281–96). The *locus classicus* for this viewpoint (at least in discussions
about Elizabethan views of revenge) is the essay from which the title of
the book is taken, Francis Bacon's "Of Revenge":

> Revenge is a kind of wild justice, which the more man's nature runs
> to, the more ought law to weed it out. For as for the first wrong, it
> does but offend the law; but the revenge of that wrong putteth the law
> out of office. Certainly, in taking revenge, a man is but even with his
> enemy, but in passing it over, he is superior; for it is a prince's part to
> pardon: and Salomon, I am sure, saith, *It is the glory of a man to pass by
> an offence.* (7–8)[6]

As befits a lawyer and judge, Bacon makes his first argument against
revenge a legal one: "the law" has been established to punish wrongdoers, and revenge against a wrongdoer is not only itself illegal but
shows contempt for the law. After his first sentence (quoted above),
Bacon never again mentions justice, though whether because he felt that
"law" and "justice" were synonymous for his purposes or because he
was not concerned with justice in this essay I cannot say.

Bacon's legal argument is unsurprising; his ethical argument is more
interesting. He again avoids the question of justice except to say, rather
oddly, that men do wrong either from self-interest, a natural phenom-
enon, or ill nature, an irreparable one. He maintains that it is better for
the victim of a wrong to forget, if not to forgive, an offense than to seek
revenge: "This is certain, that a man that studieth revenge keeps his own
wounds green, which otherwise would heal and do well" (8). Not only
the idea of justice, but the idea that extralegal punishment might lead to
exposure and reform of the wrongdoer, goes unconsidered.

I would not want it thought that I am disparaging Bacon, although I
think that in trying to determine an Elizabethan playwright's or play-
goer's attitudes toward revenge, perhaps too much weight has been
placed on one essay of less than five hundred words. Bacon's primary
concerns, as has been pointed out, were the attitude of the legal establishment toward serious revenge and the personal welfare of the victim
of the wrongdoer. He was not concerned with drama, justice, the welfare of the wrongdoer, or the welfare of society as a whole, except as

embodied in the law. And yet even in so brief an essay and with so limited a range of topics, Bacon does not express total condemnation of vengeance. Although all revenges may be equal before the law, Bacon recognizes distinctions:

> The most tolerable sort of revenge is for those wrongs which there is no law to remedy: but then, let a man take heed the revenge be such as there is no law to punish; else a man's enemy is still beforehand, and it is two for one.
> Some, when they take revenge, are desirous the party should know whence it cometh. This is the more generous. For the delight seemeth to be not so much in doing the hurt, as in making the party repent. But base and crafty cowards are like the arrow that flieth in the dark. (8)[7]

> Public revenges are for the most part fortunate; as that for the death of Caesar; for the death of Pertinax; for the death of Henry the Third of France; and many more. But in private revenges it is not so. (8)[8]

Not all Elizabethans, however, were as categorically opposed to private revenge as Bacon was. Bowers states that "the ordinary Englishman did not condemn revenge as such; it was only when the more treacherous and Italianate features were added (as in the murder of Overbury) or when accomplices were hired to revenge the deed (as by Sanquire) that he considered revenge despicable" (1934, 165). Bevan finds that "dispassionate revenge," as part of the class code, was acceptable, although rash and hasty vengeance was condemned (1967, 55–56). It seems probable, therefore, that we can reject the theory that the Elizabethans universally condemned all revenges, and it is not surprising that, as Broude asserts, the plays of the period express "a considerable range" of attitudes toward revenge (1975, 56).

In the Elizabethan Age, revenge was a theme for high literature (much of which was also popular literature), particularly in the drama. So important was revenge that Lily B. Campbell has even stated that "the great tragic theme of sixteenth—and seventeenth—century teaching is the theme of God's revenge for sin. . . . And all Elizabethan tragedy must appear as fundamentally a tragedy of revenge if the extent of the idea of revenge be but grasped" (1931, 290).[9] Revengers are clearly condemned in a majority of the revenge plays written between 1563 and 1642; but many of these plays were written after 1607, when the earlier straightforward treatment of the revenge theme had given way to plays featuring the villain-revenger, antirevenge dramas, and the decadence of the genre.[10] It would satisfy our natural desire for consistency if we could force eighty years of drama into a single mold. But the fact that the majority of plays and the legal and spiritual writings of the time condemn revenge is not convincing evidence that this attitude was universally accepted. On the contrary, one suspects that it was because the idea of revenge retained an attraction for a considerable portion of the population that the authorities felt a need to execrate it so often and so vehemently.[11] It is not surprising that many contemporary playwrights expressed the establishment's attitude, but neither would it be surprising if some were to make a subversive appeal to popular feelings and, perhaps, consequent box-office success.[12]

Whether or not some tragedies were accepted as representing justifiable revenge, it is interesting that the most justified dramatic revengers, such as Hieronymo and Hamlet, seem to have been the most popular.[13] Hamlet and Hieronymo represent the revenger who is unable to obtain justice in any other way. It can, of course, be argued that both of these heroes should, in strict morality, have awaited the just vengeance of God on the sinners they punish, and many critics have so argued; but we, as Shakespeare's audience undoubtedly did, must nevertheless feel them more justified than most other literary revengers and agree with Bacon that "the most tolerable sort of revenge is for those wrongs which there is no law to remedy" (8).

Considering the pervasiveness of various types of revenge in Elizabethan tragedy, it is surprising that except for Shakespeare, Elizabethan and Jacobean dramatists were relatively sparing in their use of revenge as a major theme in their comedies. This is not to say that the idea of revenge is absent from such works, but generally it functions merely as a minor plot device or the subject of a passing reference. In most comedies of the period, at least one character vows revenge on one or more of his or her fellows, but the revenges tend to be of a very minor sort, as, for instance, two threats directed against Touchstone in *Eastward Ho!*:

> *Quicksilver:* I have friends and I have acquaintance; I will piss at thy shop-posts, and throw rotten eggs at thy sign. Work upon that now!
>
> (2.1.176–79)

> *Gertrude:* As I am a lady, an't would snow, we'd so pebble 'em with snow-balls as they come from church. . . .
>
> (3.2.88–90)

Although many such threats are more serious, most of them remain mere threats, and have little importance except to show the pervasiveness of the idea of revenge in the drama of the time.[14]

The obvious explanation for the general absence of the revenge theme in comedy is that the theme and the genre are unsuited to each other, as

Chakravorty asserts: "It is difficult to see how the revenge motif can appear at all in a comedy. 'Revenge' is diametrically opposed to 'reconciliation' and even the presence of such a motive is ominous for a really happy ending. But Shakespeare is an exception to the general rule" (1969, 253). In fact, the paradox is only an apparent one. The comic dramatists of the era made use of many of the themes more commonly thought of as tragic: thwarted love, ambition, crime, betrayal, and death—real or imagined—are all treated in comedy, as Harbage points out:

> There is an unfounded suspicion of adultery in *The Merry Wives of Windsor* and *The Winter's Tale* as well as in *Othello*, usurpation and inordinate ambition in *As You Like It* and *The Tempest* as well as in *Macbeth*, ill-disposed parents in *A Midsummer Night's Dream* and *The Two Gentlemen of Verona* as well as in *Romeo and Juliet*. Don John of *Much Ado About Nothing* and Iachimo of *Cymbeline* traduce a pure woman as does Iago of *Othello*. Proteus projects a rape, Oliver a murder, and Angelo the equivalent of both. . . . Their story material makes most of these comedies potential tragedies. ([1947] 1961, 125–26)

Revenge is a particularly appropriate theme for comedy for the same reason it is a difficult one to use in tragedy: the necessity for intrigue. Revenge without complications not only lacks drama, it is not a subject that will sustain a five-act play. But the intrigue necessary to extend the action, as Harbage notes, works against the dignity of tragedy by stimulating our intellects rather than our emotions with its emphasis on means rather than ends: "the entertaining complication of action becomes an end in itself" (1962, 37).[15] The innovator of revenge tragedy suggested a possible solution to this dilemma by making a blackly comic scene of the Pedringano episode in *The Spanish Tragedy*, but few of his successors other than Shakespeare profited by his example, and a large number of revenge tragedies are flawed by excessively intricate plotting. But such plotting, requiring as it does schemes, confusions, delays, accomplices, and the like, is the very essence of comedy. Furthermore, although it is true that revenge is opposed to reconciliation, it is equally true that without a conflict there can be no resolution. Revenge is therefore no more unsuited to comedy than any other theme that inspires strong emotions.

Some of Shakespeare's contemporaries did on occasion make use of revenge as a major theme and plot device in comedy, including Chapman *(The Gentleman Usher)*, Greene *(Friar Bacon and Friar Bungay)*, Heywood *(The Wise-Woman of Hogsden)*, Middleton *(A Mad World, My Masters)*, and Marston *(The Fawn, The Dutch Courtesan)*. No other comic playwright, however, seems to have seized on revenge as Shakespeare did, as both a theme and a method of constructing an elaborate but well-integrated plot; as Prosser points out, "it is worth noting . . . how useful a motive Shakespeare found revenge to be" (1973, 75).

The purpose of this book is in fact to demonstrate that underlying Shakespeare's comedies is a conception of justifiable, public revenge for "wrongs there is no law to remedy," as well as occasional commentary on unjustifiable revenge. The idea of revenge pervades Shakespeare's comedies in two forms: first, as serious, often mortal, intentions of revenge that, in accordance with the conventions of comedy, must miscarry; and second, as intrinsically comic revenges intended publicly to embarrass an erring character, either to expose hypocrisy or to enforce a change in behavior, or both. Because of the wide range of meanings the Elizabethans gave to the word *revenge*, two limitations must be imposed. True revenge can be taken only for a personal injury, either to oneself or to someone for whom one feels responsible; the general hell-raising of a Puck or a Falstaff, or the common baiting of a public fool, do not really qualify, although they may resemble revenge in some respects. Furthermore, immediate return of evil for evil is not fully developed revenge, as the unplanned killing of an enemy might in the Elizabethan era be accounted manslaughter, rather than murder.[16]

A recent study of revenge-tragedy motifs describes the protagonist of revenge tragedy as a character obsessed by his need for revenge, to which he is often urged by a ghost; who views himself as an agent of God; who suffers, descends into a madness that brings him to an "utter state of depravity," and ultimately dies as a result of his quest for revenge (Hallett and Hallett 1980, 73, 77–78, 58–59, 82, 11–12). Although some critics might differ on particular aspects of this portrait, in general it accords fairly well with the standard picture of the tragic revenger, whose "experience . . . is not the deployment of a determinate character, but the assumption, and then the enactment, of a determinate *role*" (Holloway 1961, 26). This role tends to define and limit the protagonist and the play.

But comic revengers, although they too seek vengeance, have little else in common with Hieronymo, Hamlet, and their fellows. Comic revengers are seldom driven or commanded to revenge; rather, revenge is an action they choose to take. Comic revenge is emotional in its inception, but not overwhelmingly so, and it is directed by cool reason. Such comic revengers as Portia, Rosalind, and Vincentio have not been directly injured by those they punish; they assume the task of revenge not with the single aim of destroying the victim, but the multiple aims of providing aid to one or more innocent parties, limited punishment and reformation for the victim, and the restoration of harmony in society.[17] Nor are comic revengers obsessed with their self-appointed tasks; they are capable not only of rationally limiting the kind of revenge they take, but also of continuing to act as lovers, rulers, entertainers, and so on, while accomplishing their revenges.[18] "Revenger" is less a determinate role than one more aspect of character; or, if it is a role, it is one that the character is relatively free to interpret. Such characters do not describe themselves as agents of God, but the audience is able to see them as agents of good. Finally, they suffer little, if at all, in the course of the play; are generally dismissed to happiness at the play's end, rather than dying; and, far from running mad, are frequently the sanest characters in the play. Revenge, as practiced by these characters, is not an uncontrollable passion to return evil for evil, but a rational, just, and usually amusing, response to evil or folly.[19]

In discussing the popularity of revenge tragedy, the Halletts have stated: "We miss the whole point if we regard revenge as just another passion. No other passion could have been elevated to a search for justice. That search is symbolic of the individual's quest for order" (1980, 119).[20] Certainly, revenge is not "just another passion." It is possible to love or hate a person or even an object for any reason or even no reason, and neither of these passions will necessarily have any effect on anything other than the personality of the person feeling them. "Revenge," however, implies a combination of persons, history, idea, emotion, and action that makes it both more complex and more restricted than other passions. Revenge implies at least two people, a revenger and a victim; it is possible to love (or hate) an inanimate object or a concept, but it is not possible to take revenge on such. Revenge also implies a previous injury to the revenger, the idea that action may be taken to redress this injury and a sense of injustice that impels the revenger to take such action. Finally, revenge implies the action itself.

If we condemn the passion of revenge out of hand, we will naturally condemn the associated actions and their actors as well. But if we look at the comic revengers and the outcomes of their actions in Shakespeare's comedies and find them good, how can we justify condemning the passion that inspires them? To condemn all revenge simply because it is revenge is as naive a view as to approve all love (for example, Malvolio's self-love) or censure all hatred (for example, Macduff's hatred of Macbeth) without considering the objects of or reasons for those passions. Because revenge presupposes a prior wrong, it need not be much "elevated" to be seen as a search for justice; to some extent, any true revenge has some tinge of justice in it, although obviously many revenges are carried to unjust lengths (at which point, one might say, they cease to be true revenges; at any rate, such unjust revenges are unlikely to be either amusing or dramatically satisfying, and thus have no place in any moral comedy). Certainly the "quest for order" seen by the Halletts in revenge tragedy applies as well in Shakespeare's comedies, where the comic revenger functions as a restorer of the social order threatened by the actions for which he or she takes vengeance.

Although the devices of revenge are common to both tragedy and comedy, their treatment is quite different in the two genres. Revenge requires premeditation and, in the comedies as in the tragedies, is most often characterized by plotting and accomplices. But in comic revenges, accomplices are not a reason for condemnation; rather, the comic revenge is frequently a group effort by which various members of society indicate their disapproval of a character's antisocial (but generally not illegal) behavior, and unite in an effort to punish and change it. As Prosser states, "we see a social unit exposing a wrong in order to restore social health, not a private man inflicting pain in order to revenge a wrong" (1973, 75). In most instances, the society—as represented by the revengers—expresses its willingness to welcome the victim of comic revenge back into its ranks at the end of the play, although this invitation is not invariably accepted.

Although it is not my desire to impose a pattern on the development of Shakespeare's comedies, it seems to me that one is discernible. The early comedies deal mainly with attempts to take rather trivial revenges on family, friends, and lovers; the perceived injuries that provoke these revenges generally result from mistaken identities and other confusions, and all is forgiven once these confusions are cleared up. In the romantic comedies, an outsider to the spirit of the play's world tries to do serious harm to one or more characters (sometimes this attempt is itself a revenge); the comic revenge thwarts this outsider, who may be forgiven and welcomed into the play's society, although this is seldom a major concern of the revenger or of other characters. In the problem comedies, the relationships between family, friends, and lovers are again the subject, but one or more characters threatens serious harm to other characters and society in general; the revengers seem less concerned with punishing the offender than with reforming him. Obviously, such plays as *As You Like It* and *Troilus and Cressida* do not conform to this pattern, but there does seem to be a general movement from trivial to serious threats and from revenge as purely retaliatory to revenge as reformatory.

Shakespeare's romances, histories, and tragedies are beyond the scope of this book, but perhaps a few remarks would not be out of order.[21] The romances, classified as comedies by some critics, seem to me as to many other commentators to be of a different order, one well described by Robert Grams Hunter as "the Comedy of Forgiveness." For whatever reason—boredom, fashion, Christian scruples, or disenchantment with the idea of comic revenge—Shakespeare in the romances concentrates on serious revenges, rather than the generally comic revenges of the earlier plays. The seriousness of the revenge theme dictates a corresponding decrease in the use of the revenge devices and complications he exploited so successfully in earlier comedies. Generally, revenge in the romances is individual, not social; is swiftly determined and immediately acted upon; is not accomplished, but merely intended; and is ultimately a cause for regret, rather than laughter. The attitude toward revenge is entirely different from that in the comedies. Similarly, although revenge pervades the histories, it is not used, as in the comedies, in any discernibly consistent ethical scheme. Although some revenging characters are shown to be evil, we see the heroic Henry V as invading France at least in part to avenge a personal insult. While such comic revengers as Portia, the merry wives, and Touchstone represent the forces of virtue in large part through their actions as revengers, in most of the histories "we have a feeling that there is revenge but no revenger in the personal sense" (Chakravorty 1969, 61). Nor is there a single clear-cut attitude toward revengers in the tragedies. Although we see the houses of Montague and Capulet stupidly and bloodily enmired in a seemingly endless series of meaningless revenges, it is hard to believe that Shakespeare intends us to condemn Macduff, or Edgar, or Hamlet. Furthermore, to the extent that tragic revenge is motivated by malice or madness, the attitude toward revenge expressed in tragedy is virtually the antithesis of that expressed in the comedies.[22]

Although the fully developed revenge theme is not present in all of the comedies, the idea and devices of revenge are present from *The Comedy of Errors* through *Measure for Measure*. It is the more surprising that, despite the pervasiveness of revenge in the comedies, little has been written about this aspect of Shakespeare's work. Prosser refers in passing to Shakespeare's "comic revenges on folly" and Chakravorty devotes a few pages to a discussion of revenge in *The Merchant of Venice*, *Twelfth Night*, and *Measure for Measure*; these brief mentions constitute the most sustained commentary I have been able to locate on revenge in the comedies.

I believe, however, that there is a consistent conception of revenge as a useful social instrument in Shakespeare's comedies, and that the devices of revenge are significant elements in Shakespeare's comic plotting. It is to explain this conception, describe its manifestations, and analyze its effects that I have written this book.

2

Early Comedies

Cosmus, Duke of Florence, had a desperate saying against perfidious or neglecting friends, as if those wrongs were unpardonable. *You shall read* (saith he) *that we are commanded to forgive our enemies; but you never read that we are commanded to forgive our friends.*

—Francis Bacon, "Of Revenge"

Although revenge is evident in all of the early comedies, it is present primarily as a device, rather than as a theme. Even in a play in which many characters express revengeful intentions and attempt—and even accomplish—revenges, such as *The Comedy of Errors*, the audience knows all along and the characters ultimately realize that most of the revenges are due to mistaken identities and other misunderstandings. (Although mistaken identities also play a part in the revenge actions of later comedies, including *The Merry Wives of Windsor, Much Ado About Nothing*, and *Measure for Measure*, they are generally a part of a larger revenge action, not mere episodes.) Similarly, in *A Midsummer Night's Dream*, much of the revenge is instigated—and subsequently prevented from leading to serious consequences—by the intervention of the fairies. In *The Taming of the Shrew*, Petruchio uses the devices of revenge to educate Kate, but his reason for doing so is not revenge. In *Love's Labor's Lost*, the women outline a revenge against the men, but we do not see it accomplished. And in *The Two Gentlemen of Verona*, it is largely the lack of even a consideration of revenge against Proteus that makes the play's ending difficult for a modern audience to accept.

Overall, the theme of comedic revenge as a social instrument for educating and transforming the behavior of foolish or evil characters, a theme prominent in many of the later comedies, is lacking in these early plays. One obvious reason for this lack is that the early comedies contain no evil characters, nor any whose foolishness sets them much apart from the wiser characters. The nearest approach to an evil character in any of these plays is Proteus, but it seems obvious that we are to regard him as a self-deluding young man who, like the willful Katherina, is both worth reforming and capable of reformation. The foolishness of the King of Navarre and his gentlemen and that of the callow Athenian lovers is due to youth; it threatens little harm and causes none. And the multiple threats of revenge by virtually all characters in *The Comedy of Errors* are due solely to confusion and misunderstanding. In all of these plays, furthermore, those who must reform the erring characters are friends, lovers, relatives, or employers, whose aims in the long run are correction and restoration of harmony, rather than punishment.[1] Ironically, however, these close ties are apt to provoke the immediate, short-lived animosity characteristic of the early comedies. It is far more infuriating to be locked out of the house by one's own wife, defied by one's own daughter or confidential servant, or betrayed by one's best friend or lover than to be so injured by a stranger. Due to the confusions, delusions, and mistakes that we as the audience know are causing most of the threats of vengeance, though, we seldom fear for the ending. Where there is little real harm or threat of harm, it is not surprising that there is little serious consideration of revenge and its uses.

Even when revenge in the early comedies is not defused by mistakes or confusion, it is not sustained as it is in the later comedies. Although threats of serious revenge open *The Comedy of Errors* and *A Midsummer Night's Dream*, we quickly forget them until near the plays' conclusions, when they are reintroduced only to be disposed of. Many of the revenges—or revengelike activities—in the early comedies have no echoes in the later plays. The beating of servants, for example, is a commonplace in such plays as *The Comedy of Errors* and *The Taming of the Shrew*, and threats to underlings of punishment by their superiors persist throughout the early comedies; by the time of Touchstone and Feste, however, such threats are mainly facetious and the emphasis has shifted to revenges on characters of higher social standing than servants or clowns.

Nevertheless, the early comedies introduce several revenge motifs that reappear in the later comedies. Love as a vengeful god and the gods in general (or "Heaven") as vengeful are suggested in *The Two Gentlemen of Verona* and *Love's Labor's Lost*; this idea reappears in such plays as *Much Ado About Nothing* and *Troilus and Cressida*. (The idea of nondivine supernatural forces as vengeful, however, seems confined to *The Comedy of Errors*, *A Midsummer Night's Dream*, *The Merry Wives of Windsor*, and a brief mention in *Measure for Measure* [5.1.433–36].) Satire of writers and actors of the period, which some critics have found in *Love's Labor's Lost* and *A Midsummer Night's Dream*, reappears in a far more bitter key in *Troilus and Cressida*. Using the law as an instrument of revenge, a minor motif in *The Comedy of Errors*, *The Taming of the Shrew*, and *A Midsummer Night's Dream*, reappears far more prominently in *The Merchant of Venice* and *Measure for Measure*. Finally, the absence of revenge in *The Two Gentlemen of Verona* and its general condemnation by modern critics largely for that reason foreshadows similar critical dissatisfaction with *All's Well That Ends Well* and *Measure for Measure*.

Although none of the early comedies is a revenge play in the same sense as *The Merchant of Venice* or *The Merry Wives of Windsor*, there seems to be a movement in the early comedies from revenge as exemplified by the simple beating of servants in *The Comedy of Errors* and *The Taming of the Shrew* to revenge as a corrective of behavior in *Love's Labor's Lost* and *A Midsummer Night's Dream*, even though we never see the revenge against the King of Navarre and his fellows accomplished and Oberon's revenge against Titania seems purely personal and devoid of any social purpose. The move toward the revenge theme as a corrective social instrument rather than simply a farcical device is not a linear one throughout Shakespeare's comedies, but—taken as a whole—the plays do seem to evince a distinct rising and falling action. In these early comedies we see various aspects of revenge, but only for brief periods and as adjuncts to more important themes; the full development of revenge as a theme as well as a device awaits the later comedies.

Unlike the plots of some of the later comedies, the plot of *The Comedy of Errors* does not actually hinge on revenge; but while Providence in this play is wholly beneficent in bringing together Egeon's separated family, the threat of human vengeance pervades the play. Parrott has noted that "we may recall that here as in many later plays, notably in *The Merchant of Venice*, Shakespeare allows a cloud of danger, even of threatened death, to overshadow the comic action" and that "there is a certain, though limited, amount of the old physical comedy, the repeated beatings of the unfortunate servants" (1949, 107, 105). Both of these aspects of the play, the former verging on tragedy and the latter on farce, are motivated by a desire for retribution by characters who perceive themselves as wronged, largely because of the mistaken identities that underlie the action.

The opening scene outlines a history of large-scale revenge, an inter-city feud in which the innocent must suffer along with the guilty (1.1.3–25).[2] But the importance of the first scene is not only that "Egeon's story becomes the prologue or argument to the comedy of errors in the sense that the comedy will reverse his tragic fall" (Hamilton 1967, 93); this scene is also the first case of mistaken identity in the play, for Solinus believes he is passing judgment on a rather unsuccessful businessman,

not on the father of the man who saved his life, as is in fact the case.
(That this identity is significant is shown at the end of the play, when
despite his earlier protestations against disannulling his country's and
his laws, crown, oath, and dignity and recalling sentence, Solinus pardons Egeon without the fine.) Of course, in the first scene, neither
Egeon nor the audience is aware of this important aspect of his identity,
either; that information must be withheld, because in the world of this
play, the knowledge of a character's true identity brings forgiveness.

The second scene further heightens the atmosphere of violence
through the suggestion of malignant supernatural forces at work:

> S. Antipholus: They say this town is full of cozenage:
> As nimble jugglers that deceive the eye,
> Dark-working sorcerers that change the mind,
> Soul-killing witches that deform the body,
> Disguised cheaters, prating mountebanks,
> And many such-like liberties of sin.
>
> (1.2.97–102)[3]

The black arts are linked with revenge not merely because both are
generally considered snares of the devil, but because ghosts and other
supernatural beings were frequently thought to be vengeful, as
S. Dromio declares:

> This is the fairy land. Oh, spite of spites!
> We talk with goblins, owls, and sprites;
> If we obey them not, this will ensue:
> They'll suck our breath, or pinch us black and blue.
>
> (2.2.189–92)

S. Antipholus and S. Dromio recognize that they run the risk of incur-
ring such vengeance as strangers in a strange land. In fact, they fear they
may already have incurred it. They fear they are transformed, mad, and
wandering in illusions (2.2.195–96, 212–21; 4.3.42–44). Soon their only
wish is to flee. Meanwhile, their mere presence is entangling their
brothers in a similar mesh of delusions. It is only the audience who can
see the human errors and vindictive human responses causing their
confusion.

The most obvious early instance of vengeful tendencies among the
characters is the beating of the Dromios. In part, this is an outgrowth of
the older comedy, in which the Vice frequently beat clownish characters
for little or no reason; in part, it is the physical indication of mistaken
identity: a master beats another's servant, or his own, innocent, servant;

finally, it demonstrates the choleric proclivities of Adriana and E. Antipholus:

E. Dromio: The clock hath strucken twelve upon the bell:
               My mistress made it one upon my cheek.

               . . . .
               I from my mistress come to you in post:
               If I return, I shall be post indeed,
               For she will [score] your fault upon my pate.
                                 (1.2.45–46, 63–65)

Adriana: [*to E. Dromio*] Back, slave, or I will break thy pate across.
                                    (2.1.78)

E. Antipholus: To what end did I bid thee hie thee home?
E. Dromio: To a rope's end, sir, and to that end am I return'd.
E. Antipholus: And to that end, sir, I will welcome you. [*Beats Dromio.*]
                                 (4.4.15–17)

E. Dromio: [*to Adriana*] Mistress, *respice finem*, respect your end, or rather, the prophecy like the parrot, "beware the rope's end."
E. Antipholus: Wilt thou still talk? [*Beats Dromio.*]
                                 (4.4.41–44)

This is not, of course, true revenge: it is merely an immediate, infuriated response to frustration. Adriana is angry at her husband and takes it out on E. Dromio. And, while E. Antipholus is genuinely annoyed at his servant, he is also fuming at Adriana, as E. Dromio recognizes (4.4.70–78); furthermore, it appears that beating is his usual method of dealing with servants:

E. Dromio: I am an ass, indeed; you may prove it by my long ears. I have serv'd him from the hour of my nativity to this instant, and have nothing at his hands for my service but blows. When I am cold, he heats me with beating; when I am warm, he cools me with beating. I am wak'd with it when I sleep, rais'd with it when I sit, driven out of doors with it when I go from home, welcom'd home with it when I return; nay, I bear it on my shoulders, as a beggar wont her brat; and, I think, when he hath lam'd me, I shall beg with it from door to door.
                                 (4.4.29–39)

But if not vengeance, this is at least vengefulness, a generalized desire to strike out at the slightest provocation, and this spirit pervades the play until the final scene. Even the servants threaten when they dare: when E. Antipholus menaces Luce while attempting to get into his house, she threatens him with the stocks, and S. Dromio thunders "Break any breaking here, and I'll break your knave's pate" (3.1.59–60, 74).[4]

In large part, this vengefulness may have derived from *The Menaechmi*. The only true revenger in Plautus's play, Peniculus, was jettisoned by Shakespeare, but even without him vindictive behavior abounds.[5] Not only are Plautus's twins "a sorry pair of rogues" (Parrott 1949, 104), but Mulier is a shrew, Senex is an ineffectual dotard, and Medicus is a quack. Menaechmus the citizen steals from his wife, who rails at him for stealing; his brother steals from Erotium out of sheer greed, and threatens Mulier and Senex. No one trusts anyone, which is only logical, since no one in the play is trustworthy.

Shakespeare's characters are far more likeable, without, however, being less vengeful. In order to resolve this apparent paradox, Shakespeare goes to some lengths to allow both E. Antipholus and Adriana to appear justified to themselves, and in some measure to the audience. E. Antipholus's first words inform us that Adriana routinely takes a wife's revenge on his domestic lapses:

> Good Signior Angelo, you must excuse us all,
> My wife is shrewish when I keep not hours. . . .
>
> (3.1.1–2)

But there is no reason to assume that Adriana is naturally shrewish; she has in this instance some reason for anger, as Tillyard points out:

> Antipholus has indeed been laying up trouble for himself, for not only is he shockingly late for dinner but he is bringing with him two guests, probably unnotified and certainly offensive to the housewife as eating a dinner that through over-cooking does an injustice to her domestic competence. No wonder Antipholus tries to excuse himself on the ground that it was his solicitude for his wife's chain that made him late and seeks further safety by getting Angelo to father the lie. So, in their way, his sins are great, but how ludicrously different from the sins Adriana imputes to him. (1965, 55)

When E. Antipholus finds himself locked out, he immediately assumes that Adriana is avenging herself on him, and proposes his own revenge:

>   That chain will I bestow
> (Be it for nothing but to spite my wife)
> Upon mine hostess there.
>
> (3.1.117–19)

This is a far more developed vengeance than in Plautus, and yet we sympathize more with Antipholus, who really believes he has a grievance, than with Menaechmus.[6]

When next we see E. Antipholus, we find him burning for further revenge, instructing E. Dromio:

> While I go to the goldsmith's house, go thou
> And buy a rope's end; that will I bestow
> Among my wife and [her] confederates,
> For locking me out of my doors by day.
>
> (4.1.15–18)

But before he can make good this threat, his wife meets him and accuses him of madness, provoking him to attempt a more serious attack:

> Dissembling harlot, thou art false in all,
> And art confederate with a damned pack
> To make a loathsome abject scorn of me;
> But with these nails I'll pluck out these false eyes
> That would behold in me this shameful sport.
>
> (4.4.101–5)

Determined as any revenger of tragedy, he persists in this purpose until the final resolution, as the messenger of his escape reports to Adriana:

> He cries for you, and vows, if he can take you,
> To scorch your face and to disfigure you.
>
> (5.1.182–83)

The emphasis on disfigurement is apparently intended to make the punishment fit the crime, as all proper dramatic revengers try to do; since E. Antipholus thinks Adriana has been false to him (4.4.61–64), he proposes to mar her beauty, presumably an occasion of her sin.

Adriana, too, is a revenger, though both less justified and much less physically violent. Secure in her own innocence against her husband's charges, she is a loving wife whom critics have nevertheless found to be stupid, possessive, suspicious, and hysterical (Tillyard 1965, 58–61; Charlton 1938, 68–69). Her revenge for her husband's real and imagined lapses is shrewishness (5.1.63–67), for which she is properly rebuked in the final scene. But her ill temper is caused by her fear that Antipholus's love for her is waning (2.1.87–101), and in other respects she appears to be a good wife: she sends him money promptly at his request and seeks a doctor for him when he appears ill. Although not a very sympathetic character, Adriana is no more violent and only slightly less perceptive than the play's other characters, and it is clear that Shakespeare took as

many pains to differentiate her from *The Menaechmi's* Mulier as he did
the rest of the characters from Plautus's stereotypes.

Charlton finds that "the general temper of life depicted in *The Comedy
of Errors* is . . . crude, coarse, and brutal" (1938, 69) and the prevailing
thirst for immediate vengeance is not limited to domestic strife, but
extends to business, in which the law is used as an instrument of
retribution. Consider the incident in which the Merchant has Angelo
arrested for debt as Angelo tries to get the money owed him from
E. Antipholus:

Angelo:	This touches me in reputation.
	Either consent to pay this sum for me
	Or I attach you by this officer.
E. Antipholus:	Consent to pay thee that I never had!
	Arrest me, foolish fellow, if thou dar'st.
Angelo:	Here is thy fee, arrest him, officer.
	I would not spare my brother in this case,
	If he should scorn me so apparently.
Officer:	I do arrest you, sir: you hear the suit.
E. Antipholus:	I do obey thee, till I give thee bail.
	But, sirrah, you shall buy this sport as dear
	As all the metal in your shop will answer.
Angelo:	Sir, sir, I shall have law in Ephesus,
	To your notorious shame, I doubt it not.

                                                          (4.1.71–84)

Arrest for debt was, of course, a commonplace of the time; but in this
instance the arrest seems primarily a means of humiliation, just as the
financial transaction immediately becomes a personal quarrel in which
the law is seen as a means of vengeance. Clearly, the officer's presence is
all that prevents Angelo and E. Antipholus from behaving as the Merchant and S. Antipholus do in the first scene of the following act:

Angelo:	This chain you had of me, can you deny it?
S. Antipholus:	I think I had, I never did deny it.
Merchant:	Yes, that you did, sir, and forswore it too.
S. Antipholus:	Who heard me to deny it or forswear it?
Merchant:	These ears of mine thou know'st did hear thee;
	Fie on thee, wretch, 'tis pity that thou liv'st
	To walk where any honest men resort.
S. Antipholus:	Thou art a villain to impeach me thus:
	I'll prove mine honor and mine honesty
	Against thee presently, if thou dar'st stand.
Merchant:	I dare, and do defy thee for a villain.
	[*They draw.*]

                                                          (5.1.22–32)

The audience, of course, knows that this is a fight about nothing, but even for the confused participants there is little reason to quarrel, much less duel, since Angelo and the Merchant have already been paid. But in this play mistaken identity invariably leads to characters' perceiving themselves as wronged, which inevitably leads to an attempted revenge.

The play's most justified—and funniest—revenge is that taken on Doctor Pinch by E. Antipholus and E. Dromio. Although Pinch may mean well, he is described in terms that indicate that he is a quack:

> a hungry lean-fac'd villain,
> A mere anatomy, a mountebank,
> A threadbare juggler and a fortune-teller,
> A needy, hollow-ey'd, sharp-looking wretch,
> A living dead man.
>
> (5.1.238–42)

This description is E. Antipholus's, but there is other evidence that Pinch is not to be taken seriously as a medical man. For one thing, he is a schoolmaster, not only indicating little or no medical training, but also Shakespeare's favorite profession for pedantic frauds. The doctor's very name is indicative not only of discomfort and triviality, but of his character and his effect on others.[7]

This "very ineffectual Paul" is rooted in *The Menaechmi*, as is the vengeance taken on him (Hamilton 1967, 96; Craig 1948, 22, 28),[8] although in the earlier play both treatment and revenge are only suggested:

Medicus: Oh sir, I will make yee take neesing powder this twentie dayes.
Menaechmus: Ile beate yee first with a bastinado, this thirtie dayes.
(Bullough 1957, 1:34)

This exchange Shakespeare translates into action:

Pinch: Give me your hand, and let me feel your pulse.
E. Antipholus: There is my hand, and let it feel your ear.
[*Strikes Pinch.*]

(4.4.52–53)

Shakespeare further develops this incident by giving E. Antipholus another ostensible reason for seeking revenge against Pinch, as he explains to Adriana:

E. Antipholus: You minion, you, are these your customers?
Did this companion with the saffron face

> Revel and feast it at my house to-day,
> Whilst upon me the guilty doors were shut,
> And I denied to enter in my house?
>
> (4.4.60–64)

But his principal grievance against "this pernicious slave," this "doting wizard," as appears by the form of his revenge, is the diagnosis of madness/demonic possession, and his actions seem only a fair return for Pinch's malpractice. As a servant describes it to Adriana:

> My master and his man are both broke loose,
> Beaten the maids a-row, and bound the doctor,
> Whose beard they have sing'd off with brands of fire,
> And ever as it blaz'd, they threw on him
> Great pails of puddled mire to quench the hair;
> My master preaches patience to him, and the while
> His man with scissors nicks him like a fool;
> And sure (unless you send some present help)
> Between them they will kill the conjurer.
>
> (5.1.169–77)[9]

Although the actions described are cruel, they are obviously sportive (apart from the beating of the maids, who—except for the loudmouthed Luce—are presumably innocent), and not intended to be fatal; this as well as the immediate arrival of E. Antipholus and E. Dromio relieve us of any doubts we might have about Pinch's ultimate safety. In fact, he never appears again, and is promptly forgotten, but he has played his part in bringing the play's threatened violence to a head.[10] The resolution is brought about by descriptions of two proposed revenges: that sought of Solinus by E. Antipholus upon Adriana (5.1.197–254) and the legal revenge proposed for Egeon.[11]

Although it may be doubted that the audience has kept Egeon's plight in mind throughout the rapid complications of the play, his reappearance would threaten to darken the tone if the audience were not aware of his true identity. This awareness assures us that all will be well, since the discovery of true identity and the reestablishment of social relations supersede even the most certain vengeance.[12] The final scene, with its mutual recognitions and forgivenesses, establishes a new basis for a more peaceable social order, and the last lines suggest that the lesson has been learned: when the two sets of brothers make their final mistakes in identity, as Ann Barton notes, "for the first time in the play, no altercation, no ferocious exchange of words and blows results. Instead, Antipholus of Syracuse points out gently,

He speaks to me. I am your master, Dromio.
Come go with us, we'll look to that anon.
Embrace thy brother there, rejoice with him."

(The Riverside Shakespeare, 1974, 82)

And E. Dromio declines to take precedence with the play's closing lines
of amity:

We came into the world like brother and brother;
And now let's go hand in hand, not one before another.

(5.1.425–26)

Like *The Comedy of Errors, The Taming of the Shrew* maintains an atmosphere of comic vengefulness; that is, any misunderstanding,
disagreement, or mistimed foolery is apt to be perceived as a personal
insult and met by hard words or blows or both. As in *The Comedy of
Errors,* servants are particularly likely to be the objects of such violence:

Petruchio: [*to Grumio*] Villain, I say, knock me at this gate,
And rap me well, or I'll knock your knave's pate.

. . . .
Will it not be?
Faith, sirrah, and you'll not knock, I'll ring it.
I'll try how you can *sol, fa,* and sing it. [*He
wrings him by the ears.*]

(1.2.11–12, 15–17)

Clearly, Petruchio is not a patient man at best; but while he is "taming"
Kate his temper, whether real or assumed, is even shorter:

Grumio: Fie, fie on all tir'd jades, on all mad masters, and
all foul ways! Was ever man so beaten?

(4.1.1–2)

Grumio: . . . he beat me because her horse stumbled. . . .

(4.1.77)

Petruchio: Off with my boots, you rogues! You villains, when?

. . . .
Out, you rogue, you pluck my foot awry.
Take that, and mend the plucking [off] the other.
[*Strikes him.*]

(4.1.144, 147–48)

Petruchio: Where are my slippers? Shall I have some water?
Come, Kate, and wash, and welcome heartily.

You, whoreson villain, will you let it fall?
[*Strikes him.*]

(4.1.153–55)

And finally:

[*He throws down the table and meat and all, and beats them.*][13]

A further similarity to *The Comedy of Errors* is the idea that vengeance can be taken upon an individual for the faults of his state. In *The Comedy of Errors* this was a real threat, whereas in *The Taming of the Shrew* it is an imaginary one; but the idea was apparently commonplace enough (Shakespeare may have borrowed it from Gascoigne's *Supposes*), and there is no real reason to think the Pedant an idiot for being gulled by such a story:

Tranio [disguised as Lucentio]: 'Tis death for any one in Mantua
        To come to Padua. Know you not the cause?
        Your ships are stay'd at Venice, and the Duke,
        For private quarrel 'twixt your Duke and him,
        Hath publish'd and proclaim'd it openly.

(4.2.81–85)

But there are more developed schemes within this background of idle threats (2.1.404; 4.1.28–32) and idle blows (4.1.60–62). The play begins with an exchange of threats and insults, including in passing a muddled reference to the most popular early revenge tragedy:

Sly: I'll pheeze you, in faith.
Hostess: A pair of stocks, you rogue!
Sly: Y' are a baggage, the Slys are no rogues. Look in the chronicles; we came in with Richard Conqueror. Therefore *paucas pallabris*, let the world slide. Sessa!
Hostess: You will not pay for the glasses you have burst?
Sly: No, not a denier. Go by, Saint Jeronimy! go to thy cold bed, and warm thee.
Hostess: I know my remedy; I must go fetch the [thirdborough]. [*Exit.*]
(Induction.1.1–12)

Such recourse to the law as an aid to private vengeance also occurs later in the play and in what seems to some characters a more serious context. When Vincentio at first encounters Biondello, he assumes the latter is engaged in the usual servant's knavery and responds in the usual fashion:

Vincentio: What, you notorious villain, didst thou never see thy [master's] father, Vincentio?
Biondello: What, my old worshipful master? Yes, marry, sir—see where he looks out of the window.
Vincentio: Is't so indeed? [*He beats Biondello.*]

(5.1.52–57)

But when Tranio appears, disguised as Lucentio and denying Vincentio's identity, the old man turns to the law:

Lucentio! O, he hath murd'red his master!
Lay hold on him, I charge you, in the Duke's name.

(5.1.87–88)

Since Tranio continues the masquerade, it is, as Tillyard points out, "no wonder Vincentio meditates special vengeance on him" (1965, 96). Even after Lucentio's explanation, Vincentio considers personal vengeance:

I'll slit the villain's nose, that would have sent me to the jail. . . . I will in to be reveng'd for this villainy. (5.1.131–32, 136)

The major question of the play, in terms of comic revenge, is whether Petruchio can in any sense be said to be taking revenge on Kate. Certainly, several revenge elements are present. Like any good stage revenger, comic or tragic, Petruchio turns his victim's own weapons against her; as Peter puts it, "He kills her in her own humor" (4.1.180). Bianca's comment that "being mad herself, she's madly mat'd" (3.2.244) is echoed by critics who see Petruchio's actions as "comic exaggerations of her own fierce insistence upon her will" (Parrott 1949, 152; see also Craig 1948, 90). Furthermore, Petruchio announces his willingness to give her back blow for blow (2.1.220), and there is certainly no question that he makes her suffer, physically and emotionally. Finally, his actions serve the highest purpose of comic revenge: they show a misbehaving character the error of her ways, and transform her into a useful member of society.

Nevertheless, *The Taming of the Shrew* is certainly not a revenge comedy. Kate's waywardness is not primarily directed at Petruchio; he does not have a score to settle with her, and he takes prompt action to ensure that she will not be able to wrong him in any serious way. Although the play professes a moral lesson, and some critics have found one therein (although not generally the ostensible one), it is primarily knockabout entertainment.[14]

Unlike a revenger, Petruchio is not interested in the past, but only in the future. Nor is there any indication that he cares how Kate behaves

toward others, as long as she obeys him; in fact, he urges her to beat
Bianca and Hortensio's wife if they will not come to their husbands
(5.2.103–4). His only desire is to obtain a rich and tractable wife, and
while his mad pranks may be an indirect appeal to Kate's reason, he
relies largely on the deprivation methods by which one tames a wild
animal (4.1.188–96); but just as a fowler would not say he was punishing
a hawk for wildness, so Petruchio's cruelty is not an end, but merely a
means. Lacking any interest in past misdeeds or concern for society in
general, and having no desire to punish a personal affront, Petruchio
cannot properly be said to be a revenger.

Kate, on the other hand, could be the dramatic sister not of the milk-
and-water Bianca, but of such vengeful women as Bell'Imperia (*The
Spanish Tragedy*) or Franchischina (*The Dutch Courtesan*) if her misbehavior were not so obvious and so riotously funny. Certainly, she has
some cause to resent Baptista's less-than-sensitive behavior, but her far-
from-ladylike reaction indicates why she is so little sought after:

> Katherina: [*to Baptista*] I pray you, sir, is it your will
> To make a stale of me amongst these mates?
> Hortensio: Mates, maid, how mean you that? No mates for you,
> Unless you were of gentler, milder mould.
> Katherina: I' faith, sir, you shall never need to fear.
> Iwis it is not half way to her heart;
> But if it were, doubt not her care should be
> To comb your noodle with a three-legg'd stool,
> And paint your face, and use you like a fool.
>
>   (1.1.57–65)

At the opening of act 2, we see Kate at her most vengeful and least
attractive. Resentful of her younger sister's popularity, she has tied
Bianca's hands, and—having rendered her defenseless—strikes her. In-
terrupted by Baptista, she explains "Her silence flouts me, and I'll be
reveng'd" (2.1.29); rebuked by him, she storms

> Talk not to me, I will go sit and weep,
> Till I can find occasion of revenge.
>
>   (2.1.35–36)

As in *The Comedy of Errors*, Shakespeare chose to report rather than show
a scene of comic vengefulness, though a much less justified one than
that taken on Pinch:

> Hortensio: I did but tell her she mistook her frets,
> And bow'd her hand to teach her fingering;
> When, with a most impatient devilish spirit,

"Frets, call you these?" quoth she, "I'll fume with them."
And with that word she strook me on the head,
And through the instrument my pate made way,
And there I stood amazed for a while,
As on a pillory, looking through the lute,
While she did call me rascal fiddler
And twangling Jack, with twenty such vild terms,
As had she studied to misuse me so.

(2.1.149–59)

Such incidents indicate why Kate cannot properly be called a revenger. With the exception of Petruchio, all the play's characters treat her better than she treats me. She is not a rebel against the position of women in Elizabethan times; she is a nihilist. The only true revenge she takes in the entire play is hitting Grumio for teasing her with offers of food (4.3.31–35). In all other instances, before her taming, she is as the play titles her, a shrew, a remarkably vicious and bloodthirsty animal for its size, but lacking the reason necessary for true revenge.

Concerned, he says, only for wealth, Petruchio vows to wed Kate "be she as foul as was Florentius' love" (1.2.69). Tillyard states "I doubt if it is any use pointing out that in the story of Florentius his ugly bride is rejuvenated and beautified and that this reference contradicts Petruchio's apparent rejection of any concern with his bride's looks" (1965, 87). Other than passing references to Gower and Chaucer, this seems to be the extent of critical commentary on this line, but one wonders if it is not a hint of some of the play's major themes through a reference to the well-known story. Chaucer's version, "The Wife of Bath's Tale," presents a riddle—"What thyng is it that wommen moost desiren"—that is the key to the relationship between men and women throughout the play. For the answer, as Florentius learns, is that

Wommen desiren to have sovereynetee
As wel over hir housbond as hir love,
And for to been in maistrie hym above.

(*Canterbury Tales*, frag. 3, 1038–40)

This desire, in the terms of Shakespeare's play, is just what Petruchio must break Kate of. The result of his planning might also be based on the words of Florentius's wife, who delivers a sermon (as does Kate at the play's end, albeit on a different subject) on the overwhelming value of "gentillesse," in which she proves that proper behavior is all:

He nys not gentil, be he duc or erl;
For vileyns synful dedes make a cherl.

(*Canterbury Tales*, frag. 3, 1157–58)

Petruchio's faith in his own power to enforce good behavior may be a commentary on "modern" methods of achieving a transformation, while adhering to the old idea that inner beauty is essential. In Chaucer's tale, Florentius and his wife seem to attain perfect reciprocity of obedience, but that, of course, was a romance; when Chaucer used the theme for comedy without moral overtones ("The Wife of Bath's Prologue"), the woman tames the man.

Finally, one must note another critic's theory about *The Taming of the Shrew* and vengeance: Charlton suggests that the play's "prevailing temper is so rollickingly anti-romantic that one may well take it as Shakespeare's boisterous revenge on the romantic spirit which had led him the terrible dance he had trod in *The Two Gentlemen of Verona*" (1938, 76). To that "terrible dance" I now turn.

While no one has apparently claimed greatness for *The Two Gentlemen of Verona*, it would no doubt stand higher than it does in critical estimation were it not for the final scene; and it is largely because the final scene lacks any hint of vengeance that critics have frequently concluded, as Quiller-Couch put it, that there were no gentlemen left in Verona (1918, 85); that the scene cannot be Shakespeare's (Parrott 1949, 112–13, expanding on a suggestion by Quiller-Couch); or that, if authentic, it is proof that Shakespeare, like Homer, sometimes nods (Chambers 1925, 50–51; Charlton 1938, 37–38; Tillyard 1965, 112–17). The immediate forgiveness offered Proteus by the forsaken Julia and the betrayed Valentine, and especially the latter's offer of his own true love to her would-be rapist, are so foreign to modern minds that Dr. Johnson's comment on Angelo, Proteus's parallel in *Measure for Measure*, seems equally appropriate as a summary of critical reaction to *Two Gentlemen*: "[His] crimes were such, as must sufficiently justify punishment, whether its end be to secure the innocent from wrong, or to deter the guilty by example; and I believe every reader feels some indignation when he finds him spared."[15]

This lack of any hint at revenge on or even vengeful feelings toward Proteus is somewhat surprising, since the idea of vengeance is by no means foreign to the play's characters. Not only is there the usual beating of servants (2.1.79–83), but one servant sets up another for a beating:

> *Launce:* Why, then will I tell thee—that thy master stays for thee at the North-gate. . . . Thou must run to him, for thou hast stay'd so long that going will scarce serve the turn.
> *Speed:* Why didst not tell me sooner? Pox of your love-letters! [*Exit.*]

Launce: Now will he be swing'd for reading my letter—an unmannerly slave, that will thrust himself into secrets. I'll after, to rejoice in the boy's correction.

(3.1.372–73, 378–84)[16]

Love is perceived as a vengeful god, and Heaven itself may seek revenge:

Valentine: For in revenge of my contempt of love,
Love hath chas'd sleep from my enthralled eyes,
And made them watchers of mine own heart's sorrow.

(2.4.133–35)

Silvia: Urge not my father's anger, Eglamour,
But think upon my grief, a lady's grief,
And on the justice of my flying hence,
To keep me from a most unholy match,
Which heaven and fortune still rewards with plagues.

(4.3.27–31)

Even Julia, arguably the most forgiving soul in the play, shows a desire for revenge, although sublimated toward inanimate objects and actually accomplished only when directed against herself:

[*after tearing Proteus's letter*] Look, here is writ "kind Julia." Unkind Julia,
As in revenge of thy ingratitude,
I throw thy name against the bruising stones,
Trampling contemptuously on thy disdain.

(1.2.106–9)

[*to Silvia's picture*] I'll use thee kindly for thy mistress' sake
That us'd me so; or else, by Jove I vow,
I should have scratch'd out your unseeing eyes,
To make my master out of love with thee.

(4.4.202–5)

Although nearly all the revenges in *The Two Gentlemen of Verona* are limited merely to words, threats of serious vengeance abound. The only effective revenger, the Duke, is full of sound and fury, but his comparatively lenient actions seem ill proportioned to his ostensible wrath, as his punishments of Valentine and Silvia indicate:

Why, Phaeton (for thou are Merops' son),
Wilt thou aspire to guide the heavenly car,
And with thy daring folly burn the world?
Wilt thou reach stars, because they shine on thee?

> Go, base intruder, overweening slave,
> Bestow thy fawning smiles on equal mates,
> And think my patience (more than thy desert)
> Is privilege for thy departure hence.
> Thank me for this more than for all the favors
> Which (all too much) I have bestowed on thee.
> But if thou linger in my territories
> Longer than swiftest expedition
> Will give thee time to leave our royal court,
> By heaven, my wrath shall far exceed the love
> I ever bore my daughter, or thyself.
> Be gone, I will not hear thy vain excuse,
> But as thou lov'st thy life, make speed from hence.
>
> (3.1.153–69)

Silvia fares little worse, as Proteus informs Valentine:

> her intercession chaf'd him so,
> When she for thy repeal was suppliant,
> That to close prison he commanded her,
> With many bitter threats of biding there.
>
> (3.1.235–38)

That such comparatively mild punishments are levied for so serious a crime is perhaps a foreshadowing of the final scene's orgy of forgiveness. This is not to say that the Christian ideal prevails throughout the play. On the contrary, the ridiculous Thurio revels in dreams of revenge against the hapless Eglamour (5.2.51–52) only to find that Valentine, however mercifully inclined toward his ex-friend, has little clemency to spare for other rivals:

> Thurio, give back, or else embrace thy death;
> Come not within the measure of my wrath.
> Do not name Silvia thine; if once again,
> [Milan] shall not hold thee. Here she stands,
> Take but possession of her with a touch:
> I dare thee but to breathe upon my love.
>
> (5.4.126–31)

Less violent, but no less angry, is Silvia's earlier judgment on Proteus:

> my will is even this,
> That presently you hie you home to bed.
> Thou subtile, perjur'd, false, disloyal man,
> Think'st thou I am so shallow, so conceitless,
> To be seduced by thy flattery,
> That hast deceiv'd so many with thy vows?

Return, return, and make thy love amends.
For me (by this pale queen of night I swear)
I am so far from granting thy request,
That I despise thee for thy wrongful suit,
And by and by intend to chide myself
Even for this time I spend in talking to thee.

(4.2.93–104)

This tirade, the extent of the revenge taken on Proteus, seems particularly inadequate in light of his habit of calling down vengeance on himself if he proves unfaithful.[17]

Here is my hand for my true constancy;
And when that hour o'erslips me in the day
Wherein I sigh not, Julia, for thy sake,
The next ensuing hour some foul mischance
Torment me for my love's forgetfulness!

(2.2.8–12)

Longer than I prove loyal to your Grace
Let me not live to look upon your Grace.

(3.2.20–21)

Despite such deceptions and manipulations, however, Proteus does not really deserve to be called "a minor Iago" (Evans [1960] 1967, 15), for he is in no way a revenger, having not even imagined grievances against any of those he wrongs. The greater character he most resembles is Angelo; although both know they are doing evil, both are obsessed. But, while both are basically good men gone wrong, it is easier to accept Angelo's agonizing than Proteus's sudden switches, first to ruthlessness and then to remorse. It is such sudden transformations of character that, though appropriate to his name, prompt the feeling that "nothing is more conducive to contrition than getting caught" (Robert Grams Hunter 1965, 85).

Although Proteus's repentence is dramatically unsatisfying, it is probable that the Elizabethan audience had less difficulty with Valentine's complete and immediate forgiveness than does a modern one. Valentine in the final scene displays the much-discussed virtue of magnanimity as well as the central Christian virtue of forgiveness.[18] Such an overwhelming display of generosity, as well as a demonstration of the superiority of friendship to romantic love, was not original with Shakespeare, who could have found precisely the same generosity in the popular story of Titus and Gisippus in Sir Thomas Elyot's *The Governour,* book 2. Yet the hero's action is unquestionably less disturbing in Elyot than in Shakespeare. The reason is that Elyot and other writers dealing with the same situation raise the question of revenge; Shakespeare, in this play, does not. Craig has labeled the betrayal of one friend by another because of a lady one of the two main features of what "might almost be described as the most familiar plot of Renaissance comedy."[19] In fact, this betrayal plot does not seem as common as forgiveness after threats of revenge, as in *Euphues*. Even Elyot, who sets the model for friendly magnanimity, raises the question of revenge for betrayal, when Titus says to Gisippus:

> My dere and moste lovynge frende, withdrawe your frendely offers, cease of your courtaisie, refrayne your teares and regrettinges, take rather your knyfe and slee me here where I lye, or otherwise take vengeaunce on me, moste miserable and false traytour unto you, and of all other moste worthy to suffre moste shamefull dethe. . . . (Bullough 1957, 1:214)

Such a speech not only serves to convince the audience of the sincere contrition of the betrayer, but raises the natural question of revenge for the betrayed. Such a speech seems less necessary for Titus—who has done nothing wrong but fall desperately in love with his friend's fiancée—than for the scheming, constantly disloyal, and actively bad Proteus. But by raising the question, Elyot allows his hero to confront the idea of revenge and present his reasons for rejecting it; Valentine, in contrast, never considers vengeance. If like Frankford (in *A Woman Killed with Kindness*), another magnanimous Christian hero, Valentine had lost his temper for even a moment, the audience, seeing him tempted but overcoming temptation, could understand and sympathize. As it is, Valentine is less a Christian figure than a Christ-figure;[20] he loses our sympathy, and the play loses potential tragic overtones, because vengeance, although not unknown in Verona and Milan, is never seriously dealt with in a situation where our ability to identify with a major character requires its consideration.

To suggest that vengeance should have been a major topic of concern in *The Two Gentlemen of Verona* would be to ask for a different play. Tillyard is no doubt correct in his assessment that the comedy we have "does not deal with man's relations with his neighbors and his obligations to society but confines itself to his relations with one, or not more than two, other people" (1965, 134). If the preceding discussion has any value, it can only be to indicate a possible reason why, in the succeeding comedies, Shakespeare allows forgiveness and reconciliation to triumph only after vengeance—serious or comic—is expressed as a natural human desire and often effected in a socially useful way.

Love's Labor's Lost, according to some critics, is a dramatic "revenge" in the form of satire on individuals or movements (or both) in Shakespeare's society. Perhaps the best-known development of this view is Bradbrook's *The School of Night*, according to which Sir Walter Raleigh was the leader of both a group and a movement concerned with mathematics and atheism, and including among its members Christopher Marlowe, George Chapman, and Thomas Harriot. This group, according to Bradbrook, engaged in an "active literary war" with "the faction of Essex," including Shakespeare, between 1593 and 1595 (1936, 23, 7). *Love's Labor's Lost*, according to this argument, was one shot fired in that war, an attack on the behavior of the group Shakespeare termed "the school of night" (4.3.251), by means of caricature: Armado represents Raleigh, Holofernes Harriot, while the play as a whole parodies not only the movement but in particular Chapman's *The Shadow of Night* (1936, 24). But Bradbrook admits that "the satire is not sustained and consistent," and if such a satire were Shakespeare's intent it has lost its force over time.[21]

Another reading of the play, however, yields an equally biting, if less specific, "revenge":

> there is the terrible portrait of a renaissance schoolmaster, self-complacent, self-seeking, irascible, pretentious, intolerant of what he calls 'barbarism', and yet himself knowing nothing but the pitiful rudiments, the husks of learning, which he spends his life thrusting down the throats of his unfortunate pupils. . . . For we have here, not only in the figure of Holofernes, but in the play as a whole, Shakespeare's great onslaught upon the Dark Tower, the fortress of the enemies of life and grace and gaiety—
>
> The round squat tower, blind as the fool's heart, the name of which is Pedantry. (Wilson 1962, 73, 74)[22]

While Shakespeare unquestionably satirizes pedantry in *Love's Labor's Lost*, such satire is more humorous than bitter; it seems doubtful whether Shakespeare could create a schoolmaster who was not a pedantic fool, and evident that he never tried. The play is in fact full of fools, but there is no character who is in the least evil. Those characters whom critics have considered primarily satiric caricatures are not exposed or punished, since they do nothing and are obvious in their foolishness; nevertheless, Armado and Holofernes are given lines as intelligent and sensitive as any in the play (5.2.629, 660–62). There is, however, a minor theme of revenge in the play, despite the apparently static plot.[23]

The oath taken by Navarre and his lords is the first cause of threatened vengeance. It would seem to have the force of law for the common people:

King: [*to Costard*] It was proclaim'd a year's imprisonment to be taken with a wench.

(1.1.287–88)

Berowne [*reads*]: "*Item,* That no woman shall come within a mile of my court . . . on pain of losing her tongue."

(1.1.119–20, 123–24)

But the first offenders, of whom we should expect an example to be made, are instead virtually pardoned:

King: [*to Costard*] Sir, I will pronounce your sentence: you shall fast a week with bran and water.

(1.1.300–301)[24]

Jaquenetta is merely committed to Armado's custody.[25]

For the members of the court, however, the oath-taking is less a legal necessity than a personal commitment and a matter of honor; violating it is therefore an act against fellowship, which requires personal revenge.

King: Your oaths are pass'd, and now subscribe your names,
That his own hand may strike his honor down
That violates the smallest branch herein.

(1.1.19–21)

Berowne [*reads*]: "*Item,* If any man be seen to talk with a woman within the term of three years, he shall endure such public shame as the rest of the court can possibly devise."

(1.1.129–32)

The oath is, of course, immediately broken by all hands, not for Costard's excellent reason—"it is the manner of a man to speak to a woman" (1.1.209–10)—but by "necessity," which is in fact absent-mindedness (1.1.141–49). But just as the King and his lords later pretend (by concealing their loves) to have broken their oaths no more than necessity forced them, so Navarre attempts to preserve appearances at the beginning, preferring to lodge the Princess and her ladies

in the field,
Like one that comes here to besiege his court,
Than seek a dispensation for his oath.

(2.1.85–87)

The point of all the oath-taking has been, for the King, to garner fame, to make Navarre "the wonder of the world" (1.1.12); and the hypocrisy of the men "that war against [their] own affections" (1.1.9) may be in the Princess's mind when she says

And out of question so it is sometimes:
Glory grows guilty of detested crimes,

When for fame's sake, for praise, an outward part,
We bend to that the working of the heart.

(4.1.30–33)

    The Princess and her ladies, however, take no action against their
foresworn and inhospitable lovers, other than chiding (2.1.90–113;
5.2.343–61, 439–40), until the final scene. The men, meanwhile, behave
as though their shattered oath were still in force, delighting in catching
each other publicly, although privately each violates it at every opportunity. Armado reports Costard for talking with Jaquenetta (1.1.247–65),
with whom Armado promptly falls in love; Holofernes reports Berowne
(4.2.136–42); and Berowne berates the King, who has challenged Longaville, who has caught Dumaine, in a pyramid of reproach for supposed
betrayal (4.3.125–78). Since all are equally guilty, they dispense with
revenge, although not with hypocrisy. Berowne, however, sees their
subsequent embarrassments as just punishment for their sins. Of his
love for Rosaline, for instance, he says:

> It is a plague
> That Cupid will impose for my neglect
> Of his almighty dreadful little might.

(3.1.201–3)

And having discovered the trick played on them during their Russian
masquerade, he exclaims "Thus pour the stars down plagues for perjury" (5.2.394) and swears off deceit and affectation.
    Having heard the ladies' discussions, the audience knows that heav-
enly vengeance has not been necessary. The Princess has declared open
season on those who would attempt to fool her and her companions:

> The effect of my intent is to cross theirs:
> They do it but in mockery merriment,
> And mock for mock is only my intent.
> . . . .
> There's no such sport as sport by sport o'erthrown,
> To make theirs ours and ours none but our own;
> So shall we stay, mocking intended game,
> And they, well mock'd, depart away with shame.

(5.2.138–40, 153–56)

The ladies are more than able to return mock for mock; but when the
lords unleash their wits against such weak game as Nathaniel and
Armado, one can only agree with Holofernes that "this is not generous,
not gentle, not humble" (5.2.629). Although the lords are delighted with
their wit, the gracious Princess (5.2.557, 567, 587, 631, 665–66) and her

ladies do not join in the horseplay. Whether, as Tillyard speculates, Rosaline "is doubtless still feeling her disgust at [Berowne's] behavior in baiting the actors and egging on Costard in his ridiculous duel with Armado" (1965, 150), the penance she imposes on him, like that set by the Princess for the King, is a punishment perfectly designed to fit his "crime" and bring him to a realization and correction of it. Though this is not vengeance, it is nearer to it than to a traditional comic resolution, since guilt and consequent expiation through suffering are stressed:

> *Princess:* No, no, my lord, your Grace is perjur'd much,
> Full of dear guiltiness, and therefore this:
> If for my love (as there is no such cause)
> You will do aught, this shall you do for me:
> Your oath I will not trust, but go with speed
> To some forlorn and naked hermitage,
> Remote from all the pleasures of the world;
> There stay until the twelve celestial signs
> Have brought about the annual reckoning.
> If this austere insociable life
> Change not your offer made in heat of blood;
> If frosts and fasts, hard lodging and thin weeds
> Nip not the gaudy blossoms of your love
> But that it bear this trial, and last love;
> Then at the expiration of the year,
> Come challenge me, challenge me by these deserts,
> And by this virgin palm now kissing thine,
> I will be thine.
>
> (5.2.790–807)

Dumaine and Longaville, though likewise oath-breakers and mockers, are let off much more lightly, condemned only to a year's wait. It is, of course, Berowne who is most strongly indicted and harshly punished:

> *Rosaline:* Oft have I heard of you, my Lord Berowne,
> Before I saw you; and the world's large tongue
> Proclaims you for a man replete with mocks,
> Full of comparisons and wounding flouts,
> Which you on all estates will execute
> That lie within the mercy of your wit.
> To weed this wormwood from your fructful brain,
> And therewithal to win me, if you please,
> Without the which I am not to be won,
> You shall this twelvemonth term from day to day
> Visit the speechless sick, and still converse
> With groaning wretches; and your task shall be,
> With all the fierce endeavor of your wit,
> To enforce the pained impotent to smile.

Berowne: To move wild laughter in the throat of death?
            It cannot be, it is impossible:
            Mirth cannot move a soul in agony.
Rosaline: Why, that's the way to choke a gibing spirit,
            Whose influence is begot of that loose grace
            Which shallow laughing hearers give to fools.
            A jest's prosperity lies in the ear
            Of him that hears it, never in the tongue
            Of him that makes it; then, if sickly ears,
            Deaf'd with the clamors of their own dear groans,
            Will hear your idle scorns, continue then,
            And I will have you and that fault withal;
            But if they will not, throw away that spirit,
            And I shall find you empty of that fault,
            Right joyful of your reformation.

                                              (5.2.841–69)

The appropriateness of the assigned tasks is described by Tillyard:

> the two principal penances imposed are . . . perfectly fitted to expiate
> those actions. In fact they look back into the body of the play more
> than they look forward to the new life which may or may not emerge.
> It is perfectly apt that Navarre, promoter of the bogus academy,
> should have to endure the hardships he had planned in theory. . . .
> the success of Berowne's notorious sallies of satire depended on the
> applause of fools easily provoked to laughter. Let him now try his luck
> with another kind of audience. But it is a grotesque and macabre
> penance, remote from the norm of ordinary life. . . . (1965, 178–79)

Although these punishments are not revenges, they resemble typical
stage revenges in a number of ways. Not only the perfect suitability of
the penance to the sin, but the fact that the concern of the "revengers" is
at least as much with the past as the future is characteristic of both tragic
and comic revenge plays. Finally, the purpose of correcting a social evil
and the specifically comic intention of reforming the behavior of erring
characters resemble the purposes of many true stage revengers. Like
Shakespeare's other early comedies, therefore, *Love's Labor's Lost* contains hints of comic vengeance—minor social wrongs to be righted by
simultaneously punishing the transgressors and teaching them the errors of their ways—without providing a complete resolution by means of
revenge, or even, in this play, completing the transformation of the
wrongdoers while inciting us to laughter.

Although *A Midsummer Night's Dream* repeats earlier and foreshadows
later Shakespearean comic themes, the play is something of an anomaly
in its treatment of comic revenge in that, while revenge is both threatened and performed and changes certain characters' behavior, there is

no corresponding enlightenment. Not only do the affected characters fail to develop new understandings of themselves and others, as in the later plays, but they do not even learn why they have been confused, as in *The Comedy of Errors;* rather, they find themselves changed although they themselves have changed nothing. As Bullough indicates, these changes are the result of the supernatural intrusions of Oberon and Puck into human affairs: "In this Night of Errors Plautine realism is discarded, the mistakes are not mistakes of identity so much as of emotional direction. The comic 'errors' of physical resemblance are replaced by those of magic, itself sometimes erroneously used" (1957, 1:367). Despite this lack of human control and the occasional misuse of fairy magic, however, it is difficult to see the play as pervaded by "an atmosphere of fearsomeness" (Knight [1932] 1953, 152).[26]

Although Oberon controls much of the revenge in the play, he is not involved in all of it. Long before he ever appears, Egeus threatens to use Athenian law as a means of vengeance against his willful daughter, Hermia:

> Be it so she will not here before your Grace
> Consent to marry with Demetrius,
> I beg the ancient privilege of Athens:
> As she is mine, I may dispose of her;
> Which shall be either to this gentleman,
> Or to her death, according to our law
> Immediately provided in that case.

(1.1.39–45)

That Egeus intends vengeance rather than justice is shown by the fact that he omits the third legal alternative, which is, however, immediately supplied (1.1.65–66) by Theseus, another of Shakespeare's princes committed to uphold the law despite the bad uses to which it may be put and their own reluctance to impose harsh punishments on the comparatively innocent:

> Upon that day either prepare to die
> For disobedience to your father's will,
> Or else to wed Demetrius, as he would,
> Or on Diana's altar to protest
> For aye austerity and single life.

(1.1.86–90)

Egeus's threat is, of course, never fulfilled. But two other characters actually perform actions that look in some respects like revenge. Helena, having been told in confidence of Lysander and Hermia's proposed flight from Athens, promptly decides to tell Demetrius of the plan. Since

Hermia's departure from Athens would presumably leave the field open for Helena, and since her announced motive for telling him—"To have his sight thither and back again" (1.1.251)—seems rather weak, one is inclined to consider the earlier part of Helena's soliloquy as a possible reason for her treachery:

> For ere Demetrius look'd on Hermia's eyne,
> He hail'd down oaths that he was only mine;
> And when this hail some heat from Hermia felt,
> So he dissolv'd, and show'rs of oaths did melt.
>
> (1.1.242–45)

But while Helena has both motive and opportunity, it may be doubted whether she has the character for revenge. Not only do dramatic revengers generally, if not invariably, provide the audience with a direct link between their intents and their motives, but Helena does not maintain that Hermia "stole" Demetrius, even when Hermia rebukes her with "stealing" Lysander. However feeble and illogical, Helena's proclaimed reason for betraying her friend must be taken at face value.

A much more vengeful-seeming character is Puck, who has many characteristics of the stage revenger: he loves to make plots and trouble, he has dramatic imagination, and he is to some degree malicious.[27] The fairy he meets in the wood asks if he is not the spirit who likes to "mislead night-wanderers, laughing at their harm?" (2.1.39), and Puck affirms this identity:

> Thou speakest aright;
> I am that merry wanderer of the night.
> I jest to Oberon and make him smile
> When I a fat and bean-fed horse beguile,
> Neighing in likeness of a filly foal;
> And sometime lurk I in a gossip's bowl,
> In very likeness of a roasted crab,
> And when she drinks, against her lips I bob,
> And on her withered dewlop pour the ale.
> The wisest aunt, telling the saddest tale,
> Sometime for three-foot stool mistaketh me;
> Then slip I from her bum, down topples she,
> And "tailor" cries, and falls into a cough;
> And then the whole quire hold their hips and loff,
> And waxen in their mirth, and neeze, and swear
> A merrier hour was never wasted there.
>
> (2.1.42–57)

While mischief and shape-changing are traditional fairy activities, conventional representations of Robin Goodfellow often portray him as one

of the household Brownies, who, while they do work for those they like
(as does Puck, 2.1.40–41), are also more likely to be vengeful than is
Shakespeare's Puck, rather than simply making nonspecific mischief.[28]

Puck's mischief seems motivated by something else, especially since
he seems altogether impervious to injury by mortals.[29] At one point, he
actually seems driven to concoct a "human" excuse for his hell-raising:

> What hempen home-spuns have we swagg'ring here,
> So near the cradle of the Fairy Queen?
> What, a play toward? I'll be an auditor,
> An actor too perhaps, if I see cause.
>
> (3.1.77–80)

He has no "cause" at all, of course, offended artistic sense aside, but that
does not stop him from punishing the would-be actors rather horribly,
not only transforming Bottom, but pursuing the others with the declaration:

> I'll follow you, I'll lead you about a round,
> Through bog, through brush, through brake, through brier:
> Sometime a horse I'll be, sometime a hound,
> A hog, a headless bear, sometime a fire,
> And neigh, and bark, and grunt, and roar, and burn,
> Like horse, hound, hog, bear, fire, at every turn.
>
> (3.1.106–11)

Interestingly, the one time Puck suggests a real motive for involving
himself in human affairs, expressing a vengeful mood in the interests of
justice, he has been set to the task by Oberon:

> Night and silence—Who is here?
> Weeds of Athens he doth wear:
> This is he, my master said,
> Despised the Athenian maid;
> And here the maiden, sleeping sound,
> On the dank and dirty ground.
> Pretty soul, she durst not lie
> Near this lack-love, this kill-courtesy.
> Churl, upon thy eyes I throw
> All the power this charm doth owe.
> When thou wak'st, let love forbid
> Sleep his seat on thy eyelid.
>
> (2.2.70–81)

Inevitably, Puck errs in his reasonable tasks, complicating the situation
further, much to his delight (3.2.347–53). Despite similarities to vengeful
characters, however, Puck cannot be taken as one; incapable of feeling

pain, he cannot be wronged. Like Bottom, however, he is an "instrument of Oberon's revenge upon Titania" (Chambers 1925, 86).

But if Puck is impervious to human emotion, his powerful lord, Oberon, seems oddly vulnerable. He has a strange sense of justice and a certain compassion toward mortals, as when he seeks to help the forsaken Helena:

> Fare thee well, nymph. Ere he do leave this grove,
> Thou shalt fly him, and he shall seek thy love.
>
> (2.1.245–46)

His obsession with Titania's little Indian boy may spring from affection or merely a desire to dominate her; in either event, Shakespeare turns the traditional fairy king—depicted as potentially vengeful toward erring mortals (Bullough 1957, 1:391–94)—into an eager revenger against not only his own kind, but his own queen. A third possible motive is presented when Puck refers to "jealous Oberon" (2.1.24) and is developed as a possible reason for both Titania's stubbornness and Oberon's wrath in their dialogue:

> *Oberon:* Ill met by moonlight, proud Titania.
> *Titania:* What, jealous Oberon? [Fairies,] skip hence—
>   I have foresworn his bed and company.
> *Oberon:* Tarry, rash wanton! Am not I thy Lord?
> *Titania:* Then I must be thy lady; but I know
>   When thou hast stolen away from fairyland,
>   And in the shape of Corin sat all day,
>   Playing on pipes of corn, and versing love,
>   To amorous Phillida. Why art thou here
>   Come from the farthest steep of India?
>   But that, forsooth, the bouncing Amazon,
>   Your buskin'd mistress and your warrior love,
>   To Theseus must be wedded, and you come
>   To give their bed joy and prosperity.
> *Oberon:* How canst thou thus for shame, Titania,
>   Glance at my credit with Hippolyta,
>   Knowing I know thy love to Theseus?
>
> (2.1.60–76)

Their mutual accusations, Titania's desertion, and Oberon's retaliatory tactics of disturbing her revels have caused nature herself to act as if vengeful:

> *Titania:* Therefore the winds, piping to us in vain,
>   As in revenge, have suck'd up from the sea
>   Contagious fogs; which, falling in the land,

Hath every pelting river made so proud
That they have overborne their continents.
. . . .
No night is now with hymn or carol blest.
Therefore the moon (the governess of floods),
Pale in her anger, washes all the air,
That rheumatic diseases do abound.
And thorough this distemperature, we see
The seasons alter

. . . .
　　　　　　　　　　　　　and the mazed world,
By their increase, now knows not which is which.
And this same progeny of evils comes
From our debate, from our dissension;
We are their parents and original.

　　　　　　　　　　　　(2.1.88–92, 102–7, 113–17)

Although both Titania and Oberon seem to deplore the havoc wreaked by their mutual anger on nature and mortal creatures, neither is willing to make the first move toward reconciliation. Silly as the play's young human characters are, they behave much better than the ancient and powerful immortals.[30]

Though only whims control Oberon and Titania's actions, they are whims of iron. Oberon departs vowing to torment her, and immediately plots revenge (2.1.146–47, 176–85). And although the professed point of his scheme is to divert her affection from the boy, allowing him to adopt the child, his desire to hurt her keeps reappearing:

What thou seest when thou dost wake,
Do it for thy true-love take;
Love and languish for his sake.
Be it ounce, or cat, or bear,
Pard, or boar with bristled hair,
In thy eye that shall appear
When thou wak'st, it is thy dear:
Wake when some vile thing is near.

　　　　　　　　　　　　(2.2.27–34)

(Thanks to Puck's foolery, Oberon's terrible wish is not fulfilled. Bottom is ridiculous in himself, monstrous in an ass's head, and incongruous as Titania's lover; vile, however, he is not.)[31]

Oberon's mixture of motives is best shown when he has Titania fully in his power:

Welcome, good Robin. Seest thou this sweet sight?
Her dotage now I do begin to pity.

For meeting her of late behind the wood,
Seeking sweet favors for this hateful fool,
I did upbraid her, and fall out with her.
. . . .
When I had at my pleasure taunted her,
And she in mild terms begg'd my patience,
I then did ask of her her changeling child;
Which straight she gave me, and her fairy sent
To bear him to my bower in fairy land.
And now I have the boy, I will undo
This hateful imperfection of her eyes.

(4.1.46–50, 57–63)

Presumably Oberon's point in his revenge (other than obtaining the child) is to punish Titania's love for a mortal with love for a monster, her stubbornness with obsession, her disobedience to her natural lord with enslavement to an unnatural freak. But only a fairy mind could conceive of punishing his consort for giving cause for jealousy by inspiring her with passion for a monster. And only in the fairyland of this play would Oberon's solution lead to peace and harmony.

Unlike Oberon, who only promises what he can perform, the lovers constantly utter revenge threats, none of which is accomplished. The men, in particular, call down threats on themselves: "And then end life when I end loyalty" (2.2.63); on the women:

if thou follow me, do not believe
But I shall do thee mischief in the wood

(2.1.236–37);

and especially on each other (2.1.189–90; 2.2.106–7; 3.2.419–20, 426–27, et al.). The women, who have not been touched by the love potion, present quite a different picture: Helena, who has suffered most, rebukes her supposed tormentors but makes no threats. Hermia, on the other hand, loses her temper with Helena as soon as she is convinced that Lysander is not jesting:

You thief of love! What, have you come by night
And stol'n my love's heart from him?

(3.2.283–84)

But it is not until Helena, goaded beyond endurance, refers to her as a "puppet," that she threatens action:

How low am I, thou painted maypole? Speak!
How low am I? I am not yet so low
But that my nails can reach unto thine eyes.

(3.2.296–98)

The humor of so small a stimulus triggering the only effective attempt at revenge among these four is exceeded only by the departure of the two champions from the woman they are sworn to defend, leaving her to the mercies of her avowed enemy, who, however, merely remarks "I am amaz'd, and know not what to say" (3.2.344).

This chaos of crossed intents can be seen as the world's revenge on fools, as Charlton explains: "men without cool reason, who are the sport of seething brains and of the tumultuous frenzies of fancy and of sentiment, are the victims of the world, and the butts of its comedy" (1938, 122). But even though lovers, as Theseus points out, have affinities with lunatics, these lovers are less victims of their own tumultuous frenzies of fancy than of Puck's. That this is so is indicated by the fact that they do not become wiser from their ordeal—in fact, they cannot even remember it:

Theseus: I know you two are rival enemies.
            How comes this gentle concord in the world,
            That hatred is so far from jealousy
            To sleep by hate, and fear no enmity?
Lysander: My lord, I shall reply amazedly,
            Half sleep, half waking: but, as yet, I swear,
            I cannot truly say how I came here.

                                                        (4.1.142–48)

Their newfound amity seems more strange and inexplicable, not only to outsiders but to themselves, than their previous discord. Theseus, the epitome of the reasonable man in the play, suddenly finds it in him to "overbear" Egeus' will and Athens' law, and confirm legally the reality created by the fairies (4.1.179).[32] Theseus is not only the exemplar of reason in the play, but of compassion and catholicity, as he proves in the last act.

Before discussing Theseus's role in the tradesmen's production of the "tedious brief scene" of Pyramus and Thisby, however, note must be taken of Shakespeare's intent in creating these actors and their play (sheer entertainment, for the moment, aside). There seems to be general agreement among many critics that Shakespeare intended some sort of satire (literary revenge) in these scenes, even if the target of that satire is not agreed upon.[33]

But if literary revenge was Shakespeare's style, it is not Theseus's (unless he and his friends are doing the satirizing). He rejects the first two plays offered, ostensibly because they are familiar, but, however coincidentally, they are both stories of revenge, that of Hercules on the Centaurs and that of the "tipsy Bacchanals" on Orpheus. Then he rejects a "keen and critical" satire. Finally, he accepts what "simpleness and duty" can offer, despite Philostrate and Hippolyta's protestations:

> *Hippolyta:* I love not to see wretchedness o'ercharged,
>   And duty in his service perishing.
> *Theseus:*   Why, gentle sweet, you shall see no such thing.
> *Hippolyta:* He says they can do nothing in this kind.
> *Theseus:*   The kinder we, to give them thanks for nothing.
>
> (5.1.85–89)

But sheer kindness toward his subjects is not his only motive:

> Our sport shall be to take what they mistake
>
> (5.1.90);

although he reverts to *noblesse oblige:*

> And what poor duty cannot do, noble respect
> Takes it in might, not merit.
>
> (5.1.91–92)

Theseus is often taken to be the play's embodiment of reason, and he certainly seems rational; although paradoxically, a lover himself, he classes lovers with lunatics and poets. We catch a glimpse of the poet in Theseus, but nothing of the lunatic, although we have heard a description that would have him once "all as frantic" and unfaithful as any of the play's other lovers (2.1.74–80).[34] The Theseus we see, however, is rational, and something of a critic (as he shows by expatiating on "the poet" far more than "the lover" or "the lunatic"). And, in the face of his statement that the worst plays are no worse than the best "if imagination amend them" (5.1.211–12), it can only be concluded that his good taste overcomes his good manners, for he joins in the mocking of the actors with as much spirit as any auditor driven to revenge his outraged sensibilities on the outraging and outrageous performers. We know, of course, the impossibility of the sort of revenge originally feared by Quince and the others as a result of Bottom's proposed leonine sound effects:

> And you should do it too terribly, you would fright the Duchess and the ladies, that they would shrike; and that were enough to hang us all. (1.2.74–77)

But Theseus, who at first confines himself to asides (5.1.125–26, 152 et al.) and faint praise (5.1.165, 215–16), ultimately cannot help but contrib-

ute to the horseplay (5.1.227–28, 232) even though it disconcerts the
actors; and finally, he reaches the point where critical exasperation almost equals amusement: "This passion, and the death of a dear friend,
would go near to make a man look sad" (5.1.288–89).[35] But, like the
worst of the mockers—Demetrius and Lysander—Theseus retains
enough sympathy for the mechanicals to encourage them occasionally
(5.1.266, 269). Theseus concludes the mortals' portion of the play with a
speech that expresses both his critical judgment of the actors and his
kindness toward his subjects:

> No epilogue, I pray you; for your play needs no excuse. Never excuse;
> for when the players are all dead, there need none to be blam'd.
> Marry, if he that writ it had play'd Pyramus and hang'd himself in
> Thisby's garter, it would have been a fine tragedy; and so it is, truly,
> and very notably discharg'd. (5.1.355–61)

It is fitting that the fairies, who have controlled so much of the action
and who have for much of the play been obsessed by vengeful feelings,
should have the final word. And, although it comes oddly from the
unassailable and irrepressible Puck, it is likewise appropriate that this
epilogue (in lieu of that which Theseus rejected) take the form of an
explanation—that all the confused vindictiveness was but a dream—and
a plea for pardon and acceptance. After all the irrational conflict, all will
be mended merely by thought and forgiveness, and that granted, the
troublemaking Puck pledges himself to "restore amends."

3

Romantic Comedies

Revenge is wicked, & unchristian & in every way unbecoming. . . . (But it is powerful sweet, anyway.)

—Mark Twain, Letter

In the romantic comedies, revenge reaches its climax, both as theme and device.[1] The revenge plots in these plays are triggered by a character whose nature is alien to the world of the play and whose actions motivate the other characters to unite against him. Although there is frequently a gesture of reconciliation extended toward the victim of the revenge, the emphasis is on punishing the erring character in an appropriate fashion, exposing his crimes or follies both to himself and to society, and ensuring that his behavior will change. Although there is little hope that Shylock, Falstaff, Don John, or Malvolio will actually reform, by the end of their plays we are reassured that they no longer pose any threat to their societies.

Considering that revenge is generally held to be an ignoble and distasteful motive, one that most civilized and certainly all Christian people should hold in abhorrence, it is interesting to find that many of the most popular and critically acclaimed of Shakespeare's comedies are those most permeated with revenge. Not only does revenge underlie the main plot in three of these plays, and a subplot that vies in importance with the main plot in a fourth, but additional revenges flourish as well. If revenge is to be condemned out of hand, it will be difficult to find a single admirable character in *The Merry Wives of Windsor* or *Much Ado About Nothing*, and even such heroines as Portia and Rosalind will be suspect.

Clearly, in these comedies, Shakespeare does not condemn revenge; rather, when it is used to correct the behavior of a social offender, he advocates it as a method of obtaining justice through humor. Characters—sometimes themselves revengers—who seek to destroy life, livelihood, and reputation are punished by comic revengers. Bad revengers are contrasted with good revengers in various ways. Shylock and Don

John—and perhaps to some degree Malvolio, who has a grudge against
the world—are given the chance to enumerate the wrongs done to them;
but their motives are weak or nonexistent, and their revenges are dispro-
portionate to their injuries. The good revengers, on the other hand,
although they enforce justice, return good for evil by exacting far less
punishment than the malefactors deserve. Furthermore, the motives of
the alien characters (whether revengers or not) are purely personal,
while the characters who stand in opposition to them are often under no
direct threat—for example, Portia, Beatrice and Benedick, Rosalind, perhaps even Sir Toby Belch—and generally express a concern for defenseless characters or society in general. Finally, if we recognize what the
virtuous characters do in these plays as revenge, we are forced to
acknowledge that revenge can sometimes be a positive force for good,
not only because it is performed by characters who are virtuous and with
whom we are invited to identify, but because the accomplishment of
these revenges leads to the restoration of harmony in the plays' societies.

It seems safe to say, then, that these comedies present a more sophisticated attitude toward revenge than most previous commentators have
noted. Serious revenges against virtuous characters by malevolent ones
are condemned, but such revenges are punished—as are other social
offenses—by comic revenges, which are obviously of a different order.
And because these comic revenges are both apt and amusing, they are
largely responsible for making the romantic comedies among the most
satisfying and successful of Shakespeare's plays.

The Merchant of Venice is the Shakespearean comedy most often associated with revenge, and it marks the epitome of Shakespeare's use of
serious legal revenge as both theme and motivation in the comedies.[2]
After this play, revengers in the comedies tend to be either ineffectual or
frankly comic, and, in either case, to rely on extralegal means. But
Shylock has serious (which is not to say justifiable) motives, a serious
intention, and—in the law—a serious tool.

Whether he is a serious character is, of course, another and apparently
inexhaustibly controvertible question, which has been inspiring critical
comment since at least 1709, when Nicholas Rowe found Shylock an
alien not only in Venice but in the play that features him:

> tho' we have seen the Play Receiv'd and Acted as a Comedy, and the
> Part of the *Jew* perform'd by an excellent Comedian, yet I cannot but
> think that it was design'd Tragically by the Author. There appears in it
> such a deadly Spirit of Revenge, such a savage Fierceness and Fell-
> ness, and such a bloody designation of Cruelty and Mischief, as
> cannot agree either with the Stile or Characters of Comedy.[3]

Rowe's viewpoint has found many modern supporters who believe that, influenced by Christian cruelty and Jewish suffering (Wilson 1962, 105, 112), or his own "unconscious dramatic instinct" (Charlton 1938, 129), Shakespeare portrayed Shylock more or less sympathetically, thereby unbalancing the play. On the other side is the theory that Shylock is merely a stock comic character (Stoll [1927] 1942, 262–75) who "has been the victim of the great actor" (Tillyard 1965, 189). The question of the "true" Shylock is beyond the scope of this study, but consideration of Shylock purely as a revenger may reveal a new facet for discussion.

In the play, we are told that Shylock is a Jew and a usurer, but we are made to see him as a revenger. That is, he does not *do* anything on stage by which we would know, without being told, that he is a Jew or a usurer (his "pound of flesh" bargain, which it is now difficult to separate from the idea of usury, is, as he himself points out [1.3.160–64], ridiculous from a business standpoint); his behavior is entirely that of a committed revenger. There are other Jews, and presumably other usurers, in Venice, but Shylock is Shylock because he seeks revenge.

Unlike most revengers, however, Shylock does not have only one or two reasons for revenge; everything (and ultimately nothing) becomes a reason for his hatred of Antonio, and hatred, he says, justifies murder (4.1.67). In his first soliloquy he states two reasons, racial and economic, for his hatred:

> I hate him for he is a Christian;
> But more, for that in low simplicity
> He lends out money gratis, and brings down
> The rate of usance here with us in Venice.
> If I can catch him once upon the hip,
> I will feed fat the ancient grudge I bear him.
> He hates our sacred nation, and he rails
> Even there where merchants most do congregate
> On me, my bargains, and my well-won thrift,
> Which he calls interest. Cursed be my tribe
> If I forgive him!
>
> (1.3.42–52)

Although critics have been inclined to take Shylock at his word here— that his principal reason for revenge is economic (Prosser 1973, 75, n. 3; Phialas 1966, 154) (a motive reemphasized at 3.1.44–50, 127–29; 3.3.1–2, 21–24)—we are most likely to think him justified in his hatred for his debasement by Antonio. This motive is especially emphasized because Antonio, even when seeking a loan, is not in the least apologetic about his insulting and provocative behavior (1.3.106–37). Even knowing Elizabethan contempt for Jews and usurers (much less Jewish usurers), it is hard not to feel that Shylock's outrage is justified and that Antonio is something of a bully. But Antonio, unattractive as he appears in this light, is at least honest, whereas Shylock, who we know returns Antonio's hatred (with interest, naturally), proceeds to behave not as an outraged Jew or an offended usurer, but as a hypocritical, plotting revenger. His fawning lies (1.3.137–41), comically unnecessary, since they do not deceive Antonio, not only destroy the dignity he had achieved in his preceding speech, but expose him as a far worse character than we had previously imagined: a revenger who not only attempts to conceal his intentions but plans to make the state of Venice his accomplice in murder.

In his most famous speech, Shylock lists a multitude of reasons for enforcing his bond, but enunciates a new one in particular:

> *Salerio:* Why, I am sure if he forfeit thou wilt not take his flesh. What's that good for?
>
> *Shylock:* To bait fish withal—if it will feed nothing else, it will feed my revenge. He hath disgrac'd me, and hind'red me half a million, laugh'd at my losses, mock'd at my gains, scorn'd my nation, thwarted my bargains, cool'd my friends, heated mine enemies; and what's his reason? I am a Jew. Hath not a Jew eyes? Hath not a Jew hands, organs, dimensions, senses, affections, passions; fed with the same food, hurt with the same weapons, subject to the same diseases, heal'd by the same means, warm'd and cool'd by the same winter and summer, as a Christian is? If you prick us, do we not bleed? If you tickle us, do we not laugh? If you poison us, do we not die? And if you wrong us, shall we not revenge? If we are like you in the rest, we will resemble you in that. If a Jew wrong a Christian, what is his humility? Revenge. If a Christian wrong a Jew, what should his sufferance be by Christian example? Why, revenge. The villainy you teach me, I will execute, and it shall go hard but I will better the instruction.
>
> (3.1.51–73)

In this speech Shylock reveals that he has given up his identity both as a usurer, since he no longer cares about profit, and as a Jew, since he is willing to compromise his ethics by conforming to "Christian example." He has instead taken the identity of a revenger, for whom nothing matters but his self-appointed task. Even those parts of his speech which we recognize as true and with which we empathize are presented only to strengthen his case for revenge.[4] Shylock does not attempt to include himself among humanity, but rather to reduce humanity to his level. He no longer cares what else he may be called or become, if only he can become a successful revenger: he will forsake his religion to learn from the Christians;[5] he will forsake his humanity:

Thou call'dst me dog before thou hadst a cause,
But since I am a dog, beware my fangs.

(3.3.6–7)

Even Jessica's flight seems to become a motive for Shylock's revenge against Antonio, as Solanio prophetically predicts (2.8.25–26). Although he never expressly states that this is a further motive, the two events are inextricably linked for both his enemies (3.1.39–43) and his friends (3.1.97–124). Alternatively, it may be supposed that despite his grief and anger over the departure of his daughter with his ducats, his obsession with his revenge has become so great that not even such losses can long distract him.

To what extent Shylock's obsession grows may be indicated in his first speech in the trial scene, in which he ascribes his hatred of Antonio to his "humor" and relates it to other men's natural antipathies, concluding:

So can I give no reason, nor I will not,
More than a lodg'd hate and a certain loathing
I bear Antonio, that I follow thus
A losing suit against him. Are you answered?

(4.1.59–62)

Auden explains this answer (or lack thereof) by defining Shylock as a villain, like Iago, "a person with a general grudge against life and society" ("The Joker in the Pack," 247), which, of course, is difficult or impossible to articulate but which may be inferred from actions taken toward others. A more obvious reason for his silence on this subject is that his previously stated reasons could hardly be expressed in the Doge's court. But Shylock is reticent only momentarily, before his imaginative and rhetorical powers again assert themselves, although as his obsession grows stronger, his stated reasons grow weaker. During the courtroom scene he professes a grim jest, it would seem, a fear of breaking his bond:

An oath, an oath, I have an oath in heaven!
Shall I lay perjury upon my soul?
[No], not for Venice.

(4.1.228–30)

Earlier in the scene he has given a more honest answer, although expressed in the reductive terms of his earlier speech:

You have among you many a purchas'd slave,
Which like your asses, and your dogs and mules,
You use in abject and in slavish parts,

Because you bought them. Shall I say to you,
"Let them be free! Marry them to your heirs!
Why sweat they under burthens? Let their beds
Be made as soft as yours, and let their palates
Be season'd with such viands"? You will answer,
"The slaves are ours." So do I answer you:
The pound of flesh which I demand of him
Is dearly bought as mine, and I will have it.

                                                        (4.1.90–100)

Shylock's revenge at this point is not just his, it is him. And although (as
Stoll points out) it is in one way comic that when balked of it he attempts
to renegotiate for better terms, this may be seen as a last desperate
attempt to extort a measure of "satisfaction" from his defeat in addition to
simple greed. As Stoll says, Shylock "shrivels up" ([1927] 1942, 328); he
dwindles into an almost speechless figure who tamely agrees to his
decreed fate because he has lost the revenger's identity to which he had
sacrificed all others, as Jew, as usurer, and as father.

The loss of Jessica is a direct result of Shylock's growing lust for
revenge, and a foreshadowing that in crying "my deeds upon my head!"
(4.1.206) he is asking for his own just punishment. For, having declared
in his first scene (like an observing Jew) "I will not eat with you" (1.3.36–
37), his lust for revenge has so overpowered his religious scruples that by
that same evening we hear him say:

I am bid forth to supper, Jessica.
There are my keys. But wherefore should I go?
I am not bid for love, they flatter me,
But yet I'll go in hate, to feed upon
The prodigal Christian.

                                                        (2.5.11–15)[6]

It is Shylock's desire to feed his grudge that allows Jessica to escape, and
it may also be inferred that her "prodigality" is a just punishment
(though perhaps not intended by Jessica as such) for his ac-
quisitiveness.[7] As befits his identity as a revenger, Shylock seems more
concerned with getting even than with recovering either his daughter or
his ducats:

She is damn'd for it. (3.1.31)

I would my daughter were dead at my foot, and the jewels in her ear!
(3.1.87–89)

. . . the thief gone with so much, and so much to find the thief, and no
satisfaction, no revenge. . . . (3.1.92–94)

He denies his Jewishness except in the face of personal loss: "The curse never fell upon our nation till now, I never felt it till now" (3.1.85–86). His only consolation is to gloat over his projected revenge against Antonio (3.1.97–107, 113–17).[8]

Despite the mercy rendered Shylock at the end of the trial scene, some critics have found the morality of the scene "repellant" in its persecution of the "human" Shylock and in the levity of the Christians; on the other hand, it has been maintained that "Shylock, a would-be murderer, is let off remarkably lightly."[9] The aspect of the judgment most likely to repel modern readers—the enforced conversion—is, as has been pointed out, "a punishment from Shylock's point of view . . . but from Antonio's point of view, it also gave to Shylock a chance of eternal joy" (Brown, Introduction to the Arden Edition, 1955, xl) and thus functions as justice, revenge, and mercy.

Moreover, the means by which Shylock comes to judgment are peculiarly appropriate, for not only has he called down judgment upon himself ("My deeds upon my head!"), but he has craved the law, rather than justice, and he gets the law and more justice than he has sought.[10] "The victim of his own blood-thirstiness," his obsession has blinded him to the fact that "Portia's rather lengthy homily on 'mercy' is more than mere persuasion; it is a warning that for Shylock it is the last and only [*sic*] chance for salvation" (Chakravorty 1969, 255). It is significant that "his claim to his bond is not denied until he has renounced mercy" (Frye [1965] 1967, 134] not once, but three times.[11] Having offered Shylock several chances to reject revenge, Portia traps him through his own insistence on the letter of the law: "The legal quibble by which Portia saves Antonio is triumphantly and appropriately a quibble. Any sounder argument would be giving Shylock less [*sic*] than his deserts. The bare letter of the law nooses him; and mercy takes the form of another legal instrument. The deed of gift balances the 'mercy bond' " (Bradbrook 1951, 175). Even this, though, is not without an aspect of revenge, for after Antonio proposes the deed of gift and conversion, the Duke threatens:

He shall do this, or else I do recant
The pardon that I late pronounced here.

(4.1.391–92)

This is not far from, and is in fact a more serious threat than, Gratiano's interjection after Portia has asked Antonio what mercy he can render Shylock: "A halter gratis—nothing else, for God's sake" (4.1.379).

Gratiano's comic note of revenge echoes an earlier one by Shylock's *quondam* servant, Launcelot Gobbo: "My master's a very Jew. Give him a present! give him a halter. I am famish'd in his service" (2.2.104–6).

Launcelot seems to be the link between most of the comic references to revenge in the play. He combines a hint at Jessica's disguised flight with a reference to a commonplace of revenge tragedy in his speech to Shylock: "And they have conspir'd together. I will not say you shall see a masque, but if you do, then it was not for nothing that my nose fell a-bleeding on Black Monday last at six a' clock i' th' morning, falling out that year on Ash We'n'sday was four year in th' afternoon" (2.5.22–27). Launcelot may feel his part in this escape as a kind of personal revenge, since he has already declared that Shylock has done him wrong (2.2.132–34). Shylock, for his part, seems to approve Launcelot's leaving as a furtherance of revenge against Antonio and his friends:

> Drones hive not with me,
> Therefore I part with him, and part with him
> To one that I would have him help to waste
> His borrowed purse.

> (2.5.48–51)

Later, in Belmont, we find Launcelot teasing Jessica by professing to believe that she will be damned for her father's sins (3.5.1–6), and she replies by threatening to tell Lorenzo that Launcelot has criticized him for converting a Jew, thereby raising the price of pork (3.5.21–28).[12]

One major, though comic, revenge in the play remains to be dealt with: Portia and Nerissa's revenge on their husbands for giving away their rings. Although revenge may seem too strong a word for this episode, which most critics see as a coda echoing earlier themes of the play, Portia and Nerissa deceive their husbands and make them suffer, however briefly and however mistakenly. If they have no reason to do this, it is wanton cruelty; if they have a reason, it is comic revenge.

The ring is introduced by Portia as symbolizing herself and all that is hers:

> This house, these servants, and this same myself
> Are yours—my lord's!—I give them with this ring,
> Which when you part from, lose, or give away,
> Let it presage the ruin of your love,
> And be my vantage to exclaim on you.

> (3.2.170–74)

And Bassanio professes to take it even more seriously:

> when this ring
> Parts from this finger, then parts life from hence;
> O then be bold to say Bassanio's dead!

> (3.2.183–85)

But Portia and Nerissa (who has also given her husband a ring) soon learn that Bassanio and Gratiano are quick to make free with what they have been freely given:

Bassanio:	Antonio, I am married to a wife
	Which is as dear to me as life itself,
	But life itself, my wife, and all the world,
	Are not with me esteem'd above thy life.
	I would lose all, ay, sacrifice them all
	Here to this devil, to deliver you.
Portia:	Your wife would give you little thanks for that
	If she were by to hear you make the offer.
Gratiano:	I have a wife who I protest, I love;
	I would she were in heaven, so she could
	Entreat some power to change this currish Jew.
Nerissa:	'Tis well you offer it behind her back,
	The wish would make else an unquiet house.

(4.1.282–94)

After the trial, of course, Bassanio gives the disguised Portia his ring, significantly, perhaps, not because of Portia's arguments, but in response to Antonio's plea (4.1.449–51); Gratiano similarly yields up the ring Nerissa has given him. The act ends with Portia declaring her intention of punishing their husbands:

> We shall have old swearing
> That they did give the rings away to men;
> But we'll outface them, and outswear them too.

(4.2.15–17)

On their husbands' arrival in Belmont, the women immediately broach the question of the rings. Although Gratiano attempts to make light of the ring's worth, he is rebuked by his wife:

> What talk you of the posy or the value?
> You swore to me, when I did give [it] you,
> That you would wear it till your hour of death,
> And that it should lie with you in your grave.
> Though not for me, yet for your vehement oaths,
> You should have been respective and have kept it.

(5.1.151–56)

Portia concurs with this opinion and, to twist the knife, adds:

> I gave my love a ring, and made him swear
> Never to part with it, and here he stands.
> I dare be sworn for him he would not leave it,

Nor pluck it from his finger, for the wealth
That the world masters. Now, in faith, Gratiano,
You give your wife too unkind a cause of grief;
And 'twere to me I should be mad at it.

(5.1.170–76)

Poor Bassanio is so guilt-stricken at this that he says to himself:

Why, I were best to cut my left hand off,
And swear I lost the ring defending it.

(5.1.177–78)

Professing not to believe their husbands' protestations, Portia and
Nerissa vow that they will never enter their husbands' beds until they
see their respective rings; that they will sleep with the men who have the
rings; and that they have already lain with the men who had the rings
(5.1.190–92, 223–35, 258–62).

Critics have produced a multitude of explanations for this puzzling
final scene: it is a dramatic effect "created by exploitation of discrepancies
in awareness" (Evans [1960] 1967, 68); its purpose is "to introduce realistic, here bawdy, motifs into the romantic atmosphere of Belmont, and
by so doing to qualify the idealized union of the lovers" (Phialas 1966,
167); "it gives the women a teasing way to relish the fact that they have
played the parts of men as they give up the liberty of that disguise to
become wives" (Barber [1959] 1963, 186). The scene has also been perceived as a summary of the play's themes:

> The ring is the bond transformed, the gentle bond. Since "bond" has
> dinned its leaden echo into our ears for the better part of four acts,
> "ring" is now made to ring out with almost comic but still ominous
> iteration. . . . Like the bond, the ring is of a piece with flesh, so that
> we can hardly tell whether it has made flesh into metal or has itself
> become flesh. . . . Flesh, therefore, may have to be cut for it. . . . And
> in the end Antonio must once again bind himself. . . . (Burckhardt
> 1962, 261)

> . . . in getting over the difficulty, the group provides one final demon-
> stration that human relationships are stronger than their outward
> signs. Once more, Bassanio expresses a harassed perplexity about
> obligations in conflict; and Portia gaily pretends to be almost a Shylock
> about this lover's bond, carrying the logic of the machinery to absurd
> lengths before showing, by the new gift of the ring, love's power to set
> debts aside and begin over again. (Barber [1959] 1963, 187)

The explanation does not, however, appear to be quite that simple, for
even after Bassanio has apologized and promised amendment (5.1.240–
43, 246–48), Antonio has become his surety (5.1.249–53), and Portia has

returned the ring to him, she carries on the punishment by telling Bassanio that she has made him a cuckold. Not only is she quibbling and upsetting Bassanio, but merciful Portia appears to have become merciless. If she has no purpose behind it—if she is not, in fact, teaching him a lesson—her behavior is extraordinary. But what is she trying to teach him?

His prodigality, which more than one critic has deplored, seems an obvious fault in Bassanio. Not only has he given away her ring, he rashly—if rhetorically—vowed away her life in the courtroom scene, to her obvious displeasure. Furthermore, his giving away of the ring seems an obvious link with that other notorious prodigal, Jessica, who has given away her mother's ring (a gift to her father) for a monkey. But the Elizabethans do not seem to have deplored prodigality, and Jessica, far from being criticized by anyone in the play but her father, is rewarded by receiving still more money.

Another possible point of the scene is to emphasize the conflict between love and friendship, although which relationship carries the day is a matter of taste: "The play is meant to be rounded out into a complete comedy by the ring episode . . . which shows that friendship may have greater strength than love; that true love must be forgiving" (Craig 1948, 117); "love normally triumphs over friendship, as Benedick reluctantly challenges Claudio to a duel at Beatrice's command, and sometimes friendship between men is made an obstacle to the comic conclusion, the friendship of Bertram and Parolles being an example" (Frye [1965] 1967, 86). Strangely enough, both of these views, as applied to this play, confront the same difficulty: there is no evidence that any of the characters perceives a conflict between love and friendship. Bassanio appears at one point to place friendship over love, but that is a single statement made under stress. And, in spite of having heard it, Portia shows nothing but graciousness to Antonio (even aside from saving his life), while he exhibits the same attitude toward her (even apart from having risked his life to allow Bassanio to woo her). No such conflict appears in this play.

The final alternative appears to be a lesson for Bassanio in keeping his word, not, presumably, in a "letter-of-the-law" performance like that of Shylock, but in taking care what he says and fulfilling his word. Bassanio's statement that he would gladly sacrifice his wife, his own life, everything, to save Antonio is obviously no threat to Portia; her annoyance may arise less from a fear of being second in Bassanio's affections than from a fear that a man who would say that might say anything. When she discovers that he cannot be trusted to keep his solemn, voluntary oath regarding his wedding ring, she has a right to be angry, even though amused, and she is right to attempt to cure him of

the habit of speaking without thinking. This is not to say that Bassanio is
a conscious liar; he does not lie about giving away the ring, although the
possibility of doing so does occur to him. He merely, like most of
Shakespeare's comic heroes (particularly those of *Love's Labor's Lost*), has
a young person's fault, that of promising much without ever considering
whether he can perform what he promises; he is as unthrifty with words
as with money. But having assumed married status (and risked a friend's
life), it is time for him to settle down to more sober habits; he is now
responsible for more lives than his own. Portia shows him the error of
his ways not only by showing him what may depend on a word, but by
using words in such a way as to totally mislead him without lying to
him. It is a neat comic revenge, but not without a serious purpose.

The Merry Wives of Windsor is the changeling of Shakespeare's comedies. Not only is the play unloved by critics, it is sometimes not even
acknowledged.[13] One of the few critics to devote an entire book to the
play concludes that Shakespeare merely adapted an old play, "a play of
bourgeois life based on some Italian story," of which the hero was Sir John
Oldcastle; that he made a botch even of mere adaptation: "the time-
system of the Folio remains incurably irrational"; and that, finally, "it is
not a play in which Shakespeare seems to have taken much pride or
pleasure" (Crofts 1937, 108, 88, 140).

Even those critics who can tolerate the play generally perceive it as the
least of Shakespeare's comedies, hardly meriting serious discussion.[14]
Yet the play deals with a usually serious theme, although in an un-
serious way: "You might call this a revenge play in the key of farcical
comedy: bourgeois Windsor (concealing Shakespeare's own Stratford)
opposed to a fat and amorous knight from the environs of the Court"
(Trewin 1978, 120). *The Merry Wives* is, in fact, not merely concerned with
revenge: it is obsessed with it. Nearly every character in the play vows
revenge on another, three separate revenge plots (one containing three
separate revenges) are carried out, and those who are not practicing
their own revenges are frequently aiding others'. This alone would seem
enough to create interest in a play whose author was soon to deal with
the same theme in tragedy; but for the most part critics have been unable
to see beyond the bulk of the play's central character.

"What Shakespeare did to Falstaff" is the theme of most of the critical
commentary on *The Merry Wives of Windsor*, and it has driven some critics
into positive frenzies:

From among the plays so bright, so tender, so gracious of these years,
one play—*The Merry Wives of Windsor*—stands apart with a unique
character. It is essentially prosaic, and is indeed the only play of

Shakspere written almost wholly in prose. There is no reason why we should refuse to accept the tradition put upon record by Dennis and by Rowe that *The Merry Wives* was written by Shakspere upon compulsion, by order of Elizabeth, who, in her lust for gross mirth, required the poet to expose his Falstaff to ridicule by exhibiting him, the most delightful of egoists, in love. . . . *The Merry Wives of Windsor* is a play written expressly for the barbarian aristocrats with their hatred of ideas, their insensibility to beauty, their hard efficient manners, and their demand for impropriety.[15]

But, the critic who penned that diatribe concludes, the "fat rogue" of *The Merry Wives of Windsor* is not Falstaff, and this has become the standard attack of those who dislike the play.[16] Some critics take the "offense" done to Falstaff so personally that they seem to believe that Shakespeare saw him as a real person, rather than a theatrical construct:

> [Falstaff] was ruthlessly trampled into extinction by Henry V: casting him off, the King killed his heart. Even more cruelly, so too did Shakespeare. It was murder in Hal; in Shakespeare, the crime worse than parricide—the slaughter of one's own offspring.
> For Shakespeare, so the story runs, was commanded by his Queen to resuscitate the corpse whose heart had been fracted and corroborate, and to show him in love. Shakespeare obeyed: and there can be no clearer evidence of his own rejection of Falstaff. The boisterous merriment of *The Merry Wives of Windsor* is a cynical revenge which Shakespeare took on the hitherto unsuspecting gaiety of his own creative exuberance. (Charlton 1938, 192–93)

Why Shakespeare should have felt compelled to take revenge on his own genius remains an unanswered question. But there is no reason to think that Shakespeare, in *The Merry Wives of Windsor,* was demonstrating his rejection of Falstaff or that he was creating a different character with the same name. Nor does Falstaff differ much from one play to another: he remains an artist of the spoken word, a braggart, and a schemer; nor are his reversals in this play anything extraordinary.[17] One cannot help suspecting that it is not so much Falstaff's defeat per se, as his defeat, not by Hal or Poins, but by two middle-aged, middle-class women that rankles. Ironically, the glorification of the standard critical idea of Falstaff as an endearing lord of misrule has largely destroyed appreciation of the one comedy in which the actual character appears. Either the mystique of Falstaff or *The Merry Wives of Windsor* must be jettisoned, for "since Falstaff's attempt is villainous, the nature of comedy demands his discomfiture, or a repentance that to his idealizers is still more distasteful. The objection to Falstaff's defeat in the *Merry Wives* is, then, an objection to the very nature of comic drama" (Gilbert 1959, 88).

Certainly such an objection is an objection to comic revenge, and therefore unacceptable in terms of this play, which reeks of revenge and swarms with revengers of all shapes, sizes, and justifications. The play's first lines sound the note of legal revenge so often heard in the earlier comedies:

> *Shallow:* Sir Hugh, persuade me not; I will make a Star Chamber matter of it. If he were twenty Sir John Falstaffs, he shall not abuse Robert Shallow, esquire.
>
> (1.1.1–4)

But despite being a "Justice of Peace and Coram" (and *Custa-lorum* and *Rato-lorum*), Shallow would go beyond the law, if he could, to get even with Falstaff:

> Ha! o' my life, if I were young again, the sword should end it. (1.1.40–41)

All of this comes to nothing in the face of Falstaff's defiance and Evans's peacemaking, but another controversy promptly arises: Slender accuses Falstaff's companions of picking his purse, and two of them meet that accusation with threats:

> *Pistol:* . . . Sir John, and master mine,
> I combat challenge of this latten bilbo.
> Word of denial in thy *labras* here!
> Word of denial! Froth and scum, thou liest!
>
> (1.1.161–64)

> *Nym:* Be avis'd, sir, and pass good humors. I will say "marry trap" with you, if you run the nuthook's humor on me—that is the very note of it.
>
> (1.1.166–69)

None of this is developed, and it would seem to have little purpose except to introduce the theme of revenge (and perhaps to establish Pistol and Nym as potential revengers). A number of critics, however, have seen elements of this first scene as indications of personal revenges by Shakespeare in the form of satiric portraits of Sir Thomas Lucy (as Shallow) or of Surrey Justice of the Peace William Gardiner and his stepson and tool William Wayte (as Shallow and Slender, respectively), with the latter of whom, at least, Shakespeare was apparently acquainted.[18] Similar satiric topical allusions have been discovered in other characters: Oliver notes the tentative suggestion that Caius was a caricature of French gynaecologist Peter Chamberlain or a more general " 'satire on the fad for foreign doctors.' "[19] Oliver also notes that "*New*

Cambridge saw . . . a reference to 'Nym' as an alleged short form of 'Hieronimo', the hero of Kyd's *Spanish Tragedy*, and so, particularly as Nym misuses the word 'humour', interpreted him as Shakespeare's caricature of Ben Jonson, who was taunted with having played the Kyd role."[20]

Whether or not Nym is a satiric jab at Jonson, he and Pistol are caricatures:

[Nym's] humor is to terrify by deliberate understatement and vague hints of the dark deeds he could do if he would. By stuffing the word 'humour' at least once into every sentence he utters, he derides what had apparently become a ridiculous over-use of the term among Shakespeare's contemporaries.

Nym's affectation is made the funnier through its continuous contrast with the humor of Pistol. His is an irresistible impulse to form horrendous speeches out of half-remembered tags from old plays written in 'Cambyses vein'. . . . In his contemptuous treatment of Nym and Pistol, Shakespeare was probably attacking a type of petty sharper familiar to anyone who walked the streets of Elizabethan London. (Oscar James Campbell 1943, 72, 76)

Base and ridiculous as Pistol and Nym are, their revenge sets off other revenges, including the only one considered serious—if not too serious—Ford's. In a comic mode, they are classical dramatic revengers: they are injured, having been turned away by Falstaff for refusing to carry his letters to Mistresses Page and Ford. They thereupon vow revenge, in their nearest approach to stately language:

Pistol: Let vultures grip thy guts! for gourd and fullam holds,
And high and low beguiles the rich and poor.
Tester I'll have in pouch when thou shalt lack,
Base Phrygian Turk!
Nym: I have operations [in my head] which be humors of revenge.
(1.3.85–90)

They plot:

Pistol: Wilt thou revenge?
Nym: By welkin and her star!
Pistol: With wit or steel?
Nym: With both the humors, I.
I will discuss the humor of this love to [Page].
Pistol: And I to [Ford] shall eke unfold
How Falstaff (varlet vile)
His dove will prove, his gold will hold,
And his soft couch defile.
(1.3.91–99)

Nym goes so far as to claim he "will incense [Page] to deal with poison,"
(1.3.100–101) the most feared and hated of the revenger's weapons.[21]
They promptly deliver their messages and all but disappear from the
stage.

Ford and Page are left to make sense of this wholly unexpected
information; they cannot, however, come to any agreement:

> *Ford:* Do you think there is truth in them?
> *Page:* Hang 'em, slaves! I do not think the knight would offer it; but
> these that accuse him in his intent towards our wives are a yoke
> of his discarded men—very rogues, now they be out of service.
> *Ford:* Were they his men?
> *Page:* Marry, were they.
>
> (2.1.172–78)

Page correctly considers that revenge may be the motive for these accusations and therefore, incorrectly, discounts them. Ford, on the other
hand, remarks: "I like it never the better for that" (2.1.179). But Page has
a better reason for ignoring this report:

> If he should intend this voyage toward my wife, I would turn her loose
> to him; and what he gets more of her than sharp words, let it lie on my
> head. (2.1.181–84)

But Ford cannot accept this, either:

> I do not misdoubt my wife; but I would be loath to turn them together.
> A man may be too confident. I would have nothing lie on my head. I
> cannot be thus satisfied. (2.1.185–88)

Ford immediately proves that a man may be too suspicious, as well, by
arranging with the Host of the Garter to introduce him, disguised,
under an assumed name.[22] His credulity in this instance is in some part
explained by Mrs. Quickly, who tells Falstaff that Ford is "a very jealousy
man" who leads his wife "a very frampold life" (2.2.89–90). Thus, stung
on his sore point by Pistol's accusation, Ford rapidly falls into a revenger's role, utilizing disguise and trickery—having told the Host he is
doing this "only for a jest" (2.1.216), sneering at Page as "a secure fool"
and "a secure ass" (2.1.233; 2.2.300–301), and finally vowing to "detect
my wife, be reveng'd on Falstaff, and laugh at Page" (2.2.310–11).

Ford's suspicions grow progressively wilder: after meeting Mrs. Page
and Falstaff's page, Robin, on their way to visit his wife, he leaps to the
absurd—though, due to the wives' plotting, correct—conclusion that the
two women have a joint rendezvous with Falstaff. His thoughts of
revenge attain more violent expression:

Good plots, they are laid, and our revolted wives share damnation together. Well, I will take him, then torture my wife, pluck the borrow'd veil of modesty from the so-seeming Mistress Page, divulge Page himself for a secure and willful Actaeon; and to these violent proceedings all my neighbors shall cry aim. (3.2.38–44)

So sure is he of his suspicions that he invites the neighbors he has brought home with him to witness his vengeance to take revenge on him if he is wrong: "If I suspect without cause, why then make sport at me, then let me be your jest, I deserve it" (3.3.149–51). Falstaff's escape in the buck-basket (the very word "buck" causes the frenzied Ford additional mental anguish) affords both Mistress Ford ("I know not which pleases me better, that my husband is deceiv'd, or Sir John") and his neighbors ("(trust me) we'll mock him") opportunity for comic revenge on his jealousy (3.3.157–59, 178–79, 228–29).

Ford again assumes his disguise and visits Falstaff, who tells him of his escape and vows another attempt. Ford's fury increases to the point where he himself seems the principal object of his revenge: "Well, I will proclaim myself what I am. . . . If I have horns to make one mad, let the proverb go with me: I'll be horn-mad" (3.5.143–44, 150–52). The only horns he has, of course, are in his own imagination: Falstaff, honest for once, has told him he has not succeeded. But Ford will not be denied his self-induced and increasing madness, as Mistress Page describes his approach in his second attempt to catch Falstaff:

Why, woman, your husband is in his old lines again. He so takes on yonder with my husband; so rails against all married mankind; so curses all Eve's daughters, of what complexion soever; and so buffets himself on the forehead, crying, "Peer out, peer out!", that any madness I ever yet beheld seem'd but tameness, civility, and patience to this his distemper he is in now. (4.2.21–28)

Ford's neighbors also think him mad (4.2.122–27). This scene parallels the previous search: Ford offers himself as a butt of mockery if proved wrong (4.2.161–64) and is unable to find Falstaff (though he beats him nevertheless). But the wives now reveal the situation to their husbands; Ford professes to be cured of jealousy, and asks pardon, but he is able to continue as a comic revenger by joining in the final plot against Falstaff.

A standard critical reaction to this plot strand is expressed by Dowden (quoting Hartley Coleridge): " 'Ford's jealousy is of too serious a complexion for the rest of the play' " (1881, 330). Even aside from the baseless assumption that comedy cannot deal with serious subjects, this assertion is open to question. Ford's jealousy is established as a character trait antedating the events of the play; he is a comic type—the jealous husband—not an ordinary man suddenly and reasonably given cause to suspect his wife. He is not wronged; against all the evidence but the word of the lying Falstaff and his cast-off men—and even having been told by Falstaff that he has been unsuccessful—he persists in defining himself as a cuckold, his wife and Mistress Page as loose women, Page as a gull, and, most ridiculously, Falstaff as a gallant seducer. The audience knows that Ford is a fool, and this effectively nullifies his threats. As Wilson concludes, Ford's jealousy "is not taken seriously by anyone but himself" (1962, 91).

Page is free of Ford's brand of foolishness, but he exhibits a folly of his own, and with it a vengeful tendency. He believes not only that he can thwart young love, but that he has a right to do so. He will not allow his daughter to marry young Master Fenton, whom she loves and who loves her; and if they marry despite him, he is prepared to spite them:

> The gentleman is of no having. He kept company with the wild Prince and Poins; he is of too high a region, he knows too much. No, he shall not knit a knot in his fortunes with the finger of my substance. If he take her, let him take her simply. The wealth I have waits on my consent, and my consent goes not that way. (3.2.71–78)

This would not be an unreasonable speech taken in isolation; but we know that the man whom Page favors as a son-in-law is that inimitable ass Master Slender, who has not wit enough to keep him warm. That Page can be so wrongheaded as to oppose true love in favor of Slender is a clear indication that he, like his friend Ford, is headed for a fall.

Page and Ford, however, are fools only temporarily and in one respect. The play contains two revenge-obsessed characters who are fools in every respect: Caius and Evans. Much of their foolishness, of course, is shown by the way they make "fritters of English" (5.5.143); but it is not only their mispronunciation and bad grammar that is ludicrous. At one point, they unconsciously damn themselves by their misuse of the language:

> *Evans.* If there be any pody in the house, and in the chambers, and in the coffers, and in the presses, heaven forgive my sins at the day of judgment!
> *Caius.* Be-gar, nor I too. . . .
>
> (3.3.210–13)

Their behavior is of a piece with their language. They begin by quarreling over a woman, which would not in itself be absurd, except that Caius picks a quarrel with Evans, who is only an intermediary, rather than with either of his rivals, Slender and Fenton:

You jack'nape, give-a this letter to Sir Hugh. By gar, it is a shallenge. I will cut his troat in de park; and I will teach a scurvy jack-a-nape priest to meddle or make. . . . By gar, I will cut all his two stones; by gar, he shall not have a stone to throw at his dog. (1.4.107–13)[23]

In the next scene, we learn that mine Host of the Garter "hath had the measuring of their weapons" and "hath appointed them contrary places" (2.1.207–09). By the time we see them pacing their separate grounds, each is mocking the other with respect to his profession and courage (2.3.6–7, 31–32; 3.1.13–15, 65–67). Evans, clearly, is not anxious to fight; but it is not until the Host explains how he has forestalled their duel that they make up their quarrel—and then they are not only reconciled but become friends and allies in revenge (3.1.117–26). It seems rather hard on the Host that he should suffer their malice for having saved their skins, but he is to some degree convicted out of his own mouth:

Peace, I say! hear mine host of the Garter. Am I politic? Am I subtle? Am I a Machiavel? . . . Boys of art, I have deceiv'd you both; I have directed you to wrong places. (3.1.100–101, 107–8)

Though we applaud the outcome of his plotting, his means—policy and subtlety—are, conventionally, those of dramatic villains (especially villainous revengers), not heroes. And, although he obviously delights in being "a Machiavel," the term has traditional dramatic overtones of hypocritical evil. This is not to say that the Host is evil, but by this self-description he has set the stage for a performance of "the biter bit," with himself in the title role. By the end of 3.3, Caius and Evans have planned their revenge, although as Oliver notes, "the audience still does not know what form the vengeance is to take" (the Arden edition, 1971, 90, n. 221–25).

In fact, according to some critics, the audience never does learn the form of this revenge, for the only possible candidate for that episode in the play is what has been called "surely the worst-handled episode in all Shakespeare's plays" (Bullough 1957, 2:11): the horse-stealing subplot. One theory is that the scene linking the Caius-Evans plot to the horse-stealing scene has been lost:

To reconstruct this lost episode is of course impossible, but its outline can at least be guessed at from certain indications that remain in the text. In the scenes that led up to it we find that Caius and Sir Hugh are vowing vengeance on the Host, that Pistol and Nym have a grudge against Falstaff, and that the two merry wives have decided to give Falstaff "a show of comfort in his Suit, and lead him on with a fine baited delay, till he hath pawn'd his horses to mine host of the Garter." (II.i.88) In later scenes the Host is complaining of heavy loss (IV.vi.1), the horses have been arrested at the suit of Ford (V.v.111), and the revenges are apparently complete, since we hear no more about them.

Taking these indications at their face-value we should infer that there had been some device by which Falstaff's horses, pawned to the Host as security for a debt, had been taken from his possession in such a manner as to leave him no means of redress. (Crofts 1937, 44–45; see also Bullough 1957, 2:11)

Another theory holds that the scene "comes out of nothing and goes nowhere":

A rereading of [the relevant lines] from IV.v . . . . will reveal that the lines that Caius and Evans utter when they warn the Host about the Cozen-Germans and the Duke who is not to come do not in any way give a hint that the horse-stealing episode is the revenge plan which the two duelists have executed. It is, of course, possible not to accept at face value the words of Caius and Evans when, after giving their news to the Host, they tell him respectively, " 'tis not convenient you should be cozoned" and "I tell you for good will." The interlinking, then of the two incidents—the trick played on the Host and the revenge scheme—comes not on the authority of text but from the interpretations of editors seeking a resolution of the revenge scheme, which otherwise dies in III.iii. (Green 1962, 151, 159–60)

As a coup de grâce, this critic adds that "to steal these horses—no doubt post horses—is a scheme that is completely incompatible with the characters of the doctor and parson as well as with Shakespeare's portrayal of village life in the play. With the value of horses so great in Elizabethan days, the theft of these would have been a major crime, far out of line with the degree of revenge Caius and Evans might have planned" (1962, 160–61).

Critics who hold either of these views—lost scene or inexplicable excresence—generally maintain that the horse-stealing scene functioned mainly as a topical reference. There is, however, little agreement as to the subject of the reference.[24]

"Now this is like the mending of highways / In summer when the ways are fair enough!" As Oliver points out, the horse-stealing subplot is "not connected in any way with the two main 'intrigue' plots—other than that they are all variations on the tale of the biter bit and that all these involve the deflating of a character who thinks himself safe from deception" (Introduction to the Arden edition, 1971, lxxv). The wives' reference to forcing Falstaff to pawn his horses and Ford's arrest of those horses have nothing to do with the Host's horses, nor do Nym and Pistol, who have already taken revenge on Falstaff by reporting his intended amours, necessarily come into it (although they might as easily enact "Germans" as Pistol enacts a fairy in the final scene).[25] The Host complains of "heavy loss" after learning of the cozen-Germans' flight with his horses. Furthermore, it is not only "possible not to accept at face value the words of Caius and Evans" (4.5.75–82, 86–89), it is impossible to do otherwise. Not only do we know that Caius and Evans are nursing a grudge against the Host that makes honest concern for his welfare improbable, but their knowledge of the plot and the timing of their warnings are inexplicable unless they are behind the scheme; finally, Evans's language—"gibes" and "vlouting-stocks"—echoes his language when he and Caius discuss the trick played on them (3.1.117–18; 3.3.242–43).[26]

As for the theft of horses being too great a revenge, such an assertion is hard to justify in two characters willing to duel over so slight a quarrel. Nor do we know that the horses are permanently gone, though the Host naturally leaps to that conclusion. At any rate, we know that the Host will suffer no real loss, for Fenton promises him "a hundred pound in gold more than your loss" (4.6.5) for his assistance, which is given.[27]

Granted, the episode is untidy, principally because the revengers don't reveal themselves and gloat over the Host's discomfiture. But the circumstantial evidence is strong: Evans and Caius feel wronged by the Host; they make a plan and vow to put it into operation "to-morrow" (3.3.239–40); in the next act, a trick is played on the Host, immediately after which the two revengers appear with sarcastic warnings that come too late.

The one serious difficulty in accepting this obvious explanation is the time scheme. Evans and Caius plan their revenge for "to-morrow," although at 4.3.9–10, the Host declares the Germans "have had my [house] a week at command." But in this scene, the Host is clearly addled; although Bardolph refers to a single man with whom he assumes the Host to be acquainted—"Sir, the German desires to have three of your horses" (4.3.1–2)—the Host, although not questioning this reference, takes it to mean a group of men with whom he has never spoken: "Let me speak with the gentlemen. They speak English?" (4.3.5–6). Bardolph grants that at least one of them does; the Host then announces that he will rent them his horses, although they owe him a week's room and board. How could it be that the voluble Host would refrain from speaking to guests who have taken over his house for a week and yet trust them to leave him on his own horses? It is inexplicable except by assuming that the scene, as we have it, is faulty, an assumption supported by the obvious incongruity in number of Germans between the Host's speeches and Bardolph's.[28]

So permeated with revenge is *The Merry Wives* that even the slightest characters express vengeful feelings, if only on themselves (Slender, 1.1.248) or, like Mistress Quickly, on imaginary beings: "Vengeance of

Jinny's case! Fie on her! never name her, child, if she be a whore"
(4.1.62–63). Mistress Quickly also professes to see a divine vengeance in
Falstaff's vexation: "Sure, one of you does not serve heaven well, that you
are so cross'd" (4.5.125–26). In this statement, she is unconsciously
echoing Falstaff's earlier conclusion that heaven is punishing him for his
sins: "I never prosper'd since I forswore myself at primero" (4.5.101–2).
Unable to discern an earthly cause for his troubles, Falstaff—the object of
so many revenges—becomes generally vengeful. He vows specific revenge on Ford (5.1.26–29), but he also calls down maledictions on the
wives, even though he does not yet suspect them: "The devil take one
party and his dam the other! and so they shall be both bestow'd"
(4.5.106–7). His vengefulness reaches even further: he wishes ill on the
world, not only for what has happened to him, but out of fear of the
malicious comic revenge that will be taken on him if the court learns of
his misadventures:

> I would all the world might be cozen'd, for I have been cozen'd and
> beaten too. If it should come to the ear of the court, how I have been
> transform'd, and how my transformation hath been wash'd and
> cudgell'd, they would melt me out of my fat drop by drop, and liquor
> fishermen's boots with me. I warrant they would whip me with their
> fine wits till I were as crestfall'n as a dried pear. (4.5.93–100)[29]

The principal revenge of the play, that of the wives on Falstaff, does
not begin until act 2. Following the rantings of Pistol, Nym, and Caius
over their imagined wrongs, the responses of the wives to the genuine
insult of Falstaff's propositions appear entirely justified as well as consciously witty:

Mrs. Page: What a Herod of Jewry is this! O wicked, wicked world!
One that is well-nigh worn to pieces with age to show
himself a young gallant! What an unweigh'd behavior
hath this Flemish drunkard pick'd (with the devil's name!)
out of my conversation, that he dares in this manner assay
me? Why, he hath not been thrice in my company! What
should I say to him? I was then frugal of my mirth.
Heaven forgive me! Why, I'll exhibit a bill in the parlia-
ment for the putting down of men. How shall I be reveng'd on him? for reveng'd I will be! as sure as his guts
are made of puddings.

                                              (2.1.20–32)

Mrs. Ford: I shall think the worse of fat men, as long as I have an eye
to make difference of men's liking: and yet he would not
swear; [prais'd] women's modesty; and gave such orderly
and well-behav'd reproof to all uncomeliness, that I

would have sworn his disposition would have gone to the truth of his words; but they do no more adhere and keep place together than the hundred Psalms to the tune of "Green-sleeves." What tempest, I trow, threw this whale (with so many tuns of oil in his belly) ashore at Windsor? How shall I be reveng'd on him? I think the best way were to entertain him with hope, till the wicked fire of lust have melted him in his own grease.

(2.1.55–68)

Mrs. Page: To thy great comfort in this mystery of ill opinions, here's the twin-brother of thy letter; but let thine inherit first, for I protest mine never shall. I warrant he hath a thousand of these letters, writ with blank space for different names (sure, more!); and these are of the second edition. He will print them, out of doubt; for he cares not what he puts into the press, when he would put us two. I had rather be a giantess, and lie under Mount Pelion.

(2.1.71–80)

In these speeches the wives provide a host of reasons for their revenge. Falstaff is fat and old, past the suitable time for courting. He is only slightly acquainted with them and they have given him no reason to think they would welcome his advances. He has hypocritically represented himself as an honorable man while a guest in their houses. Above all, his assumption that they would yield to him is an insult to their honor, while his simultaneous wooing of them is an insult to both their self-respect and their intelligence. Their instantly conceived plan for revenge—"let's appoint him a meeting, give him a show of comfort in his suit, and lead him on with a fine-baited delay till he hath pawn'd his horses to mine host of the Garter" (2.1.90–94)—is perfectly designed to trap Falstaff by means of his overweening self-esteem and punish him in his most tender spot: his purse.[30]

On the way to their ultimate, economic vengeance, the wives also manage a series of lesser revenges. Not only do they arrange for Falstaff to be thrown in the river and beaten, but each woman teases him by suggesting that he loves the other (3.3.75–76, 139–40), and Mrs. Ford skewers him with sharp irony: "Well, heaven knows how I love you, and you shall one day find it" (3.3.80–81). Nor are the wives above delighting in a bit of revenge on Ford, for his unwarranted jealousy: "I know not which pleases me better, that my husband is deceiv'd, or Sir John" (3.3.178–79), says Mrs. Ford after Falstaff's departure in the buck-basket, adding a few lines later, "I think my husband hath some special suspicion of Falstaff's being here, for I never saw him so gross in his jealousy till now" (3.3.187–89). Mrs. Page's reply is, "I will lay a plot to try that"

(3.3.190), although we never learn that she does so. But Ford's unexpected appearance during Falstaff's second visit does allow them to "try" Ford's intelligence by again presenting him with the buck-basket (4.2.91–96).

The wives show a mixture of attitudes toward their own activities. At first they appear to be set on revenging the insult to their honesty (2.1.98–100); then they begin to discuss their plots in terms of teaching or curing Falstaff (3.3.42, 190–92). Vengeance continues to be a motive— "Hang him, dishonest varlet! we cannot misuse [him] enough" (4.2.102– 3)—but by the time of the second plot, Mrs. Page is characterizing their revenge as a dramatic proof of the virtue of all merry wives:

> We'll leave a proof, by that which we will do,
> Wives may be merry, and yet honest too:
> We do not act that often jest and laugh;
> 'Tis old, but true: still swine eats all the draff.
>
> (4.2.104–7)

After Falstaff's beating, the wives conclude they have taken sufficient vengeance, for "the spirit of wantonness is sure scar'd out of him" (4.2.209–10). But after deciding to tell their husbands what they have done, "if it be but to scrape the figures out of [Ford's] brains" (4.2.215– 16), the wives seem loath to conclude the jest:

> *Mrs. Page:* If they can find in their hearts the poor unvirtuous fat
> knight shall be any further afflicted, we two will still be the
> ministers.
> *Mrs. Ford:* I'll warrant they'll have him publicly sham'd, and methinks
> there would be no period to the jest, should he not be
> publicly sham'd.
> *Mrs. Page:* Come, to the forge with it, then shape it. I would not have
> things cool.
>
> (4.2.216–24)

The good wives do not allow things to cool, for after revealing the story to their husbands, hearing Ford repent, and receiving their husbands' assent to a public disgrace for Falstaff, they once more fall to plotting. Ford and Page, while enthusiastic, are not very helpful: Mrs. Ford tells the men to

> Devise but how you'll use him when he comes,
> And let us two devise to bring him thither.
>
> (4.4.26–27)

But after the women describe their portion of the plan, Page asks, "What shall be done with him? What is your plot?" (4.4.46). No matter: the women have formed the plot to its last detail (4.4.47–65), and all conclude, in Evans's words, "It is admirable pleasures and fery honest knaveries" (4.4.80–81).[31]

This final plot centers around "fairies," who are clearly regarded as capable of revenge, though in this instance, at least, not such serious revenge as Falstaff images:

> *Pistol* [*as Hobgoblin*]: Elves, list your names; silence, you aery toys!
>   Cricket, to Windsor chimneys shalt thou leap;
>   Where fires thou find'st unrak'd and hearths unswept,
>   There pinch the maids as blue as bilberry;
>   Our radiant Queen hates sluts and sluttery.
> *Falstaff:* They are fairies, he that speaks to them shall die.
>   I'll wink and couch; no man their works must eye.
>   (5.5.42–48)[32]

The "Welsh devil Hugh" having instructed the fairies to pinch "those as sleep and think not on their sins" (5.5.53), the action leads naturally into the trial of the discovered Falstaff's chastity and his consequent punishment of pinching and burning (5.5.84–102). Mrs. Page appears ready to call a halt to the jest (5.5.105), but she, like the others, including Evans, cannot resist mocking Falstaff and gloating over him for some time (5.5.106–69). When Page finally seeks to cheer Falstaff up, he does so by attempting to turn the laughter at the victim of another plot: "Yet be cheerful, knight. Thou shalt eat a posset to-night at my house, where I will desire thee to laugh at my wife, that now laughs at thee. Tell her Master Slender hath married her daughter" (5.5.170–73). In the series of discoveries that follow, Slender and Caius receive the just rewards of fools,[33] the Pages the disappointed expectations of parents who try to thwart true love, and Falstaff, at long last, gets a laugh at two of his tormentors: "I am glad, though you have ta'en a special stand to strike at me, that your arrow hath glanc'd" (5.5.234–35).

Ultimately, as Prosser states, "the sanity of Windsor welcomes Falstaff back with laughter" (1973, 75), and justly so; Ford has been jealous without cause, Page has preferred money to love, even Mrs. Page has lied to Fenton (3.4.88–92; 4.4.88–90): "Hence as an individual Falstaff has as much right to be at the final party as Ford and Page have" (Frye [1965] 1967, 91). The only remaining outsider is Caius, who storms off in a rage.[34]

In *The Idea of Revenge in Shakespeare*, Chakravorty asserts that "one thing that emerges prominently from Shakespeare's plays is that Shakespeare is never keen on celebrating the triumph of revenge as such. He always stresses values which are higher than crude revenge" (1969, 257). "Crude revenge" is the significant phrase here, for the plotting of the wives, judged by their motivations, intent, and outcome, is anything but crude. Despite the broad humor of the revenges, there is no sustained ill will in the play, with the exception of Caius; Page, while waiting to help play the final trick on Falstaff, speaks a line that summarizes the play: "No man means evil but the devil" (no, nor woman neither) (5.2.12–13). In the context of comedy, Falstaff is justly punished, and despite our humane (as, perhaps, opposed to human) distaste for revenge and its underhanded means, it is impossible to disagree with Mrs. Page:

> Against such lewdsters, and their lechery,
> Those that betray them do no treachery.
>
> (5.3.21–22)

In its use of revenge to punish immorality (possibly, in Falstaff's case, amorality), expose folly, and restore social harmony, *The Merry Wives of Windsor* represents a triumph of sophisticated comic revenge.

Much Ado About Nothing is almost as obsessed with revenge as *The Merry Wives of Windsor,* although in *Much Ado* the various revenges are much more tightly interwoven than in *The Merry Wives.* Don John seeks to revenge himself on his brother's favorite, Claudio, and thereby on Don Pedro himself; he attempts to accomplish this by falsely accusing Claudio's fiancée, Hero, of infidelity. Claudio, with Don Pedro in support, takes revenge on Hero, an action that inspires Hero's cousin, Beatrice, to incite her fiancé, Benedick, to take revenge on Claudio. Hero's father, Leonato, vows his own revenge on Hero if the accusation is true, and on Claudio and Don Pedro if it is false.

Such dependence on revenge is unusual in a comedy, and may suggest why one critic has described *Much Ado* as a play "which sights tragedy without reaching it" (Trewin 1978, 132). In particular, Don John's plot, which inspires all the others in the series, has been viewed as "a complication potentially as grave as that of 'Othello,' and indeed analogous to it" (Van Doren 1939, 143). As in such earlier comedies as *A Midsummer Night's Dream* and *The Merchant of Venice,* vengeance is thwarted by law, but in *Much Ado* the vengeance is extralegal, and the law is represented not by a figure of authority but by a rabble of muddleheaded clowns.

All of the revenge in *Much Ado* begins with Don John, whose character, as Bullough points out, is an invention of Shakespeare (1957, 2:72). Don John's prototypes in the sources—Ariosto, Bandello, and Spenser—do what they do for love of the Hero figure. While this clearly is not Don John's motive, his causes and his character have both been the subjects of critical disagreement. Bullough sees Don John as "a Malcontent of a kind just emerging in satire and the theatre" (1957, 2:72). Smith describes him as "a kind of devil . . . but . . . not a devil conceived in the spirit of tragedy" (Introduction to the Arden edition, xvii). Bradbrook sees Don John as a "very mechanical" villain (1951, 179). George Bernard Shaw finds him more evil than Shakespeare's other villains and therefore less developed: "William's villains are all my eye: neither Iago, Edmund, Richard nor Macbeth have any real malice in them. When William did a really malicious creature, like Don John, he couldnt take any real interest in him" ([1903] 1961, 172).[35]

Each of these descriptions contains elements of truth, but in addition, Don John is perhaps Shakespeare's nearest approach to the traditional stage revenger. Wronged, as he feels, before the play opens, his object is of more concern to him (and to the audience) than his motives. Unlike most of Shakespeare's revengers, but like many revengers of contemporary drama, he has no interest, in himself or for us, outside of revenge. He is surrounded by the trappings of the conventional dramatic revenger—intrigue, treachery, accomplices. Although he is not a tragic figure, he may be seen as a character from the conventional revenge tragedy who has somehow strayed into the comic world. His easy defeat by Dogberry et al. may be Shakespeare's commentary on the inferiority of the standard stage revenger, with his limited imagination and his limitless thirst for blood.

Both of these conventional characteristics are attributable to Don John. His limited imagination is apparent from his first speech, as barren an introduction to a character as any in Shakespeare: "I thank you. I am not of many words, but I thank you" (1.1.157–58). Though his companion, Conrade, recognizes that it is to Don John's advantage to dissemble, Don John insists he cannot:

> I cannot hide what I am: I must be sad when I have cause, and smile at no man's jests; eat when I have stomach, and wait for no man's leisure; sleep when I am drowsy, and tend on no man's business; laugh when I am merry, and claw no man in his humor. (1.3.13–18)

Not only does Don John see himself as a slave to his own appetites and emotions, but he presents himself as a slave of his fortune as well; the extent of his activity is to be publicly miserable and dream of what he would do if he could:

> I had rather be a canker in a hedge than a rose in his grace, and it better fits my blood to be disdain'd of all than to fashion a carriage to rob love from any. In this (though I cannot be said to be a flattering honest man) it must not be denied but I am a plain-dealing villain. I

am trusted with a muzzle, and enfranchis'd with a clog, therefore I
have decreed not to sing in my cage. If I had my mouth, I would bite;
if I had my liberty, I would do my liking. In the mean time let me be
that I am, and seek not to alter me. (1.3.27–36)

Don John has not even the assertiveness of "Misery loves company," for
when Conrade asks him "Can you make no use of your discontent?" he
replies, "I make all use of it, for I use it only" (1.3.38–39).

So passive a villain is Don John that if we were not told that he has
lately rebelled against his brother, we could never have imagined he had
it in him. Luckily for the play's plot development, he has a more active
and inventive accomplice in Borachio, who brings him news of "an
intended marriage" (1.3.42–45). The limitlessness of Don John's malignity is demonstrated by his asking "Will it serve for any model to build
mischief on?" (1.3.46–47) even before he knows that the marriage is to be
that of his "enemy" Claudio. But once he learns this fact, he determines
to see if the opportunity can be turned to account:

Come, come, let us thither, this may prove food to my displeasure.
That young start-up hath all the glory of my overthrow. If I can cross
him any way, I bless myself every way. (1.3.65–68)

Don John's final speech in this scene highlights both his bloodthirstiness
and his lack of imagination. He is going to supper with people who, to
the extent that they give him any thought at all, seem willing to let his
past bad behavior be forgotten; and he is presented with an opportunity
for revenge that, from any of Shakespeare's other villains, would have
produced a full-blown plot in an instant. Yet all Don John can manage to
think of at this moment is a totally undeserved "vengeance" of which he
dares not even imagine himself the perpetrator:

Let us to the great supper, their cheer is the greater that I am subdu'd.
Would the cook were a' my mind! Shall we go prove what's to be
done? (1.3.71–74)[36]

The incompetence of the plotters becomes obvious at their next appearance. Not only is it difficult to imagine what they expect to gain by
deceiving Claudio about Don Pedro's intentions toward Hero, but—
despite the fact that Borachio has overheard Don Pedro's plot to "woo
Hero for himself, and having obtain'd her, give her to Count Claudio"
(1.3.62–64) and has reported it to Don John—they now inexplicably
appear to believe that Don Pedro is in fact "amorous on Hero" (2.1.155–
57).[37] They do succeed in the not-very-difficult task of convincing
Claudio to doubt what he knows, but the only result is to make him
unhappy for a short time.

At the plotters' next appearance, Don John is again passive; Borachio takes the active role. Don John seems to have regressed even further since the opening scenes: he is now so dull that everything must be explained to him (2.2.7–29). Don John becomes Borachio's henchman in this plot; Borachio tells him what to do and how to do it (2.2.33–50). Don John performs his messenger's task without incident, largely owing to Claudio's readiness to believe whatever anyone tells him. The Bastard makes his final appearance at the first wedding scene, where as accuser he plays a very weak third fiddle to Claudio and Don Pedro, and then this most passive of Shakespearean villains disappears. We are told that he has fled from Messina (4.2.61 and again at 5.1.190–91) for no very obvious reason, since Borachio's confession has not yet been made public; and in the last lines of the play a messenger appears to report his capture and Benedick promises to devise "brave punishments for him" on the morrow (5.4.125–28).

This is rather ungrateful of Benedick, since, as Smith points out, "it is Don John's plot, not his brother's, which finally unites [Beatrice and Benedick] and makes one match where it has aimed at ruining another" (Introduction to the Arden edition, xx). In fact, it would seem that Don John was less interested in simply thwarting the marriage than in making all of the play's virtuous characters as unhappy as possible. In the interests of justice, it is necessary that we know Don John will be punished; but as either a character or an effective force of evil, Shakespeare might as well have let him go. He has "the will but not the wit to conceive" (Smith, Introduction to the Arden edition, xvii).[38] Without such a tool as Borachio, Don John is helpless. Nor can we expect that punishment will make him more miserable than he already is, for he has never shown any joy either in the accomplishment of his revenge or in plotting for its own sake. Unlike Shakespeare's other villains—and even his mere comic butts—Don John has no soliloquies, virtually no character, in fact, apart from his sheer anhedonia. The perfectly correct revenge taken on the character of Don John is that, in spite of his malice and "his" machinations, no one—in the play or out of it—really cares enough about him to worry about what will happen to him. To the extent that the "ado" of this play is caused by Don John, it is indeed "about nothing."

Much more disturbing than the conventional vengefulness of Don John is the unconventional vengefulness of Claudio and Don Pedro. Just as Shakespeare provides a revenge motive for Don John, so he heightens Claudio's revenge upon the "faithless" Hero by inventing the scene of her public shaming.[39] This scene presents Claudio and, to a lesser extent, Don Pedro as dramatic revengers. Their revenge is honorable in that it is public and, as they believe, justified, but it appears dishonorable in that it is taken on a helpless and, as we know, innocent woman. To some degree, this revenge may be seen merely as a function of the central plot device, "the alacrity of persons to perpetrate practices and to be deceived by others' practices" (Evans [1960] 1967, 72). On the other hand, while all of the play's major characters (except, perhaps, Hero) at least attempt to become revengers, all but Claudio have motives based in fact; he alone undertakes a "successful" revenge for an imaginary injury. (The credulity of Don Pedro—older, presumably wiser, and certainly less emotionally involved—is explained by himself in terms of his honor and friendship [4.1.64–65] but is really explicable only in terms of the exigencies of the plot.) Claudio is therefore the only virtuous character in *Much Ado* to be presented as an unjustified revenger, and it is a triumph of Shakespeare's portraiture that we do not see him as the villain of the piece.

The explanation of Claudio's behavior, like that of so many of Shakespeare's flawed comic heroes, is youth and the natural limitations of youth.[40] Our first report of Claudio is of a young hero; but before the first scene of the play is finished we have seen him as a young lover too insecure to do his own wooing. He is, therefore, a figure of fun from his first appearance. His gullibility in the face of Don John's scheme, the suddenness of his decision to seek revenge (even before the accusation against Hero is tested), and his vehemence in carrying it out are well prepared for by our earlier glimpses of him.[41]

At least one critic sees in Claudio another characteristic popularly considered common to youth—idealism—and therefore finds the time and place of his denunciation peculiarly appropriate:

> He chooses to denounce her at the wedding ceremony because there mere words are to stand for deepest thoughts and bridal garments for inward beauty: it will enable Claudio to say effectively that which he can scarely think. His choice is not due to heartlessness as Beatrice too readily assumes, but to the uncertainty he had always striven against, to the purity of his ideal, and to the blind, destructive rage of his disappointment in which he can pity but not feel for Hero. (Brown 1962, 114–15)[42]

It must also be said, however, that if Claudio is an exemplar of youth's idealism, he is equally an exemplar of its cruelty:

> If I see any thing to-night why I should not marry her, to-morrow in the congregation, where I should wed, there will I shame her. (3.2.123–25)

This is a perfect stage revenger's credo, expressing as it does a desire to transform the victim's perfect joy to complete misery at a time and place symbolizing her "crime."

The first scene at the church (4.1) is painful, yet it remains, at least in part, comic, because we can see Claudio the revenger as neither heroic nor villainous, but merely as a baffled young man who weeps while he accuses (4.1.152–54). His position itself is somewhat ridiculous: "Wounded self-esteem, at best, is difficult to express with dignity, and the indignation of the chaste male, however righteous, is rarely pre-possessing" (Smith, Introduction to the Arden edition, xxi). Further-more, the audience "is by [this] time accustomed to smile at Claudio, an absurdly solemn victim of young love's egotism" (Fergusson [1954] 1966, 19). Finally, of course, "the audience knows that it is all a mistake" (Fergusson [1954] 1966, 19), and since this play is a comedy, we antici-pate that justice will prevail.

But though the audience can rest assured that it will all come right, the characters, of course, have no such assurance, and Claudio's accusation naturally leads to threats of revenge.[43] Leonato's first thought is to avenge the loss of his honor on Hero:

> Do not live, Hero, do not ope thine eyes;
> For did I think thou wouldst not quickly die,
> Thought I thy spirits were stronger than thy shames,
> Myself would, on the rearward of reproaches,
> Strike at thy life.
>
> (4.1.123–27)

Hero, upon reviving from her swoon, calls down both Leonato's and Heaven's vengeance upon herself if she is guilty:

> If I know more of any man alive
> Than that which maiden modesty doth warrant,
> Let all my sins lack mercy! O my father,
> Prove you that any man with me convers'd
> At hours unmeet, or that I yesternight
> Maintain'd the change of words with any creature,
> Refuse me, hate me, torture me to death!
>
> (4.1.178–84)

Faced with this declaration, the belief of the Friar and Beatrice in Hero's innocence, and Benedick's perceptive suggestion that Claudio and Don Pedro are the victims of Don John's trickery, the bewildered Leonato can only declare that he will be revenged on *someone*:

> I know not. If they speak but truth of her,
> These hands shall tear her; if they wrong her honor,
> The proudest of them shall well hear of it.
> Time hath not yet so dried this blood of mine,
> Nor age so eat up my invention,
> Nor fortune made such havoc of my means,

Nor my bad life reft me so much of friends,
But they shall find, awak'd in such a kind,
Both strength of limb, and policy of mind,
Ability in means, and choice of friends,
To quit me of them throughly.

(4.1.190–200)

Following this avowal, however, the distracted Leonato allows himself to
be persuaded by the Friar to "publish it that she is dead indeed"
(4.1.204). The Friar himself seems not entirely clear on the final result of
such a false report, but he anticipates that the immediate effect will be
not only to increase Claudio's suffering, but to redirect his emotions from
self-pity to compassion:

When he shall hear she died upon his words,
Th' idea of her life shall sweetly creep
Into his study of imagination,
And every lovely organ of her life
Shall come apparell'd in more precious habit,
More moving, delicate, and full of life,
Into the eye and prospect of his soul,
Than when she liv'd indeed. Then shall he mourn,
If ever love had interest in his liver,
And wish he had not so accused her;
No, though he thought his accusation true.
Let this be so, and doubt not but success
Will fashion the event in better shape
Than I can lay it down in likelihood.

(4.1.223–36)

But Leonato's desire for more tangible vengeance is only temporarily
allayed; now convinced of Hero's innocence, his suffering does not
abate, and when his brother counsels "Make those that do offend you
suffer too," he promptly agrees: "There thou speak'st reason; nay, I will
do so" (5.1.40–41). When Claudio and Don Pedro appear, the two old
men insult and challenge Claudio, whose refusal to take them seriously
drives them into such a frenzy that they seem to forget not only the
suggestion that Claudio and Don Pedro may have been tricked by Don
John, but even that Hero is not really dead. Antonio in particular is so
carried away with indignation that he attacks Claudio as a representative
of all the old man despises in the younger generation, including traits of
which Claudio has given no sign:

Boys, apes, braggarts, Jacks, milksops!
. . . .
Scambling, outfacing, fashion-monging boys,

That lie and cog and flout, deprave and slander,
Go anticly, and show outward hideousness,
And speak [off] half a dozen dang'rous words,
How they might hurt their enemies—if they durst—
And this is all.

(5.1.91, 94–99)

Antonio's outbursts, Leonato's attempts to calm him, and Antonio's insistence that Leonato not "meddle" in his own quarrel are all comic, but the scene ends on a more serious note, as Don Pedro refuses to listen to Leonato, who storms out, declaring "No? Come, brother, away! I will be heard," to which Antonio adds "And shall, or some of us will smart for it" (5.1.108–9).

The Friar's plan for the correction of Claudio seems to have no effect until Borachio reveals the plot against Hero. But once Claudio learns of her innocence, he is stricken with remorse:

Sweet Hero, now thy image doth appear
In the rare semblance that I lov'd it first.

(5.1.251–52)

And now at last Leonato has a chance to take revenge:

I thank you, princes, for my daughter's death;
Record it with your high and worthy deeds.
'Twas bravely done, if you bethink you of it.

(5.1.268–70)

That Claudio regrets his rashness as well as his loss is shown by his submissiveness and willingness to make amends:

I know not how to pray your patience,
Yet I must speak. Choose your revenge yourself,
Impose me to what penance your invention
Can lay upon my sin; yet sinn'd I not,
But in mistaking.

(5.1.271–75)

Don Pedro seconds the sentiment, and Leonato imposes his conditions: that they proclaim Hero's innocence; that Claudio compose an epitaph, hang it on Hero's tomb, and "sing it to her bones" (5.1.285); and that Claudio marry Leonato's niece. With that, Leonato concludes, "so dies my revenge" (5.1.292). Claudio's immediate acceptance of this match seems unromantic, but presumably he is subordinating himself to Leonato's just revenge. The reality of his grief for Hero may be demonstrated by the fact that he vows to exceed Leonato's demands by

annually performing rites at her tomb (5.3.23). When he is reunited with
the resurrected Hero he is all but struck dumb with amazement, understandably in the circumstances. Since Claudio has only been something
of a fool, and by no means a villain, we can safely assume that he has
learned his lesson, even though he gives little obvious sign of it. That
lesson is summarized by Don Pedro: "What a pretty thing man is when
he goes in his doublet and hose and leaves off his wit!" (5.1.199–200).

Messina has a plenitude of such pretty fellows, and a group of them
constitute the watch. In *Much Ado*, as in *The Merchant of Venice*, the law is
the means of foiling serious revenge; but both the revengers and the
representatives of the law are much more comic figures in the later play:
"the knaves [are] caught out by the fools . . . it makes the fools feel much
more important than they are, it makes the villains much less villainous;
or villainous in a way that disturbs us less" (Storey [1959] 1966, 43).[44] It is
indeed the fact that Don John's revenge can be thwarted by a gang of
ninnies that robs it of most of its seriousness. Our only early hint that
these are comic villains is the name of Don John's principal accomplice:
"Borachio's very name of 'Drunkard' is a guarantee of failure" (Smith,
Introduction to the Arden edition, xvii). But it is not quite accurate to say,
as Smith does, that "the solution . . . is left, as in Comedy it may
legitimately be left, to chance. Borachio's advertised weakness makes the
chance probable" (Introduction to the Arden edition, xviii). True,
Borachio's babbling makes the watch suspicious and leads to his arrest.
But Dogberry and Company misunderstand what he says to such a
degree that their accusations against him are sheer nonsense. Although
the news of his arrest does lead to Don John's flight, it is only when
Borachio himself confesses that he stands accused of what he has actually done; his confession and repentance can be viewed as either alco-
holic weakness or true remorse, but there is some reason to see it as the
latter, for it is not only the drunkard in this play who is overheard and
caught by his own words.

Every one of the play's important characters overhears or is overheard,
frequently both. Don Pedro and Claudio overhear Borachio and Margaret and are overheard by Borachio and Benedick. Leonato is also
overheard by Benedick, and Don John also overhears Borachio and
Margaret. Benedick overhears Beatrice, as well as Don Pedro and
Claudio. Beatrice overhears Hero and Ursula. The fascinating aspect of
all of this eavesdropping is that, with the exception of Borachio's over-
hearing of Don Pedro and Claudio, all of the listeners hear lies, which
they devoutly believe to be true.[45] The eventual outcome of each of the
overheard plots is confession by all hands and a happy ending. Borachio
is a weak and not entirely well-disposed character, but in a play so full of
plotting and eavesdropping he is not far from the norm, and there is

little reason to doubt the sincerity of his remorse. As for whether his "discovery" by the watch is due to chance, we are reminded late in the play of the great plotter and eavesdropper; Claudio's taunt at Benedick, "All, all! and moreover, God saw him when he was hid in the garden" (5.1.179–80), suggests through its echo of *Genesis* that God works in a mysterious way His wonders—among them justice—to perform.

And God knows that Dogberry's watch is as wonderful and mysterious a way as even poetic justice ever worked. They are immediately associated with divine justice, albeit in a garbled fashion, upon their introduction:

> Dogberry: Are you good men and true?
> Verges: Yea, or else it were pity but they should suffer salvation, body and soul.
> Dogberry: Nay that were a punishment too good for them, if they should have any allegiance in them, being chosen for the Prince's watch.

> (3.3.1–6)

Clearly, the apprehension of anyone by this watch can only be due to divine intervention, considering the charge they are given (3.3.24–34, 42–60, 80–82). But if divine intervention is responsible for the arrest of Borachio and Conrade, surely divine inspiration is responsible for the charges leveled against them by the watch. Before Borachio has even uttered anything incriminating, the Second Watchman suspects "treason" (3.3.106). And even though the Second Watchman becomes confused by Borachio's disquisition on the "deformed thief this fashion," his description of the thief Deformed is in fact a description of fashion: " 'a goes up and down like a gentleman" (3.3.124–27). They conclude that they have "recover'd the most dangerous piece of lechery that ever was known in the commonwealth" (3.3.167–68) and make the arrest that assures the audience all will be well. They even attempt to bring the matter to Leonato's attention, but being unable to tell him how their arrest of two "arrant knaves" and "aspicious persons" "decerns him nearly," they are sent off to examine the prisoners by themselves (3.5.32, 46, 3, 49–50). Before the conspirators are even formally charged, Dogberry accuses them of being "villains" and "false knaves" (4.2.20, 21, 28), and he is quite right; for just as they are guilty of treason (insofar as their plot is directed against Don Pedro) and lechery (insofar as it not only affects Hero's reputation but poisons Claudio's mind), so they are also guilty of perjury and burglary, just as Dogberry says, although not quite for the reasons he alleges. It is sometimes hard to know if there is any sense behind Dogberry's words, but his commentary on the description of Don John as a "villain" is correct in one sense: it is perjury to call a

gentleman "lowborn"; however, we know that Don John is both a bastard and evil, so "villain" is appropriate, and therefore no perjury.
Nevertheless, we also know that Borachio is guilty of perjury, since he
has falsely "confess'd [to Claudio and Don Pedro] the vile encounters" he
and Hero have supposedly had (4.1.93). Similarly, there seems to be
nothing felonious about Borachio's thousand ducats: if he cannot be said
to have obtained them honestly, neither did he steal them—they are the
fruit of dishonest labor. But he has come to Leonato's house like a thief in
the night with felonious intent; and if what he steals—Hero's reputation—is intangible, it is valuable and hers, and he has no right to take it
from her.

Hard upon the watch's final accusation, Borachio learns of Don John's
flight and Hero's supposed death. This, presumably, is the turning point
for him, since in contrast to the struggling Conrade, he does not speak
again until 5.1, when his first lines are "Sweet Prince, let me go no
farther to mine answer; do you hear me, and let this count kill me" (230–
31). But Claudio makes no move to take any such revenge, perhaps
because although Borachio seems eager to take sole responsibility for
Hero's death (5.1.263–64), he also feels some guilt. His confession
finished, Borachio disappears from the play (not, however, before leaving a further indication of his sincerity in his exoneration of Margaret
from any guilty intention); his remorse seems sincere enough that we
can only hope he is indeed "condemned into everlasting redemption for
this" (4.2.56–57).

Dogberry also leaves the play at this point, having first summarized
the charges against Borachio and Conrade:

> Marry, sire, they have committed false report; moreover they have
> spoken untruths; secondarily, they are slanders; sixt and lastly, they
> have belied a lady; thirdly, they have verified unjust things; and to
> conclude, they are lying knaves. (5.1.215–19)

Despite all this, Dogberry remains a merciful man. He does, indeed,
seek punishment for Borachio, but only "for the example of others"
(5.1.322–23).[46] It is natural that Dogberry be both just and merciful, since
these are divine attributes and God's name is ever on Dogberry's lips.
Dogberry and his companions are themselves the *dei ex machina* of *Much
Ado*, and though they may not add much to the sense of the play, as
representatives of good intentions overcoming wit they certainly em-
body one of its themes.[47]

The principal example of characters whose wits are overcome by their
feelings (though their wits are dulled and their feelings stimulated by
others' plotting) are Beatrice and Benedick. They have been engaged in
what Leonato terms "a kind of merry war" (1.1.62) even before the play

opens, so that Beatrice's insults before Benedick appears have the character of revenges for earlier engagements:

> I pray you, how many hath he kill'd and eaten in these wars? But how many hath he kill'd? for indeed I promis'd to eat all of his killing. (1.1.42–45)

Even the onlookers of this combat recognize its nature as a series of comic revenges, as Leonato notes:

> Faith, niece, you tax Signior Benedick too much, but he'll be meet with you, I doubt it not. (1.1.46–47)

Benedick has not been on the scene a minute (although he has had time to try conclusions with, and be bested by, Leonato) before the exchange begins:

> *Beatrice:* I wonder that you will still be talking, Signior Benedick, nobody marks you.
> *Benedick:* What, my dear Lady Disdain! are you yet living?
> *Beatrice:* Is it possible disdain should die while she hath such meet food to feed it as Signior Benedick? Courtesy itself must convert to disdain, if you come in her presence.
> *Benedick:* Then is courtesy a turncoat. But it is certain I am lov'd of all ladies, only you excepted; and I would I could find in my heart that I had not a hard heart, for truly I love none.
> *Beatrice:* A dear happiness to women, they would else have been troubled with a pernicious suitor. I thank God and my cold blood, I am of your humor for that: I had rather hear my dog bark at a crow than a man swear he loves me.
> *Benedick:* God keep your Ladyship still in that mind! so some gentleman or other shall scape a predestinate scratch'd face.
> *Beatrice:* Scratching could not make it worse, and 'twere such a face as yours were.
>
> (1.1.116–36)

And so on and so on. Since there is no real animosity between these two, this would appear to be another instance of "much ado about nothing," but in fact this mock combat and the initially unexpressed feelings underlying it shape the actions of these characters throughout much of the play:

> In the wit-combats between Benedick and Beatrice, it is easy to see that each of them is anti-pathetic to persons of the opposite sex, because there is the subconscious feeling that an alliance with the opposite sex will mean the end of independence. It is this intellectual pride which makes Beatrice a male-hater and Benedick a misogynist, but they are

mutually attracted, because each finds in the other, in spite of a superficial antagonism, a kindred spirit whom it is a pleasure to meet and subdue. This mutual attraction which, in their pride of intellect, they do their best to repress, takes its revenge in a strangely tortuous manner. It colours their ideas, distorts their arguments and determines the very symbols in which their thoughts are expressed. (Sen Gupta 1950, 145–46)

Certainly all sorts of revenge are much on their minds; but when parted from one another each considers revenge not so much on the other as on him- or herself. Benedick sets himself up as the proper object of a wide range of revenges should he ever fall in love:

Don Pedro:	I shall see thee, ere I die, look pale with love.
Benedick:	With anger, with sickness, or with hunger, my lord, not with love. Prove that I ever lose more blood with love than I will get again with drinking, pick out mine eyes with a ballad-maker's pen, and hang me up at the door of a brothel-house for the sign of blind Cupid.
Don Pedro:	Well, if ever thou dost fall from this faith, thou wilt prove a notable argument.
Benedick:	If I do, hang me in a bottle like a cat, and shoot at me, and he that hits me, let him be clapp'd on the shoulder, and call'd Adam.
Don Pedro:	Well, as time shall try: "In time the savage bull doth bear the yoke."
Benedick:	The savage bull may, but if ever the sensible Benedick bear it, pluck off the bull's horns, and set them in my forehead, and let me be vildly painted, and in such great letters as they write "Here is good horse to hire," let them signify under my sign, "Here you may see Benedick the married man."

(1.1.247–68)[48]

Beatrice's musings are no less bizarre, but she contemplates divine (if comic) retribution, rather than human mockery:

Leonato:	By my troth, niece, thou wilt never get thee a husband, if thou be so shrewd of thy tongue.
Antonio:	In faith, she's too curst.
Beatrice:	Too curst is more than curst. I shall lessen God's sending that way, for it is said, "God sends a curst cow short horns"—but to a cow too curst he sends none.
Leonato:	So, by being too curst, God will send you no horns.
Beatrice:	Just, if he send me no husband, for the which blessing I am at him upon my knees every morning and evening.

(2.1.18–29)

Beatrice: He that hath a beard is more than a youth, and he that hath no beard is less than a man; and he that is more than a youth is not for me, and he that is less than a man, I am not for him; therefore I will even take sixpence in earnest of the berrord, and lead his apes into hell.

Leonato: Well, then, go you into hell.

Beatrice: No, but to the gate, and there will the devil meet me like an old cuckold with horns on his head, and say, "Get you to heaven, Beatrice, get you to heaven, here's no place for you maids." So deliver I up my apes, and away to St. Peter. For the heavens, he shows me where the bachelors sit, and there live we as merry as the day is long.

(2.1.36–49)

Leonato: Well, niece, I hope to see you one day fitted with a husband.

Beatrice: Not till God make men of some other mettle than earth. Would it not grieve a woman to be overmaster'd with a piece of valiant dust? to make an account of her life to a clod of wayward marl? No, uncle, I'll none. Adam's sons are my brethren, and truly I hold it a sin to match in my kinred.

(2.1.57–65)

That flat denial and theological quibbles are the best explanations two such articulate characters can offer for their behavior is surprising only if we assume that their behavior is based on their real beliefs and feelings. If it is not, it becomes easier to understand why they acquiesce in their own "fall."[49]

For despite the weakness of their defenses, Benedick and Beatrice have engaged in another round (2.1.125–54), which has ended with Beatrice winning the honors of the encounter and Benedick vowing revenge (2.1.209–10). Don Pedro's realization that Beatrice and Benedick are two of a kind, Claudio's desire to laugh at Benedick, and Leonato and Hero's hope of finding Beatrice a good husband bring them together in a plot, of which it has been noted that "though the purposes of Don Pedro and Don John stand in direct contrast, their means are parallel" (Evans [1960] 1967, 74). The means in both instances is to convince the victim that he or she has discovered a secret, when in fact what is overseen or overheard is a carefully contrived fiction. Although Claudio will suspect his friend Don Pedro even when he is aware of the plot to woo Hero by proxy, and Beatrice and Benedick will quibble over almost anything said to them straightforwardly, none of them ever really doubts what they learn by eavesdropping; "secret" information obtained by underhanded means is perceived as much less questionable than public statements of fact or expressions of feeling. To the degree that Beatrice and Benedick conceal their own feelings and believe that other characters also do so, the deceptions played upon then "are also beautifully-managed examples of a favourite Elizabethan device: the over-reacher over-reached, the 'engineer hoist with his own petar,' the marriage-mocker and husband-scorner taken in by—to us—a transparently obvious trick" (Storey [1959] 1966, 40). More seriously, however, the overreached overreachers are Don Pedro and Claudio, who are taken in by the same kind of plot they arrange. As for the "transparent obviousness" of these plots, it must be remembered that they are directed primarily at their victims' strongest passions: love, honor, self-doubt, and pride.

Part of the motivation behind the plotting—at least "against" Benedick—is a desire for comic revenge: as Claudio says, "we'll fit the [hid]-fox with a pennyworth" (2.3.42); and Don Pedro, although evincing no previous sign of even comic vengefulness toward Benedick, cannot resist in the course of their conversations making a jest about Benedick's courage (2.3.189–92).[50] Basically, however, Don Pedro hatches this plot *pour le sport* (or so he says, 2.3.215–18); Benedick, taken in though he is by the plot, recognizes this attitude among his friends and knows the consequences of changing his behavior:

> I may chance have some odd quirks and remnants of wit broken on me, because I have rail'd so long against marriage; but doth not the appetite alter? A man loves the meat in his youth that he cannot endure in his age. Shall quips and sentences and these paper bullets of the brain awe a man from the career of his humor? No, the world must be peopled. When I said I would die a bachelor, I did not think I should live till I were married. (2.3.235–44)

Hero and Ursula catch Beatrice in the same fashion, and although Hero does not, like Claudio, avow a desire to get even with her more articulate friend, she makes use of the opportunity not merely to praise Benedick and discuss his supposed unrequited love, but also to accuse Beatrice of being proud, scornful, and "self-endeared" (3.1.47–56); she adds that Beatrice is a slanderer and announces that she herself will "devise some honest slanders / To stain my cousin with" (3.1.59–70, 84–85). Beatrice is horrified to find herself so "condemn'd for pride and scorn" and decides to "requite" Benedick's love (3.1.108, 111–12). Thus "as Claudio is deceived into thinking Hero false, [Benedick and Beatrice] are entrapped into thinking each other fond" (Smith, Introduction to the Arden edition, xix).

Benedick and Beatrice's friends continue to have their fun with the reluctant lovers (3.2.7–69; 3.4.41–92) until Claudio's accusation of Hero briefly sobers the play's tone. Shakespeare allows the generally humorous characters to express elaborate reactions in this scene, while the real victim, Hero suffers mostly in silence. Although Leonato expresses a desire for vengeance on whomever is responsible, he is too baffled and despairing to be very convincing. It is Beatrice, who is in no doubt about Hero's innocence, who is the most serious exponent of revenge not only in this scene, but in the entire play. Revenge suddenly becomes of paramount importance to her: "Ah, how much might the man deserve of me that would right her!" (4.1.261–62). It is even possible to read her role in this scene as a willingness to use Benedick's love for her in the service of revenge; but it is also possible, and perhaps more dramatically effective, to see her as a character so moved by hatred of the attacker of someone she loves that not even her own prospects for happiness can distract her for long. At any rate, the two-word close to her first exchange of avowals with Benedick is arguably the most striking note of vengeance to be sounded in any of Shakespeare's plays:

Benedick:	By my sword, Beatrice, thou lovest me.
Beatrice:	Do not swear and eat it.
Benedick:	I will swear by it that you love me, and I will make him eat it that says I love not you.
Beatrice:	Will you not eat your word?
Benedick:	With no sauce that can be devis'd to it. I protest I love thee.
Beatrice:	Why then God forgive me!
Benedick:	What offense, sweet Beatrice?
Beatrice:	You have stay'd me in a happy hour, I was about to protest I lov'd you.
Benedick:	And do it with all thy heart.
Beatrice:	I love you with so much of my heart that none is left to protest.
Benedick:	Come, bid me do anything for thee.
Beatrice:	Kill Claudio.

(4.1.274–89)

When Benedick objects to this cool proposition, Beatrice's response reveals the depth of her vengefulness.

Is 'a not approv'd in the height a villain, that hath slander'd, scorn'd, dishonor'd my kinswoman? O that I were a man! What, bear her in hand until they come to take hands, and then with public accusation, uncover'd slander, unmitigated rancor—O God, that I were a man! I would eat his heart in the market-place. (4.1.301–7)

On her own behalf, this might seem monstrous, but because it is generous indignation on behalf of someone else, we like Beatrice the better for it, as we do Benedick, whose challenge of a friend in any cause other than that of an innocent and otherwise helpless woman would also

appear deplorable. Lest we forget that no help is really required since
nothing is really wrong, however, Shakespeare immediately decreases
the tension: "Benedick's resolve to challenge Claudio in response to
Beatrice's command serves not only to confirm their love but also to
present Benedick in the self-dramatizing, seriocomic attitude of the
would-be avenging hero who, the audience knows, has nothing to
avenge" (Phialas 1966, 177).

Certainly in his next appearance Benedick's high seriousness is most
uncharacteristic:

> [*aside to Claudio.*] You are a villain. I jest not; I will make it good how
> you dare, with what you dare, and when you dare. Do me right, or I
> will protest your cowardice. You have kill'd a sweet lady, and her death
> shall fall heavy on you. Let me hear from you. (5.1.145–50)

There is nothing intrinsically funny in this speech; but not only is the
audience aware that the challenge is superfluous, but the attitude of
Claudio and Don Pedro makes Benedick's grimness laughable. They
simply cannot take the challenge seriously:

> Claudio: Well, I will meet you, so I may have good cheer.
> Don Pedro: What, a feast, a feast?
> Claudio: I' faith, I thank him, he hath bid me to a calve's-head and a
>   capon, the which if I do not carve most curiously, say my
>   knife's naught. Shall I not find a woodcock too?
>
> (5.1.151–57)

Don Pedro and Claudio, unaware that their accusation of Hero has
precipitated a mutual avowal of love between Beatrice and Benedick (and
thus, indirectly, the challenge) are lighthearted enough to continue to
twit Benedick about Beatrice (5.1.159–78). Not only is their timing poor,
but they have the bad taste to make Hero part of the joke (5.1.178).[51] The
honors for wit are entirely theirs; but Benedick, after all, is no longer
playing.[52] If his parting speech is amusing in its disorganization and
excessive formality, it nevertheless delivers a blow, in its news about
Don John, that jolts his hearers out of their complacency. In addition, it
delivers a few well-aimed shots at Claudio's youth and inexperience
(although we have no reason to consider Benedick his superior in these
respects):

> Fare you well, boy, you know my mind. I will leave you now to your
> gossip-like humor. You break jests as braggarts do their blades, which,
> God be thank'd, hurt not. My lord, for your many courtesies I thank
> you. I must discontinue your company. Your brother the bastard is
> fled from Messina. You have among you kill'd a sweet and innocent

lady. For my Lord Lack-beard there, he and I shall meet, and till then peace be with him. (5.1.185–93)

For Don Pedro and Claudio, of course, the challenge is immediately nullified by Borachio's confession. But even Beatrice is much in her own humor again before she knows that the challenge has been made (5.2.42–46); and once this is confirmed, she is back to quibbling with Benedick, although she professes to be doing "very ill" (5.1.91–92).

The play's final scene is, naturally, one of reconciliation, but echoes of revenge ring throughout it. Benedick expresses his relief that he does not have to "call young Claudio to a reckoning" (5.4.8–9);[53] but when Claudio again teases him about taking on the yoke of marriage, the restored Benedick has no hesitation in striking back:

Bull Jove, sir, had an amiable low,
And some such strange bull leapt your father's cow
And got a calf in that same noble feat
Much like to you, for you have just his bleat.

(5.4.48–51)

Claudio's reply to this is "For this I owe you: here comes other reck'nings" (5.4.52).

The other reckonings include forgiveness and restoration of Hero for Claudio and "brave punishments" for Don John. Greater complexity naturally characterizes the reckoning between Benedick and Beatrice. Neither will be the first to make a public declaration of love; but Hero and Claudio get some of their own back at the mockers of love by revealing purloined affirmations of each satirist's love for the other. Even then, they will not yield entirely, out of fear of giving an advantage either to the other or to their friends, or both. But Benedick, at least, has learned something from the manifold confusions wrought upon him and his clever friends. Wit is a game, which he can take or leave alone; in the serious business of life he will be guided not by others' quips, but by his own feelings. He still cannot quite bring himself to a straightforward, unqualified declaration of love for Beatrice, but he has learned the truth of the truism that actions speak louder than words:

Benedick: A miracle! here's our own hands against our hearts. Come, I will have thee, but by this light, I take thee for pity.
Beatrice: I would not deny you, but by this good day, I yield upon great persuasion, and partly to save your life, for I was told you were in a consumption.
Benedick: Peace, I will stop your mouth. [*Kissing her.*]
Don Pedro: How dost thou, Benedick the married man?
Benedick: I'll tell thee what, Prince: a college of wit-crackers cannot

flout me out of my humor. Dost thou think I care for a
satire or an epigram? No, if a man will be beaten with
brains, 'a shall wear nothing handsome about him. In brief,
since I do purpose to marry, I will think nothing to any
purpose that the world can say against it, and therefore
never flout at me for what I have said against it; for man is a
giddy thing, and this is my conclusion.

(5.4.91–109)

In terms of revenge, *As You Like It* is an anomaly among the romantic
comedies. Although the most commonly accepted date for the composi-
tion of the play places it between the multiple revenges of *The Merry
Wives of Windsor* and what might be called the apotheosis of comic
revenge in *Twelfth Night, As You Like It* almost completely dispenses with
revenge either as theme or as plot device. The absence of revenge is
particularly strange, since two major characters are unjustly treated by
their own brothers and might be expected to mention (at least) a desire
for revenge. Furthermore, the outsider, the focus of revenge in the
romantic comedies, has not one, but two, representatives in this play,
Jaques and Touchstone. Yet no serious and very little comic revenge is
attempted in *As You Like It*, and even the idea of revenge is almost
forgotten. Why Shakespeare, in the midst of a period of plays characterized by revenge, wrote a play almost totally lacking in references to
this theme seems to me an ultimately unanswerable question. But perhaps some suggestions can be made.

The most obvious explanation would seem to be that the play is a
pastoral, in which revenge would be out of place. It would obviously be
disconcerting if Duke Senior, after finding

tongues in trees, books in the running brooks
Sermons in stones, and good in every thing

(2.1.16–17)

were to announce his intention to be revenged upon his brother. Similarly, it would be difficult for Orlando to immerse himself in the worship
of Rosalind if he were obsessed with evening the score against Oliver.
Not only the tone, but the action of the play would be upset by even a
significant subplot dealing with vengeance; pastoral is static, for the
most part, while vengeance usually requires conspiracy, plotting, trap-
setting, punishment—activity of all kinds. The little revenge in *As You
Like It* is undertaken by individuals, rather than groups, and although it
is essential to the plot, little is made of it.[54]

The satirists of the play—Jaques and Touchstone—are rarely personal in their satire, and when they are it amounts merely to teasing.[55] They cannot be even comic revengers, for they have no wrongs to avenge. Touchstone's threats to William are mere braggadocio, and although Duke Senior claims that Jaques has a personal motive behind his plan to "cleanse the foul body of th' infected world" (2.7.60), Jaques denies it plausibly. Jaques and Touchstone, the outsider figures in *As You Like It*, unlike parallel figures in the other Shakespearean comedies, have little to do with revenge.

Perhaps it is not strange in terms of this play that the outsider characters provide no focus for revenge, since most of its characters are outsiders in one way or another. Rosalind and Orlando have both been deprived of their proper stations in the world of the play's opening, and once the scene shifts to Arden, everyone but the rustics is a stranger in a strange land. The fact that most of the play is set in this edenic wood might seem sufficient reason for the absence of revenge in *As You Like It*; yet Shakespeare's principal source, Thomas Lodge's pastoral romance *Rosalynde*, positively revels in revenge. A close comparison of the treatment of revenge in the play and this source, to which Shakespeare adhered so closely in plot and from which he deviated so profoundly in tone, may suggest another reason for the lack of revenge in *As You Like It*.

That much of the difference between the two works may simply be attributable to the characters or personalities of their authors is one immediate possibility. The very title of Shakespeare's play may be seen as a suggestion of the complaisant playwright's attempt to give the public what it wanted; but although the title may have been suggested by Lodge's preface "To the Gentlemen Readers," Lodge's use of a very similar phrase is not a promise, but a challenge:

> If you like it, so: and yet I will be yours in duetie, if you be mine in favour. But if *Momus* or anie squint-eied asse that hath mightie eares to conceive with *Midas*, and yet little reason to judge; if hee come aboord our Barke to find fault with the tackling, when he knows not the shrowdes, Ile downe into the hold, and fetch out a rustie pollax, that sawe no sunne this seaven yeare, and either will bebast him, or heave the cockscombe over boord to feede cods. (160)[56]

Lodge's attitude toward revenge throughout *Rosalynde* may have been based on personal experience, as Bradbrook points out: "Lodge depicted his own wrongs in the character of Orlando and what he considered the perfidy of his elder brother in the behavior of Oliver" (1951, 230; in *Rosalynde*, of course, "Orlando" is named Rosader, and "Oliver" Saladyne). Certainly, in Lodge's work the relationship of the brothers is characterized by vengeful feelings on both sides. Saladyne seeks revenge against Rosader for a clearly stated reason: "So fared it with *Saladyne*, for after a months mourning was past, he fell to consideration of his Fathers testament, how he had bequeathed more to his younger brothers than himselfe, that *Rosader* was his Fathers darling" (165). Oliver, on the other hand, claims not to know why he hates Orlando, although he follows this statement with another suggesting a motive for his malignity:

> I hope I shall see an end of him; for my soul (yet I know not why) hates nothing more than he. Yet he's gentle, never school'd and yet learned, full of noble device, of all sorts enchantingly belov'd, and indeed so much in the heart of the world, and especially of my own people, who best know him, that I am altogether mispris'd. (1.1.162–69)[57]

Oliver's confession of the baselessness of his hatred occurs immediately after he has contrived at Orlando's death. Although Oliver is not a revenger, having nothing to revenge against the innocent Orlando, his actions resemble those of a villain-revenger. He treacherously plots a death that is intended to appear accidental, and provides himself with an accomplice by claiming that Orlando is a classic revenger:

> I'll tell thee, Charles, it is the stubbornest young fellow of France, full of ambition, an envious emulator of every man's good parts, a secret and villainous contriver against me his natural brother. . . . And thou wert best look to't; for if thou dost him any slight disgrace, or if he do not mightily grace himself on thee, he will practice against thee by poison, entrap thee by some treacherous device, and never leave thee till he hath ta'en thy life by some indirect means or other. (1.1.141–45, 147–53)

Although Lodge created the wrestling scene in which Rosader/ Orlando is victorious after others have fallen to the professional champion, Shakespeare's use of it to characterize Oliver as a treacherous villain is brilliantly original. He further altered Lodge's presentation by presenting Orlando in this scene only as an innocent seeker after honor. In *Rosalynde*, Rosader, although no doubt perfectly honorable, shows a taste for revenge similar, if not equal, to that of the novel's more villainous characters. Lodge's presentation is more bloodthirsty altogether; the wrestler kills the elder of a franklin's two sons, which makes the other son "thirstie after the revenge." When this son meets the same end, Rosader says to the franklin: "stand a while and either see mee make a third in their tragedie, or else revenge their fall with an honourable triumph." He then proceeds to kill the wrestler, an action that "highlie contented the *Francklin*, as a man satisfied with revenge" (170–71).

Rosader brings some friends home with him to help celebrate his victory, but finds himself locked out of the house. His friends leave, and "assoone as they were gone, *Rosader* growing impatient of the abuse, drewe his sworde, and swore to be revenged on the discurteous Saladyne" (173), but Adam Spencer dissuades him. (Earlier, the enraged Rosader has chased Saladyne and his guests with a rake.) Finally, "when Saladyne had a long while concealed a secret resolution of revenge" (191), he has Rosader seized and bound to a pillar, intending to have him starved to death. Adam frees Rosader, however, and as soon as Rosader recovers, "straight his thoughts aymed at revenge" (192). He attacks Saladyne and his guests, who escape; Rosader flees, although not without the pursuit of the local Sheriff, to whom Saladyne has complained and who has made "a determined resolution to revenge the Gentlemens wrongs" (192).[58]

In contrast, Orlando cannot be provoked into taking up arms against his own flesh and blood; although he will defend himself against Oliver (1.1.53–54), he does not pursue his advantage. And when Adam reveals Oliver's plot to burn him to death in his sleep, Orlando considers (if only to reject them) beggary and thievery, but not revenge. Since we know by this time that Orlando has both courage and a proper sense of the wrongs Oliver has done him, it can only be that he is too good a man to stoop to plotting revenge against his brother. The time does come, of course, when the thought of revenge occurs to him, but it is significant that he simply happens upon a situation where his mere failure to act will accomplish his revenge. Shakespeare takes the incident from Lodge, but again discards or weakens the revenge motifs. Rosader, finding the sleeping Saladyne watched by a lion (the attractively described "green and gilded snake" being a Shakespearean addition), soliloquizes about "sweet revenge," attempting to convince himself that the situation is an indication of the gods' intention of "revenging his rigour, and thy injuries" (216). Ultimately, of course, he rejects "so dismall a revenge," concluding that "more honour shalt thou purchase by pleasuring a foe, than revenging a thousand injuries" (217). Saladyne, upon awaking, agrees with Rosader's views on divine retribution, attributing his misfortunes to "the Gods, not able to suffer such pietie unrevenged," but congratulates Rosader on his more-than-divine mercy in showing "how highly he held revenge in scorne" (219).

This incident—the wronged man confronted by his oppressor, whom he need merely ignore to destroy—is highly dramatic, and yet Shakespeare chose not to stage it. To be sure, the snake was probably impossible to stage, but the snake is no more than a charming aesthetic, and perhaps symbolic, afterthought; the lioness could easily have been changed to a much more probable bear, which was subsequently considered feasible in *The Winter's Tale*. Shakespeare seems to have chosen to tell, rather than show, this incident to decrease the emphasis on the serious theme of revenge. We can assume, with Phialas, that "Orlando's momentary hesitation to save his sleeping brother menaced by the lioness is due to vengeful impulse rather than thought of material profit, as in Lodge" (1966, 222) (although this judgment seems a little hard on Rosader), but in fact we never hear anything about Orlando's thoughts on the matter. All we have is Oliver's statement that

> Twice did he turn his back . . .
> But kindness, nobler ever than revenge,
> And nature, stronger than his just occasion,
> Made him give battle to the lioness. . . .
>
> (4.3.127–30)

By deemphasizing Orlando's motives, Shakespeare avoids complicating Orlando's character or darkening the play's tone; we see no inner struggle, merely a little blood on a handkerchief. Oliver's description colorfully summarizes the event to give us the necessary information and allow the characters to get on with the important aspect of the play—the complications of their love lives.

Lodge's other great vengeful character is the usurping Duke, Torismond, and Shakespeare's comparable character, Frederick, is again generally less vengeful than his original. In one instance, however, Shakespeare adds a revenge motif: Frederick resents Orlando as soon as he discovers him to be the son of Sir Rowland de Boys, whom he regarded as an enemy (1.2.224–28). So quickly does this resentment grow, that soon Le Beau warns Orlando to leave the court (1.2.261–67). The link that Rosalind describes between Sir Rowland and Duke Senior will soon be matched by Frederick's similar treatment of their children, making them parallel characters. This parallelism is a distinct change from Lodge, whose Torismond shows no distaste for Rosader, and whose exile of Rosalynde is much better motivated than Frederick's of Rosalind, largely because Torismond expresses his fear of revenge; he fears, he says, that Rosalynde "will proove to me as *Helen* did to *Priam*" (176). And when Alinda (Celia) defends Rosalynde, saying that she has not contemplated revenge (not, strictly speaking, quite true, for Rosalynde has at least regretted that she cannot avenge her father's injuries [175]), Torismond banishes his own daughter. In contrast, Frederick presents no good reason for banishing Rosalind. According to Le Beau, Frederick's "displeasure 'gainst his gentle niece" (1.2.278) is

> Grounded upon no other argument
> But that the people praise her for her virtues,
> And pity her for her good father's sake. . . .
>
> (1.2.279–81)

This assessment is confirmed out of Frederick's own mouth, for when Rosalind asks the reason why he has banished her on pain of death, he can only reply, "Let it suffice thee that I trust thee not" (1.3.55). When she asks the reason for this distrust, he answers, "Thou art thy father's daughter, there's enough" (1.3.58). And when Celia defends her, Frederick uses Rosalind's virtues as accusations:

> She is too subtile for thee, and her smoothness,
> Her very silence, and her patience
> Speak to the people, and they pity her.
> Thou art a fool; she robs thee of thy name,
> And thou wilt show more bright and seem more virtuous
> When she is gone.
>
> (1.3.77–82)

But if Shakespeare's alterations in this instance make Frederick more of a villain than Torismond, the reverse is true with regard to Frederick's relationship with his daughter. For Frederick does not revenge her threat to parental authority with banishment, and his treatment of Oliver (3.1) appears to be motivated primarily by the belief that Oliver can help him find Celia, rather than by greed masked with hypocrisy, as in Lodge. Shakespeare establishes Frederick as an unconsciously ironic revenger here: believing, incorrectly, that Orlando has fled with Rosalind and Celia, and assuming, also incorrectly, that Orlando's brother will know where to find him, he punishes Oliver, who deserves punishment, but not for the crime he is accused of. And the confession that Oliver hopes will absolve him,

> O that your Highness knew my heart in this!
> I never lov'd my brother in my life

produces, from a man who has also wronged his brother, only the laconic judgment,

> More villain thou.
>
> (3.1.13–15)

Finally, Frederick's relationship with his brother differs from that between Torismond and Gerismond (who are not brothers). At the conclusion of *Rosalynde,* Gerismond and the other men leave the wedding feast to battle with—and ultimately kill—Torismond, Gerismond declaring: "let us shew that we carrie revenge and honour at our fawchions points" (255). Frederick, on the other hand, is like Oliver converted, leaving no need for revenge in a world where all the characters have become virtuous.

What little serious revenge there is in *As You Like It* is contemplated by men; the much more successful comic revenges are the province of women. Rosalind is, of course, the chief figure of comic revenge in the play, but her cousin Celia also shows a disposition toward well-deserved mockery. Celia's teasing seems motivated by a concern for justice, whether she is criticizing the injustice of life in general,

> Let us sit and mock the good huswife Fortune from her wheel,
> that her gifts may henceforth be bestow'd equally. (1.2.31–32)

or acknowledging Touchstone's protest of her suggestion that he will someday be whipped for "taxation":

> By my troth, thou sayest true; for since the little wit that fools have was silenc'd, the little foolery that wise men have makes a great show. (1.2.88–90)

Celia's principal target, however, is the love-struck Rosalind. This is perhaps not quite fair, for although Rosalind has suggested falling in love as a sport, she discards the idea after Celia entreats her not to love "in good earnest" (1.2.24–29), and never dissembles her love for Orlando except to him. Perhaps it is Rosalind's hyperbole in regard to her love that Celia finds laughable (3.2.163–246; 3.4.1–46), which would be understandable, for the tender emotion takes Celia quite differently; after the scene in which she meets Oliver, we hear of her love for him (5.2.7–9, 32–39), but we never hear another word out of her. More easily explicable as even-handed comic revenge is her threat following Rosalind's description of married life (4.1.143–76):

> You have simply misus'd our sex in your love-prate. We must have your doublet and hose pluck'd over your head, and show the world what the bird hath done to her own nest. (4.1.201–4)

Celia, though she talks of comic revenge, performs none. Nor does Rosalind, though she mocks Orlando's protestations of love (3.2.163–78, 358–424; 4.1.38–108) and Jaques's affectations of melancholy (4.1.1–38), do so with any comic-vengeful intent; as Bradbrook notes:

> Her two great scenes with [Orlando], the first and second encounter [sic] in the forest, are full of lively satire upon lovers; the forlorn state of the "unfortunate he" and the capriccios of the weathercock she are mercilessly mocked. But the ridicule itself by its very vivacity demonstrates Love's power. (1951, 220)

In fact, both Rosalind and Orlando are playing roles, and know it; their self-awareness allows us to laugh with them at least as much as at them.

It is more accurate to say, as Bradbrook does, that "the lesser characters of *As You Like It* are varying parody upon simpler modes" (1951, 224), but even these characters are dealt with gently and affectionately. If this is satire, it is of a far different mode than that directed at Dr. Pinch or Holofernes.

But Rosalind does accomplish a revenge on a character who outrages her sense of justice, perhaps not least by scorning the emotion to which Rosalind finds herself in thrall:

> Phebe is the first real victim of Rosalind's mockery. She looks on to Olivia, innocent victim of Viola's disguise, but she differs from Olivia in deserving to be humiliated. Presumptuous, pretentious, proud, she scorns the poor slave of a shepherd who dotes on her, killing him over and over with darted looks—all the while insisting that "there is no force in eyes / That can do hurt" . . . Phebe deserves the corrective medicine of ridicule which Rosalind, of all Shakespeare's heroines, is best qualified to administer. (Evans [1960] 1967, 91)

By scorning love in general and Silvius in particular, Phebe sets herself up as a proper target for a comic revenge that will correct her thinking and behavior. This is recognized by the characters of both *Rosalynde* and *As You Like It*, but while the revenge is the same in both works, the reason for the revenge is different. In *Rosalynde* the characters recognize Phebe's actions as an offense against the gods. Phebe declares "justly have the Gods ballanst my fortunes, who being cruell to *Montanus* [Silvius] found Ganimede, as unkinde to my selfe" (245). Rosader tells Gerismond of "the love of *Montanus* to *Phebe*, his great loyaltie and her deepe crueltie: and how in revenge the Gods had made the curious Nymph amorous of young Ganimede" (251). And Phebe concludes "Yet *Venus* to adde revenge, hath given me wine of the same grape, a sippe of the same sawce, and firing me with the like passion, hath crost me with as ill a penaunce" (251).

The only similar reference in *As You Like It* is Rosalind's description of "that same wicked bastard of Venus that was begot of thought, conceiv'd of spleen, and born of madness, that blind rascally boy that abuses every one's eyes because his own are out" (4.1.211–14), and this reference is to herself, not to Phebe. The gods are not involved in the comic revenge of this play. Silvius suggests that in the natural course of events Phebe may suffer the pangs of love, but he seems to desire this only to excite her pity for him, not out of any desire to see her suffer; and Phebe's reply is to invite him to take vengeance if this happens:

Silvius: O dear Phebe,
       If ever (as that ever may be near)
       You meet in some fresh cheek the power of fancy,

> Then shall you know the wounds invisible
> That love's keen arrows make.
> *Phebe:*   But till that time
> Come not thou near me; and when that time comes,
> Afflict me with thy mocks, pity me not,
> As till that time I shall not pity thee.

> (3.5.27–34)

It is at this point that vengeance begins, though Silvius has nothing to do with it. Rosalind—no immortal, though under the alias of the gods' cupbearer—attempts to bring Phebe to a sense of her proper self with a furious and very funny speech:

> And why, I pray you? Who might be your mother,
> That you insult, exult, and all at once,
> Over the wretched? What though you have no beauty—
> As, by my faith, I see no more in you
> Than without candle may go dark to bed—
> Must you be therefore proud and pitiless?
> Why, what means this? Why do you look on me?
> I see no more in you than in the ordinary
> Of nature's sale-work. 'Od's my little life,
> I think she means to tangle my eyes too!
> No, faith, proud mistress, hope not after it.
> 'Tis not your inky brows, your black silk hair,
> Your bugle eyeballs, nor your cheek of cream
> That can entame my spirits to your worship.
> You foolish shepherd, wherefore do you follow her,
> Like foggy south, puffing with wind and rain?
> You are a thousand times a properer man
> Than she a woman. 'Tis such fools as you
> That makes the world full of ill-favor'd children.
> 'Tis not her glass, but you that flatters her,
> And out of you she sees herself more proper
> Than any of her lineaments can show her.
> But, mistress, know yourself, down on your knees,
> And thank heaven, fasting, for a good man's love;
> For I must tell you friendly in your ear,
> Sell when you can, you are not for all markets.
> Cry the man mercy, love him, take his offer;
> Foul is most foul, being foul to be a scoffer.

> (3.5.35–62)

Phebe's response to this derogatory catalog of her appearance and behavior is to fall in love with her critic, a fact that Rosalind immediately recognizes, while making explicit her purpose and leading Phebe on even in rejection:

> *Rosalind:* [*to Phebe*] He's fall'n in love with your foulness—[*to Silvius*]
> and she'll fall in love with my anger. If it be so, as fast as she

> answers thee with frowning looks, I'll sauce her with bitter
> words.—[*to Phebe*] Why look you so upon me?
> *Phebe:* For no ill will I bear you.
> *Rosalind:* I pray you do not fall in love with me,
> For I am falser than vows made in wine.
> Besides, I like you not. If you will know my house,
> 'Tis at the tuft of olives here hard by.
>
> (3.5.66–75)

Rosalind's disclosure of her address is clearly calculated to lead Phebe on
to further punishment, and Phebe, smitten—

> Dead shepherd, now I find thy saw of might,
> "Who ever lov'd that lov'd not at first sight?"
>
> (3.5.81–82)

—takes the bait. Anatomizing "Ganymede" as "he" did her, she finds his
appearance pleasing but suddenly recalls his behavior, a recollection that
allows her to communicate with him without sacrificing her pride, under
cover of revenge for his public vivisection of her:

> There be some women, Silvius, had they mark'd him
> In parcels as I did, would have gone near
> To fall in love with him; but for my part
> I love him not, nor hate him not; and yet
> Have more cause to hate him than to love him,
> For what had he to do to chide at me?
> He said mine eyes were black and my hair black,
> And, now I am rememb'red, scorn'd at me.
> I marvel why I answer'd not again.
> But that's all one; omittance is no quittance.
> I'll write to him a very taunting letter. . . .
>
> . . . .
> I will be bitter with him and passing short.
>
> (3.5.124–34, 138)

Despite Rosalind's willfully perverse misreading of it, however, Phebe's
epistle is purely and simply a love letter. The only note of revenge it
sounds is a denial:

> "Whiles the eye of man did woo me,
> That could do no vengeance to me."
>
> (4.3.47–48)

Rosalind continues her scorn of Phebe by reading the letter to Silvius
and sending him back with a message:

> Well, go your way to her (for I see love hath made thee a tame snake)
> and say this to her: that if she love me, I charge her to love thee; if she
> will not, I will never have her unless thou entreat for her. (4.3.69–73)

At their next meeting, Phebe expresses her annoyance, and "Ganymede" continues the same combination of scorn and exhortation:

> *Phebe:*   Youth, you have done me much ungentleness,
>   To show the letter that I writ to you.
> *Rosalind:* I care not if I have. It is my study
>   To seem despiteful and ungentle to you.
>   You are there followed by a faithful shepherd—
>   Look upon him, love him; he worships you.

$$(5.2.77-82)$$

Finally, however, Rosalind entraps Phebe. The bait is Rosalind's statement "I will marry you, if ever I marry woman, and I'll be married tomorrow" (5.2.113–14); the trap is not revealed to the audience until the final scene:

> *Rosalind:* You say you'll marry me, if I be willing?
> *Phebe:*   That will I, should I die the hour after.
> *Rosalind:* But if you do refuse to marry me,
>   You'll give yourself to this most faithful shepherd?
> *Phebe:*   So is the bargain.

$$(5.4.11-15)$$

When Rosalind reappears as herself, Phebe naturally (and rather pathetically) renounces her:

> If sight and shape be true,
> Why then my love adieu!

$$(5.4.120-21)$$

and Rosalind, in the best tradition of comic revengers, cannot resist at least one little laugh at Phebe's expense (5.4.124). But Phebe has indeed learned her lesson and seems content with her lot as she joins the other couples, saying to Silvius:

> I will not eat my word, now thou art mine,
> Thy faith my fancy to thee doth combine.

$$(5.4.149-50)$$

None of the foregoing completely answers the question of why Shakespeare, in the midst of a group of comedies in which vengeance plays a significant part, wrote one in which vengeance is minimized. Although it is true, as Harbage states, that *As You Like It* is a play of reconciliation like *The Tempest* and *A Midsummer Night's Dream*, neither of those plays lacks revenge ([1947] 1961, xiii–xiv). Further, to some degree all of Shakespeare's comedies are plays of reconciliation, and the reconciliation is frequently brought about by means of comic revenge. I am not prepared to argue that the pattern of revenge I perceive in the comedies proves that *As You Like It* must be a reworking of an earlier play written when Shakespeare's interest in dramatic revenge was less developed than it became by the time of the romantic comedies, although, combined with the play's similarities to *Love's Labor's Lost* as pointed out by Wilson (1962, 159), and the references to Marlowe, this seems to me a possibility. The alternative is that, in the middle of a group of plays concerned with and utilizing revenge, Shakespeare simply wrote a different kind of play.

Twelfth Night contains the most famous of Shakespeare's comic revenges, the vengeance taken on Malvolio by Sir Toby Belch and his pack of revelers. But this revenge is merely a subplot (though a beautifully integrated one), and apart from it and the minor episode of Sir Andrew Aguecheek's "revenge" on "Cesario," the play is surprisingly lacking in developed revenges (or even vengeful intentions) among the major characters, compared to most of the earlier comedies and *Twelfth Night*'s sources.

Although serious revenge is never taken in any of the play's sources, it is certainly threatened. In the original basis for Shakespeare's story, *Gl'Ingannati* (1531), Flamminio (the Orsino figure), on learning of the supposed treachery of Fabio (Cesario), exclaims: " 'Let me not be thought a man if I do not take such a revenge as, so long as the world endures, will be an example to all servants not to betray their masters! . . . I'll have such a revenge!' " (Bullough 1957, 2:312). Subsequently, he explains to a servant of Isabella (Olivia) the kind of revenge he has in mind: " 'Tell her that one day she will repent of [falling in love with Fabio]. Tell [Fabio], that if I find him (and I carry this dagger in my hand on purpose) I shall cut off his lips and his ears, and dig out one of his eyes, and put them all in a dish and send him in to give it to her' " (Bullough 1957, 2:329).

Somewhat less gruesome, but no less intent on serious revenge, is the parallel character in Barnabe Riche's version of the story, "Of Apolonius and Silla": "the Duke hymself . . . was verie well assured that it could bee no other then his owne manne, that had thrust his Nose so farre out of ioynte, wherefore without any further respect, caused hym to be thrust into a Dongeon, where he was kept prisoner, in a verie pitifull plight" (*Twelfth Night*, the Arden edition, 1975, appendix 1, 170). When his servant denies the disloyalty, appearing to desert Iulina (Olivia), Apolonius orders him "to make such satisfaction as she requireth . . . or I sweare by god, that thou shalt not escape the death which I will minister to thee with my owne handes" (*Twelfth Night*, the Arden edition, 1975, appendix 1, 176).

Orsino, too, contemplates bloody revenge, and not merely against his servant:

> Why should I not (had I the heart to do it),
> Like to th' Egyptian thief at point of death,
> Kill what I love? (a savage jealousy
> That sometime savors nobly), but hear me this:
> Since you to non-regardance cast my faith,
> And that I partly know the instrument
> That screws me from my true place in your favor,
> Live you the marble-breasted tyrant still.
> But this your minion, whom I know you love,
> And whom, by heaven I swear, I tender dearly,
> Him will I tear out of that cruel eye,
> Where he sits crowned in his master's spite.
> Come, boy, with me, my thoughts are ripe in mischief.
> I'll sacrifice the lamb that I do love,
> To spite a raven's heart within a dove.
>
> (5.1.117–31)

Orsino, however, shows himself nobler than Flamminio or Apolonius, who relinquish their desire for revenge only after they learn the true identities of their supposed servants. Orsino, though not reconciled to Cesario or Olivia, spares them as soon as he hears that they are formally contracted:

> O thou dissembling cub! What wilt thou be
> When time hath sow'd a grizzle on thy case?
> Or will not else thy craft so quickly grow,
> That thine own trip shall be thine overthrow?
> Farewell, and take her, but direct thy feet
> Where thou and I (henceforth) may never meet.
>
> (5.1.164–69)

For Orsino to act out a revenge (or even to threaten such a revolting one as Flamminio's) would upset the balance of the play, and destroy our image of him as an admirable ruler, if a bit of the madman and the poet as a lover. A serious threat of revenge would be particularly out of place, since the audience knows how deceived Orsino is. Revenge must be raised as an issue here so that it can be dealt with and renounced, and Orsino's renunciation is especially laudable because of his perception of himself in love as the innocent victim of divine vengeance, like Actaeon (1.1.18–22).[59] That—suffering for love as he does—Orsino pardons Olivia and Cesario demonstrates the magnanimity of his character.

Unlike Orsino, Olivia seems to have no sense that her acute attack of lovesickness is a form of revenge, and given her situation this is somewhat surprising. Her vow to waste her youth in an unnaturally long period of mourning for her dead brother is much more extreme than that taken by the young men in *Love's Labor's Lost*; but, unlike them, when love overcomes her resolution she seems to have no sense that her "fall" is the natural revenge of "outraged nature."[60] Even when the possibility of such revenge is suggested—ironically, by the object of her affections— Olivia displays no sense that she deserves what has happened to her:

> Viola: Love make his heart of flint that you shall love,
> And let your fervor like my master's be
> Plac'd in contempt! Farewell, fair cruelty.
> Olivia: . . . .
> How now?
> Even so quickly may one catch the plague?
> Methinks I feel this youth's perfections
> With an invisible and subtle stealth
> To creep in at mine eyes. Well, let it be.
>
> (1.5.286–88, 294–98)

Although she characterizes love as a "plague," Olivia's prompt and unprotesting surrender to this disease indicates even less resistance than that shown by the plebeian but parallel Phebe. But even though she fails to personify love as her enemy, Olivia is nevertheless a victim of comic revenge: "The spectacle of a woman thus yielding to the dictates of the heart she wanted to tyrannize over shows that this play, too, contains its own ironical commentary and reminds the reader of what the Fool says in another context, '. . . the whirligig of time brings in his revenges' (V.i.389)" (Sen Gupta 1950, 164). Despite her exalted position and the high seriousness of her intention, the audience is quickly made aware that her mourning is fated to dissolve in laughter: "It is not only Orsino's suit that threatens her solemn purpose; the stamp of futility is set on her vow by the lunatic character of her household: vain dream, to pass seven years in weeping under the same roof with Malvolio, Maria, Belch, and Aguecheek!" (Evans [1960] 1967, 129).

The other characters in the main plot likewise have little to do with revenge, at least until the final scene. Antonio, indeed, goes in fear of Orsino's vengeance (2.1.45–48; 3.3.25–37) and revenges himself for the supposed Sebastian's ingratitude by reproaches (3.4.347–70); Sebastian revenges Sir Andrew's blow by beating him and is prepared to duel with Sir Toby for interfering (4.1.24–43). But Shakespeare has been careful to assure us that Antonio's offense is not of a nature to call for the gravest penalty, even if we could imagine Orsino as a blood revenger against so worthy an opponent; and the other revenges are a result of mistaken identities, and therefore unlikely, according to the rules of comedy, to lead to serious consequences. So, although revenge is central to *Twelfth Night*, it is to the subplot that we must turn to find it.

At the center of the subplot stands another of those Shakespearean characters so powerfully imagined that for some readers they unbalance the plays they inhabit. The alien Malvolio, both in himself and in his effect on criticism, makes one think of the alien Shylock;[61] and, like Shylock, Malvolio has his defenders.[62] Nevertheless, despite Bradbrook's contention that "a great deal of sympathy has been wasted on Malvolio" (1951, 231), most critics do not find him a sympathetic character. This is not to say, however, that there is general agreement about him. There is disagreement over whether he may be a satire on a particular person or type of person, or whether he may be Shakespeare's satiric portrait of a Puritan.[63]

Whether or not Malvolio is to be seen as a Puritan, critics generally agree that he is representative of a new order of values to which Shakespeare in this play shows himself unsympathetic.[64] But there is less agreement about the plot against Malvolio: one theory holds that the steward is the victim of a sadistic plot that has no redeeming social value; on the other hand, some commentators maintain that the revenge taken on him is justifiable.[65] Even among critics who agree that Malvolio deserves the revenge taken on him, however, there is disagreement about the effect of that revenge, both on our feelings toward Malvolio and on the character himself.[66]

Like Shylock, Malvolio has become the focus for criticism of the play he inhabits, especially among his defenders; but sympathy for both characters seems to stem primarily from a modern distaste for the forms of revenge taken on them. A modern audience or reader cannot justify enforced conversion or false imprisonment of a sane person as insane; but our inability to justify such punishments does not absolve the characters who suffer them. Although Malvolio is a far less serious threat to Illyria than Shylock is to Venice and Belmont, he also has less reason for his objectionable actions. No one spits upon Malvolio; no one insults him until he has established himself as an obnoxious intruder. And while Shylock shows what may be interpreted as flashes of feeling for his daughter and late wife, Malvolio never shows the slightest charitable impulse toward anyone but himself.

Malvolio's very name alerts us to the ill will that is his hallmark, and his first lines set the tone from which he never deviates. The clown has been attempting, with both wit and wisdom, to persuade Olivia to give over her excessive mourning for her brother, and Olivia seeks Malvolio's opinion:

Olivia: What think you of this fool, Malvolio? doth he not mend?
Malvolio: Yes, and shall do till the pangs of death shake him. Infirmity, that decays the wise, doth ever make the better fool.

(1.5.73–77)

Malvolio is, in fact, perfectly content that the house should stay in a state of mourning, however excessive. He associates fun and laughter with weakness. Although this attitude is unattractive, especially in a comedy, we might view Malvolio as merely the obverse of the irrepressible Feste, if he did not immediately condemn himself:

Clown: God send you, sir, a speedy infirmity, for the better increasing your folly! Sir Toby will be sworn that I am no fox, but he will not pass his word for twopence that you are no fool.
Olivia: How say you to that, Malvolio?
Malvolio: I marvel your ladyship takes delight in such a barren rascal. I saw him put down the other day with an ordinary fool that has no more brain than a stone. Look you now, he's out of his guard already. Unless you laugh and minister occasion to him, he is gagg'd. I protest I take these wise men that crow so at these set kind of fools no better than the fools' zanies.

(1.5.78–89)

By his attack on Feste, who has won our sympathy with his humor and good sense regarding Olivia, Malvolio offends us. Not only has he criticized Feste, but—if his opinion were taken seriously—he would endanger the clown's livelihood. Luckily, there is no chance that Malvolio's feelings in this matter will be respected, for Olivia, whose taste Malvolio has thoughtlessly disparaged, passes judgment on him for all of us:

O, you are sick of self-love, Malvolio, and taste with a distemper'd appetite. To be generous, guiltless, and of free disposition, is to take those things for bird-bolts that you deem cannon-bullets. There is no slander in an allow'd fool, though he do nothing but rail; nor no railing in a known discreet man, though he do nothing but reprove. (1.5.90–96)

Prior to the revenge taken on him, Malvolio hardly speaks of another character but to malign, or to one but to threaten. He describes the disguised Viola as "of very ill manner" (1.5.153) and speaking "very shrewishly" (1.5.160). When we see him actually dealing with her, his behavior is contemptuous, certainly exceeding the bounds of his commission to return the ring (1.5.300–306):

Come, sir, you peevishly threw it to her; and her will is, it should be so return'd. If it be worth stooping for, there it lies, in your eye; if not, be it his that finds it. (2.2.13–16)

Typically, after an appearance by Malvolio, one or more of the sympathetic characters comments on his behavior; in this instance, Viola describes Malvolio as a "churlish messenger" (2.2.23). Clearly, Shakespeare is taking some pains not only to show us Malvolio, but to direct our response to him.

Significantly, we have seen Malvolio's insolence toward Olivia, Viola, and Feste before seeing his more justifiable behavior toward Sir Toby's merry band. We are therefore more ready to side with the roisterers against Malvolio, especially since the injured and charming Feste is among them. Some critics have argued that, as Olivia's steward, Malvolio is merely performing his duty in attempting to quell what even Maria describes as "caterwauling" (2.3.72). There may be a degree of truth in this contention, although we do not in fact know what Olivia told Malvolio to tell Sir Toby and the others. True, he delivers a message as coming from her, but we know from his scene with Viola that he is capable of infusing his lady's messages with his own mean spirit. Even if he is delivering Olivia's sentiments, he does so in as offensive a manner as possible:

> My masters, are you mad? Or what are you? Have you no wit, manners, nor honesty, but to gabble like tinkers at this time of night? Do ye make an alehouse of my lady's house, that ye squeak out your coziers' catches without any mitigation or remorse of voice? Is there no respect of place, persons, nor time in you? . . . Sir Toby, I must be round with you. My lady bade me tell you, that though she harbors you as her kinsman, she's nothing allied to your disorders. If you can separate yourself and your misdemeanors, you are welcome to the house; if not, and it would please you to take leave of her, she is very willing to bid you farewell. (2.3.86–92, 95–101)

When all of this has no effect on the "three merry men," Malvolio rounds on Maria, who seems rather an innocent bystander at this point, having attempted to calm the rioting and, after all, having no authority to control her lady's cousin:

> Mistress Mary, if you priz'd my lady's favor at any thing more than contempt, you would not give means for this uncivil rule. She shall know of it, by this hand. (2.3.121–24)

Although we cannot entirely approve of Sir Toby—a sort of bush-league Falstaff—we can hardly keep from applauding his most coherent reply to Malvolio:

> Art any more than a steward? Dost thou think because thou art virtuous there shall be no more cakes and ale? (2.3.114–16)

Not only must the cakes-and-ale party prevail in Illyria, but Sir Toby's first question reminds us that Malvolio is the type of the biblical statement that "For thre things the earth is moved: yea, for foure it can not susteine it self," the first of which is "a servant when he reigneth" (Prov. 30:21, 22; although it is hardly likely that Sir Toby has this in mind). Malvolio in his pretensions *is* unbearable, and, aptly, these pretensions are the key to the revenge taken on him.

Maria, by far the clearest-headed of the lot, provides the most complete description of Malvolio even while plotting how to use his pretensions against him:

> The dev'l a puritan that he is, or anything constantly but a time-pleaser, an affection'd ass, that cons state without book, and utters it by great swarths; the best persuaded of himself, so cramm'd (as he thinks) with excellencies, that it is his grounds of faith that all that look on him love him; and on that vice in him will my revenge find notable cause to work. (2.3.147–53)

Maria's plot is a notable comic revenge just because it does play off of the self-love that is Malvolio's principal comic flaw. Some of his other flaws, however, abet and extend the revenge. Fabian joins the plotters because Malvolio has gotten him into trouble with Olivia over a bear-baiting (2.5.7–8).[67] As the plot is being put into action, Maria provides another of her vivid descriptions of Malvolio:

> Get ye all three into the box-tree; Malvolio's coming down this walk. He has been yonder i' the sun practicing behavior to his own shadow this half hour. Observe him, for the love of mockery; for I know this letter will make a contemplative idiot of him. Close, in the name of jesting! *[The men hide themselves.]* Lie thou there *[throws down a letter]*; for here comes the trout that must be caught with tickling. (2.5.15–22)

The remainder of this scene beggars all description. It need only be said that Malvolio in soliloquy, as he thinks, reveals an insolent, overweening, and self-deluding character. If he had not previously revealed himself as such an unpleasant person, we might be moved to pity such total self-delusion; as it is, the fact that he aids in his own entrapment, by making sense of "M.O.A.I." and resolving to follow the insane advice given in the letter, only adds to the fun. The only faintly pathetic note is sounded by a single word, "now," in "I do not now fool myself, to let imagination jade me" (2.5.164); the implication seems to be that Malvolio has just enough self-awareness to realize that his imagination can run away with him, and perhaps has done so in the past. But his faith in the forged letter only adds irony to his situation.

In his next appearance, spurred on by Maria's advice, Malvolio gives

his unattractive character free rein. He makes indecent suggestions to
Olivia, sneers at Maria and Sir Toby, and interprets Olivia's use of the
word "fellow" in a manner complimentary toward himself (3.4.29–31,
34–36, 88–90, 75–78).[68] Finally, he reveals his contempt for all of them:

> Go hang yourselves all! You are idle shallow things, I am not of your
> element. You shall know more hereafter. (3.4.123–25)

But Malvolio in adversity is quite a different character; then the "barren
rascal" Feste becomes "good fool" repeatedly and is begged for favors
(4.2.84–119). Although this is understandable behavior, it does not suit
with Malvolio's previous pride, and it reinforces our image of him as a
"time-pleaser."

The nature and intent of the plot against Malvolio have been the
subject of considerable controversy. One theory is that the roisterers'
revenge is an almost instinctive reaction against their opposition:

> Doubtless they have never thought it out. They only know that the
> sight of Malvolio, like the sound of his voice, threatens death to their
> existence. His own existence somehow challenges their right to be
> freely what they are. He is of a new order—ambitious, self-contained,
> cold and intelligent, and dreadfully likely to prevail. That is why Sir
> Toby and his retinue hate him. Feste at the end provides too simple an
> explanation. The humiliation of Malvolio, he says, was his personal
> revenge upon one who had discounted him to his mistress as "a
> barren rascal," a jester unworthy of his hire. But the others had been
> as active as Feste, and they had had no such motive. (Van Doren 1939,
> 139–40)

Feste's explanation is, of course, not the whole truth—though neither is
it quite accurate to say that all the other plotters have been as active as he.
One, in fact, is a good deal more active: Maria develops and directs the
scheme, although she eventually relinquishes control of it. But because
the original idea is hers, her character is important to understanding the
meaning of the revenge taken on Malvolio. There seems to be, however,
little agreement as to what her character is.[69]

Part of the difficulty of analyzing Maria is that, while a major plotter,
she is only a minor character. She does not tell us her feelings; she
speaks only to characters such as Olivia and Sir Toby, from whom she
may be concealing her true intentions. But what she says and what she
does are of a piece. She says that she will "gull [Malvolio] into a ayword,
and make him a common recreation," make him an ass (she has previously told him "Go shake your ears"), and "turn him into a notable
contempt" (2.3.134–35, 168–70, 125; 2.5.203–4); all of this she does. In
addition, she provides hilarity for her fellow conspirators (3.2.68–69).

When Olivia calls for Malvolio, Maria prepares her to assume that he is mad (3.4.8–13). Whether or not Maria is sincere in her unconcern for Malvolio's sanity, it is Sir Toby who extends the jest to the dark room; in the same speech, however, he reassures us that they will eventually "have mercy on him" (3.4.135–41, a reassurance repeated, this time out of fear of Olivia's anger, at 4.2.66–71).

Certainly, "[Maria's] device is adapted precisely to that singular lack of self-perspective which is Malvolio's whole vice and whole virtue" (Evans [1960] 1967, 130). The device of the letter, in which he finds himself "most feelingly personated" (2.3.159) by one who hates but understands him, is simply brilliant, and the appeal to him of the supposed love letter perfectly accords with Maria's description of his vanity. Whether she has any intent to reform him must remain an open question, although her reference to "my physic" may indicate some such aim, however secondary to the "sport royal" that is the main object of the plot (2.3.172–73). That her revenge, whatever its purpose, is approved within the world of the play is proved by the fact that Maria is rewarded for it; true, her reward—marriage to Sir Toby—may not be an unmixed blessing, but presumably it is to Maria's taste.

Feste, who has perhaps the best reason to hate Malvolio, takes little part in the revenge until Malvolio is imprisoned. Then the "fool" mocks the "madman," nonsensically as Sir Topas and rationally as himself.[70] Ultimately, however, the revenge taken on Malvolio is simply to force him to see himself as others see him.[71] However cruel this revenge may seem to us, and regardless of its effectiveness in altering Malvolio's behavior, it is a just revenge. For, by the standards of Illyria, Malvolio, with his self-love and self-delusions, and his lack of a generous, guiltless, and free disposition, *is* mad. And it is a measure of the disregard in which Shakespeare holds him that the revenge plot against him is conceived and carried out, not by a significant character of the stature, for example, of Portia, but by a comic cabal of a gentlewoman, a servant, a fool, a clown, and a drunkard.

Like many of Shakespeare's comic revengers, the plotters frequently refer to revenges distinct from their own scheme, as though vengeance were a natural mode of behavior in their world. Such references may be rational, like Maria's caution to Sir Toby, or the wildest hyperbole, like her "warning" to Feste:

> By my troth, Sir Toby, you must come in earlier a' nights. Your cousin, my lady, takes great exception to your ill hours. . . . . That quaffing and drinking will undo you. (1.3.4–6,14)

> Nay, either tell me where thou hast been, or I will not open my lips so wide as a bristle may enter, in way of thy excuse. My lady will hang

thee for thy absence. . . . Yet you will be hang'd for being so long absent, or to be turn'd away—is not that as good as hanging to you? (1.5.1–4, 16–18)

References to vengeance in the form of curses are frequent: Sir Toby curses his boots (1.3.11–13) and Sir Andrew (1.3.61–62, 102–4); and he, Fabian, and Sir Andrew all define particular vengeances that should be taken on them under certain conditions (1.3.63–64; 2.3.186–87; 2.5.2–3); Sir Andrew even unconsciously damns himself (3.4.166–69).

Sir Andrew is unique among Shakespeare's characters in being both a revenger in two separate revenge plots and a victim of revenge, although it is clear that he lacks the intelligence to understand the concept of revenge. His idea of a suitable revenge on Malvolio might be sheer cowardice: " 'Twere as good a deed as to drink when a man's a-hungry, to challenge him the field, and then to break promise with him, and make a fool of him" (2.3.126–28); but he immediately makes it clear that his wit is not adequate to comprehend the idea of having a reasonable motive for revenge:

Maria: Marry, sir, sometimes he is a kind of puritan.
Sir Andrew: O, if I thought that, I'd beat him like a dog!
Sir Toby: What, for being a puritan? Thy exquisite reason, dear knight?
Sir Andrew: I have no exquisite reason for't, but I have reason good enough.

(2.3.140–46)

So little a natural revenger (in anything but muddled language) is Sir Andrew that, confronted with a rival in his love for Olivia, his instinct is to leave. Fabian and Sir Toby must persuade him to revenge, and even then he is averse to the intrigue expected of revengers: "And't be any way, it must be with valor, for policy I hate. I had as lief be a Brownist as a politician" (3.2.30–32). But even though Sir Andrew sees the projected duel as both revenge and a means of gaining Olivia's favor, the real reasons behind it are quite different: "Toby incites Andrew to challenge 'Cesario', not because he thinks there are grounds for his gull's jealousy but merely for the love of the game" (Evans [1960] 1967, 135). Equally important to Sir Toby, this plot distracts Sir Andrew from his proposed departure. It is certain, however, that Sir Toby and Fabian do not expect anything serious to come of this duel:

Sir Toby: I think oxen and wain-ropes cannot hale them together. For Andrew, if he were open'd and you find so much blood in his liver as will clog the foot of a flea, I'll eat the rest of th' anatomy.

Fabian: And his opposite, the youth, bears in his visage no great presage of cruelty.

(3.2.59–65)

Sir Toby manages to hale the antagonists together, although not without difficulty, and manages to improve on the jest by getting a horse from Sir Andrew as a bribe to stop the fight. But the intervention and arrest of Antonio put Sir Toby out of temper and appear to change his intention. Craig maintains that "Sir Toby sees that Caesario is an acknowledged coward; even Sir Andrew sees it, and they resolve to pursue their vengeance" (1948, 167), but this is not strictly accurate: Sir Toby has suspected all along that Cesario is a coward, and Cesario has frankly admitted as much; nor does Andrew show any recognition of this fact until both Sir Toby and Fabian have told him of it. More probably, Sir Toby is incensed at Cesario's supposed ingratitude:

A very dishonest paltry boy, and more a coward than a hare. His dishonesty appears in leaving his friend here in necessity, and denying him; and for his cowardship, ask Fabian. (3.4.385–88)

Certainly Sir Toby, whatever his other faults, is no coward, and being the man he is, he naturally makes fun of those who are less brave then he. But cowardice is understandable, while such a betrayal of friendship as Cesario is thought to be guilty of is truly contemptible. It is therefore little wonder that Sir Toby urges Sir Andrew to follow and beat Cesario, although he is careful to forbid swordplay. That this blatant display of ingratitude is Sir Toby's true quarrel with Cesario is demonstrated when he intervenes in Sebastian's beating of Sir Andrew. Sir Andrew is only a gull, but he is Sir Toby's gull, and Sir Toby protects him, although there is no indication that Sebastian will seriously injure Sir Andrew. But before Sir Toby, who is not at all averse to dueling (having just attempted it with Antonio, and immediately taking up Sebastian's challenge), can effect any serious revenge, Olivia, summoned by Feste, breaks up the duel. In the meantime, Sir Andrew has given another indication of his desire for and misunderstanding of revenge, by threatening a lawsuit, despite his having struck the first blow (4.1.33–36).

The intervention of Olivia at this point means that "the natural release by a just revenge on the bullies is suspended," (G. K. Hunter [1962] 1966, 99), since Olivia is more concerned with "Cesario" than with the punishment Feste has anticipated (4.1.30–31). But the revenge is accomplished, offstage, in act 5, when Sebastian beats both Sir Andrew and Sir Toby. Sir Toby takes his punishment philosophically, while Sir Andrew continues to misunderstand the link between revenge and justice:

'Od's lifelings, here he is! You broke my head for nothing, and that that I did, I was set on to do't by Sir Toby. (5.1.184–86)

Sir Andrew is, of course, addressing the still-disguised Viola; and although she is innocent of the assault, her reply emphasizes the justice of the revenge that her brother has unwittingly taken on her behalf:

Why do you speak to me? I never hurt you.
You drew your sword upon me without cause,
But I bespake you fair, and hurt you not.

(5.1.187–89)

Minor as this revenge is, it provides the impetus for the unraveling of the main plot, since Sebastian's immediate appearance onstage to explain his behavior to Olivia brings him face to face with Viola. Orsino's desire to see Viola in her "woman's weeds" brings up the name of Malvolio (who has had her friend the Captain imprisoned) and thus neatly leads to the resolution of the subplot.

Olivia asks Feste about Malvolio's condition; his reply indicates that he, at least, has not tired of revenge:

Truly, Madam, he holds Belzebub at the stave's end as well as a man in his case may do. H'as here writ a letter to you; I should have given't you to-day morning. But as a madman's epistles are no gospels, so it skills not much when they are deliver'd. (5.1.284–88)

Malvolio's letter is both ill-bred and foolish. In it he falsely accuses and threatens a lady who is not only his social superior and employer, but who has always treated him graciously and now has him entirely in her power (as he thinks):

"By the Lord, madam, you wrong me, and the world shall know it. Though you have put me into darkness, and given your drunken cousin rule over me, yet have I the benefit of my senses as well as your ladyship. I have your own letter, that induc'd me to the semblance I put on; with the which I doubt not but to do myself much right, or you much shame. Think of me as you please. I leave my duty a little unthought of, and speak out of my injury.
The madly-us'd Malvolio."
(5.1.302–11)

Although, as Orsino remarks, "this savors not much of distraction" (5.1.314) as far as the sense of the message, it is surely a mad letter as coming from a servant to his mistress, a commoner to a great lady, or a prospective suitor to his beloved. That Malvolio can take such a tone toward Olivia, no matter what his injuries, can only increase our distaste for him, as do his accusations when he finally confronts her:

Malvolio: Madam, you have done me wrong,
                Notorious wrong.
Olivia: Have I, Malvolio? No.
Malvolio: Lady, you have. Pray you, peruse that letter.
          You must not now deny it is your hand;
          Write from it if you can, in hand or phrase,
          Or say 'tis not your seal, not your invention.
          You can say none of this. Well, grant it then,
          And tell me, in the modesty of honor,
          Why you have given me such clear lights of favor,
          Bade me come smiling and cross-garter'd to you,
          To put on yellow stockings, and to frown
          Upon Sir Toby, and the lighter people;
          And acting this in an obedient hope,
          Why have you suffer'd me to be imprison'd,
          Kept in a dark house, visited by the priest,
          And made the most notorious geck and gull
          That e'er invention play'd on? Tell me why!

                                                    (5.1.328–44)

In giving Olivia the lie, Malvolio is wrong in courtesy, in deference, and
in fact. But Olivia nevertheless responds to him with her customary
graciousness:

Alas, Malvolio, this is not my writing,
Though I confess much like the character;
But out of question 'tis Maria's hand.
And now I do bethink me, it was she
First told me thou wast mad. Then cam'st in smiling,
And in such forms which here were presuppos'd
Upon thee in the letter. Prithee, be content.
This practice hath most shrewdly pass'd upon thee;
But when we know the grounds and authors of it,
Thou shalt be both the plaintiff and the judge
Of thine own cause.

                                                    (5.1.345–55)

This generous response, however, draws no answering generosity—nor
even an apology—from Malvolio. Instead, generosity is shown by one of
the revengers, who takes the burden of blame on himself, defends the
justice of the plot, and expresses hope for reconciliation:

Fabian: Good madam, hear me speak,
          And let no quarrel nor no brawl to come
          Taint the condition of this present hour,
          Which I have wond'red at. In hope it shall not,
          Most freely I confess, myself and Toby
          Set this device against Malvolio here,
          Upon some stubborn and uncourteous parts

We had conceiv'd against him. Maria writ
The letter at Sir Toby's great importance,
In recompense whereof he hath married her.
How with a sportful malice it was follow'd
May rather pluck on laughter than revenge,
If that the injuries be justly weigh'd
That have on both sides pass'd.

(5.1.355–68)

Lest this speech fail to justify the revenge taken on Malvolio, he is made to condemn himself in his final response to Olivia's sympathy and Feste's explicit moralizing:

Olivia: Alas, poor fool, how have they baffled thee!
Feste: Why, "some are born great, some achieve greatness, and
            some have greatness thrown upon them." I was one, sir, in
            this enterlude—one Sir Topas, sir, but that's all one. "By the
            Lord, fool, I am not mad." But do you remember? "Madam,
            why laugh you at such a barren rascal? And you smile not,
            he's gagg'd." And thus the whirligig of time brings in his
            revenges.
Malvolio: I'll be reveng'd on the whole pack of you. [*Exit*]

(5.1.369–77)

Feste, who has been repeatedly praised throughout the play (2.4.11–12; 3.1.60–68; 5.1.24), has proved that this revenge, at least from his standpoint, was no more than justice; as Malvolio has denigrated his fooling, so he has helped to undermine Malvolio's reputation for rationality.[72] And although the last sentence of Feste's speech provides a perfect lead-in for Malvolio's final line, it does more than that—it presents a view of Fate: "The 'whirligig of time' only for a moment appears to be a light-hearted and irreverent way of referring to Fortune's wheel: the fun evaporates with the word 'revenges.' This is a vindictive Fortune, a Fortune who not only turns her wheel but punishes. Her spokesperson is the clever and engaging Fool" (Leech [1965] 1968, 72).

In fact, though arguably irreverent, Feste's theory of Fortune is an uncommonly benign one. This is not an evil fate that ultimately and inevitably befalls those who have been fortunate; this is a vision of a fate merry as a whirligig, inexorable as time, that nevertheless takes account of justice. Just as the world of *Twelfth Night* is not that of *The Mirrour for Magistrates*, so the whirligig of time is not the medieval Wheel of Fortune. The latter was a representation of the tragic fate of a gifted individual; Feste's formulation is comic and social: though linked with the older idea, it has more in common with "turning the tables" than the turn of the wheel. What has been done to Malvolio is relatively harmless and altogether deserved, and it is this kind of revenge that Feste is describing.

Feste's idea of revenge, however, is not Malvolio's, and many critics have found Malvolio's exit line a disturbing element, often on the assumption that the (self-)expulsion of Malvolio is somehow a judgment on Illyria and its inhabitants.[73] But it seems a bit harsh to condemn Illyrian society on the basis of Malvolio's dissatisfaction with it. Although Shakespeare weaves his plots together with great skill, the happiness of the lovers has in fact nothing to do with the revenge taken on Malvolio. Nor is it correct to call this revenge mere "practical jesting": each of the major plotters has a score to settle with Malvolio, and that is what they do. But their revenge has a limit; in the end "Illyria seeks only Malvolio's goodwill, and with such charming people it may win him over" (Prosser 1973, 75–76). Whether or not Malvolio can be "converted" is a moot point; but if it is assumed that he cannot be, the assumption condemns him, rather than Illyria, whose inhabitants go much farther than those of any other comedy to make peace with the outsider in their midst.[74]

The contrast between the behavior of Malvolio and that of Olivia and Orsino could hardly be more pronounced, and it is this contrast that damns Malvolio and finally prevents him from being a sympathetic character. Malvolio rejects the offered reconciliation and threatens the innocent as well as the guilty, whereas Olivia and Orsino, who have in no way wronged Malvolio, continue even after his vow of vengeance to placate him. Such charity speaks well for Olivia and Orsino, but by this point it is difficult to care what happens to Malvolio. Even if it can be argued that Malvolio did not, because of his injuries to Feste, Fabian, and the others, deserve what was done to him, certainly he earns his punishment retroactively in the last scene. He is freely offered forgiveness and refuses it, and for this he cannot be forgiven: "No one in *Twelfth Night* entirely escapes the darkness of ignorance, but at least those who come to know generous love and friendship escape time's harshest revenges. Those who escape make it clear why the others suffered, for comedy thrives on poetic justice" (Williams [1961] 1968, 42). And poetic justice, in *Twelfth Night*, is accomplished through comic revenge.

4

Problem Comedies

Revenge is a dish which people of taste prefer to eat cold.
—Robert Hamer and John Dighton, *Kind Hearts and Coronets*

Troilus and Cressida, All's Well That Ends Well, and *Measure for Measure* have been identified as three of Shakespeare's "problem plays" because they present ethical problems they do not solve to the satisfaction of many critics. A large part of the "problem" of these plays, it seems to me, is that too little revenge is felt to be taken on erring or evil characters, although the dissatisfaction is seldom stated in precisely those terms.[1] In *Troilus and Cressida,* we are dissatisfied because Cressida is not punished for deceiving Troilus and, more important, Achilles is not punished for murdering Hector. In *All's Well* and *Measure for Measure,* the consensus seems to be that Bertram and Angelo get off much too lightly.

Although critics prefer to assert that in these plays justice is not served rather than that revenge is not exacted, it is difficult to see how "justice" could be established in these plays without recourse to revenge. *Troilus and Cressida* is concerned with the two areas in which "all's fair"—love and war—and so is entirely outside the pale of law. Similarly, love and war are the two areas within which Bertram offends in *All's Well,* and although he disobeys his king in fleeing to the war, there is nobility as well as disobedience and obstinacy in his flight into danger, and we are told that he behaves heroically in Italy; his remaining offenses are sins or errors, but they are not crimes, and it is hard to imagine what suitable punishment the king or any other character could impose for them. Finally, in *Measure for Measure,* crimes are committed; but the principal criminal is also the principal legal authority in the city. The Duke, having temporarily abdicated after having in effect allowed the laws to lapse for many years, prefers to restore justice by extralegal means. Furthermore, since Angelo's crimes remain merely intents, as Isabella points out, they are not suitable objects for the legal retribution that Vincentio threatens.

Whether justice is in fact adequately served in *All's Well* and *Measure for Measure* remains a matter of personal opinion, but such justice as

126

there is is brought about by the devices of revenge. (Justice is, of course, not served in *Troilus and Cressida,* which I take to be a satire in part on the possibility of justice in wartime.) The theme of revenge is deemphasized in *All's Well* and *Measure for Measure* and combined with the themes of justice and mercy. But the devices of revenge—plotting, accomplices, and the use of the victim's faults against him—are much in evidence. And, as in the romantic comedies, the use of these devices leads to the restoration of social harmony.

One major difference between these two plays and the romantic comedies is linked to the fact that the devices rather than the theme of revenge predominate in the later plays. Bertram and Angelo are not aliens in their societies like Shylock, Falstaff, Don John, and Malvolio. Although Bertram seems much less intelligent and Angelo much more malicious than anyone else in their respective plays, they are, when the plays open, living well-adjusted lives in their societies; they are surrounded by people who love and respect them, and they are not without admirable qualities. Even at the nadir of their fortunes, virtuous characters come forward to plead for them. They are not, therefore, to be made fun of, nor do we wish to see them excluded from their societies, even at their own wish. The characters who plot against them are plotting only against their errors, in the hope that their better selves will allow them to reform their behavior.

In a sense, therefore, the plotters plot not against but for Bertram and Angelo who, once they repent, are proper objects for mercy. It is therefore not surprising if, lacking an alien focus for unalloyed feelings of vengeance (such as Shylock or Malvolio), the characters of these plays are somewhat less passionate in their pursuit of revenge than their predecessors. Perhaps this moving away from alien objects of revenge while preserving the devices of revenge is part of the reason why these plays are such problems. Neither whole-hearted acceptances of revenge nor yet rejections of it, the problem comedies look back at the cheerfully vengeful comedies that preceded them and ahead to the merciful worlds of the romances to come.

Considering that it is a Trojan War play and that the Trojan War was the Greeks' revenge on the Trojans for the abduction of Helen, *Troilus and Cressida* gives remarkably little emphasis to the theme of revenge. This is not to say that revenge is absent from the play; the story demands the mention of revenge as a motive in subplots (Achilles' vengeance for Patroclus' death and the Greek leaders' resentment of Achilles' mockery of them) as well as the war itself. But the subject matter makes comic revenge unsuitable—the death of Hector is hardly an object for merriment—while Shakespeare's treatment of the material makes serious revenge equally impossible—the assassin Achilles cannot be viewed as a tragic revenger. Consequently, one way of interpreting *Troilus and Cressida* is as an "anti-revenge" play, not so much in rejecting revenge as in presenting the idea that other motives, among them pride, honor, lechery, jealousy, and self-interest, may be of more importance than revenge in what is ostensibly a revenge story.

Whether or not *Troilus and Cressida* is "(with *Timon*) the least liked of Shakespeare's mature works" (Rossiter 1961, 129), certainly it is "a puzzle for classifiers" (Sen Gupta 1950, 186). To begin with, it is probably the only play in the canon that can generate reasonable debate over whether it is a comedy, a tragedy, or a history.[2] Other than a disinclination to classify it as either a tragedy or a history, perhaps the principal reason to identify the play as a comedy is that the characters are reduced from heroic size, rather than exalted, although critics disagree on the reason for the characters' trivialization.[3] This trivialization has led to suggestions that the play is a satire, but the object(s) of the satire are likewise manifold and subject to dispute.[4]

Just as critics have disagreed over the classification of the play and the objects of its satire, so too have they disagreed over the ethical values it upholds—surely an odd state of affairs for a satire. On the one hand, Tillyard insists that the morality of the play is that of all Shakespearean drama: "Finally, it cannot be asserted too strongly that Shakespeare in writing *Troilus and Cressida* did not alter his moral standards. . . . The same ethical standards prevail as in the rest of Shakespeare" (1950, 85–86). On the other hand, Knowland maintains that it is hard to sort out the values presented in the play: "Indeed, the more closely we look at the play in the hope of extracting from it a clearly defined set of opposing values, the more difficult the task becomes" (1959, 355). With regard to the ethical treatment of revenge in this play, both views are to some degree accurate: Shakespeare continues, in *Troilus and Cressida*, to make use of comic revenge for the purpose of delighting the audience and teaching the victim; at the same time, revenge is less developed and dwelt upon than in earlier comedies, and other motivations—some parallel in effect with revenge and some in opposition to it—take up the slack left by the relaxation of the revenge motif. *Troilus and Cressida* is, therefore, a pivotal play in any examination of Shakespeare's use of comic revenge. The move to forgiveness has not yet been made (Hector's mercy is merely a reprieve, not a pardon; but then Shakespeare could hardly introduce Christian forgiveness into the story, even if he had felt so inclined). Yet there is a shift away from the madcap antics of the merry wives or Sir Toby's crew (again, the subject matter may be a constraint).

The play begins with a Prologue in armor that, if not conventional, is neither completely anomalous (being similar to the Prologue of *The Poetaster*) nor unsuited to a play about war. Likewise, his speech is appropriate to a play based on the major revenge story of antiquity:

> In Troy, there lies the scene. From isles of Greece
> The princes orgillous, their high blood chaf'd,
> Have to the port of Athens sent their ships
> Fraught with the ministers and instruments
> Of cruel war. Sixty and nine, that wore
> Their crownets regal, from th' Athenian bay
> Put forth toward Phrygia, and their vow is made
> To ransack Troy, within whose strong immures
> The ravish'd Helen, Menelaus' queen,
> With wanton Paris sleeps—and that's the quarrel.
>
> (1--10)

One critic has noted of this speech that "*Troilus* opens, like a Senecan tragedy, with a Prologue, composed somewhat in the quasi-epic manner of the Pyrrhus speech in *Hamlet*" (Thomson 1952, 141). But the Prologue ends on a note much more natural and appropriate to comedy than to tragedy:

> Like or find fault, do as your pleasures are,
> Now good or bad, 'tis but the chance of war.
>
> (30–31)

The Prologue, in fact, foreshadows the uneasy juxtaposition of revenges throughout the play: serious revenges contained in a comedy, and comic revenges contained in a play about war and betrayal. Both serious and comic revenges (or threats of revenge), as is usual in Shakespeare's comedies, may be presented as major incidents or minor ones. Since the minor ones are for the most part straightforward, and have the greatest similarities to revenges in earlier plays, it seems logical to deal with them first.

As is typical in the comedies, characters in this play make frequent, often comic, reference to revenges that they wish would befall other characters. Helen, for instance, says to Pandarus, "You shall not bob us out of our melody. If you do, our melancholy upon your head!" (3.1.68–69). Cressida repeatedly curses Pandarus for "mocking" her: "A pestilence on him!" "Go hang yourself, you naughty mocking uncle!" "Come, come, beshrew your heart" "Would he were knock'd i' th' head!" (4.2.21, 25, 29, 34). Pandarus facetiously curses Troilus ("A bugbear take him!" [4.2.33]) and, in a more serious vein, curses Cressida ("Would thou hadst ne'er been born! I knew thou wouldest be his death" [4.2.85–

86]) and Antenor ("The devil take Antenor! the young prince will go
mad. A plague upon Antenor! I would they had broke 's neck!" [4.2.74–
77; echoed at 4.2.87]). Most seriously, Troilus curses Pandarus:

> Hence, broker, lackey! [*Strikes him.*] Ignominy, shame
> Pursue thy life, and live aye with thy name!
>
> (5.10.33–34)

Also as in other comedies, in *Troilus and Cressida* characters revile
themselves or call down revenges on their own heads for real, imagined,
or possible faults:

> *Troilus:*   And when fair Cressid comes into my thoughts—
> So, traitor, "When she comes"! When is she thence?
>
> (1.1.30–31)

> *Troilus:*   I speak not "be thou true" as fearing thee,
> For I will throw my glove to Death himself
> That there is no maculation in thy heart. . . .
>
> (4.4.62–64)

> *Cressida:*   O heavens, you love me not.
> *Troilus:*   Die I a villain then!
>
> (4.4.82–83)

> *Cressida:*   O you gods divine,
> Make Cressid's name the very crown of falsehood,
> If ever she leave Troilus!
>
> (4.2.99–101)

The most important occurrence of characters calling down vengeance on
themselves is the scene (3.2) in which Troilus, Cressida, and Pandarus
take oaths that present them as the symbols they will become in after
ages: "as true as Troilus," "as false as Cressid," "and all brokers-between
Pandars." The scene is well summarized by Palmer in his Introduction to
the Arden edition:

> Troilus affirms his faith that Cressida will indeed prove to be what he
> believes she is: a woman not subject to time and change, whose
> constancy is of another order than the physical decline of her bodily
> beauty, and who will answer him with a love as pure and simple as his
> own. And having said it, he prophesies, and turns himself into a
> proverbial comparison for good faith. Cressida likewise prophesies;
> but her vision is of future obloquy. What she sees, beyond the wrack
> of cities and the death of history, is a time when (should she now
> prove untrue) she will be still the archetype of all unfaithful women.
> Troilus' prophecy was simple, and his own name a climax to all

fidelity; but Cressida's is conditional, and the curse which she utters is prophecy as well. The "handfasting" which Pandarus then performs becomes itself an irony. It looks like a legal betrothal; it looks like a wedding; but it sounds, in context, as if its power as a contract derived from the prophecies just spoken; so that the truth in Cressida's vision (which we know for truth) asserts the truth of Pandarus' own prophecy—he will be the first pander, if either lover proves untrue. It is an odd situation. (1982, 52–53)

It is, in fact, a little odder even than Palmer's description, because what Pandarus says is "If ever you prove false one to another . . . let all constant men be Troiluses, all false women Cressids" (3.2.199, 202–3). The possibility that Troilus could be the false lover is not even considered, as though by her own self-vengeful words Cressida has defined her fate and Pandarus', which he accepts.

Other conventional revenges mentioned in passing concern abstractions, rather than characters. Troilus attributes his loss of Cressida to vengeance by the gods:

Cressid, I love thee in so strain'd a purity
That the blest gods, as angry with my fancy,
More bright in zeal than the devotion which
Cold lips blow to their deities, take thee from me.

(4.4.24–27)

Earlier, he has cursed for its brevity the night he has spent with Cressida:

Beshrew the witch! With venomous wights she stays
As tediously as hell, but flies the grasps of love
With wings more momentary-swift than thought.
You will catch cold and curse me.

(4.2.12–15)

Earlier still, Ulysses has ascribed the loss of all good things to the malice of "envious and calumniating Time" (3.3.174).

Several of the minor revenges in the play, however, are less conventional than the foregoing. Diomedes and Aeneas exchange death threats mingled with compliments; they "know each other well . . . and long to know each other worse" (4.1.31–32). Ulysses insults Cressida by declining to kiss her, saying that he is disgusted by "her wanton spirits" (4.5.56). Hector breaks off his duel with Ajax, explaining, however, that if it were possible for him to destroy the Greek half of Ajax without harming the Trojan half, he would be glad to do so (4.5.124–35). Although each of these incidents is amusingly phrased, each also reminds us of the history of the war. Ajax is half Trojan because his mother was a Trojan princess.[5] To avenge her loss, Paris seduced Helen, in Shakespeare's version of the story a wanton woman like Cressida. And to avenge the loss of Helen, noble princes with no personal animosity toward one another have fought and died for years. And, we are also reminded, since there has been no resolution of the central issue, when this lull in the fighting ends, the dying will resume.

Ostensibly, both the past and future are determined by what Prosser calls "the revenge theme at the core of the play." As she sees it, "the original cause of the pointless conflict was not Paris's lust for Helen, but simple revenge. Paris had been commissioned merely to take a Greek captive, any captive, in retaliation for the Greeks' capture of some 'old,' and in the play nameless, 'aunt.' Hector surely gives Shakespeare's evaluation of the ensuing events when he charges that 'pleasure and revenge / Have ears more deaf than adders to the voice / Of any true decision' (II.ii.171–73). The issue was tainted from the beginning" (1973, 82).

Whether or not Hector expresses Shakespeare's attitude, it is certain that all of the characters express an unusual attitude toward a "theme at the core of the play." When they comment upon it at all, it is generally to express contempt and cynicism; but, for the most part, they cannot seem to keep their minds on this central revenge, being continually distracted by other, more personal, motives. Their feelings toward the major revenge theme are reflected in their comments on the actors in the drama that embodies it: Helen, Menelaus, and Paris. When Menelaus partially avenges himself by wounding Paris, Troilus remarks of his brother's injury

> Let Paris bleed, 'tis but a scar to scorn;
> Paris is gor'd with Menelaus' horn.

$$(1.1.111–12)$$

Cressida describes Helen as "a merry Greek" (1.2.109). Menelaus is mocked by Patroclus and Cressida, criticized (in an aside) by Ulysses, and even insulted by the usually gracious Hector (4.5.26–46, 176–80). The most thorough condemnation of these three—and thus of the whole war and its cause—is made by Diomedes when asked by Paris, "Who, in your thoughts, deserves fair Helen best, / Myself, or Menelaus?":

>   Both alike.
> He merits well to have her that doth seek her,
> Not making any scruple of her soil,
> With such a hell of pain and world of charge;
> And you as well to keep her that defend her,

> Not palating the taste of her dishonor,
> With such a costly loss of wealth and friends.
> He like a puling cuckold would drink up
> The lees and dregs of a flat tamed piece;
> You like a lecher out of whorish loins
> Are pleas'd to breed out your inheritors.
> Both merits pois'd, each weighs nor less nor more,
> But he as he, the heavier for a whore.
> *Paris:* You are too bitter to your country-woman.
> *Diomedes:* She's bitter to her country. Hear me, Paris:
> For every false drop in her bawdy veins,
> A Grecian's life hath sunk; for every scruple
> Of her contaminated carrion weight,
> A Troyan hath been slain. Since she could speak,
> She hath not given so many good words breath
> As for her Greeks and Troyans suff'red death.
>
> (4.1.54–75)

If we can accept Diomedes' words as true—and although he is no very exalted character, there is nothing in the play to contradict what he says here—then "the issue was tainted from the beginning," not necessarily by revenge but by the characters and motives of the actors in the initial situation. Paris is a lecher, Menelaus a cuckold, and Helen a whore. The revenges of such characters will necessarily be as ignoble as they themselves, but that fact does not constitute a general condemnation of revenge.

Since what is ostensibly the reason for the central revenge—that taken for the "rape" of Helen—is presented as being beneath contempt, it is not surprising that none of the characters except Paris and Menelaus (who play very small parts) pays it much attention. Both Greeks and Trojans are continually distracted from the reason for and prosecution of the war by more personal concerns, some of which involve minor revenges but none of which has much to do with "the" revenge. The Greeks are primarily concerned with "degree" and satiric attacks that undermine it; the Trojans are primarily interested in various questions of honor and chivalry. Both groups degrade revenge by making it either comic or contemptible or—in the case of Thersites—both.

Critics differ as widely in their estimation of Thersites as about any other aspect of the play. On the one hand, he is seen as the voice of truth; on the other, as expressing ideas that are both valueless and offensive.[6] That Thersites' sentiments are offensive is inarguable, but that they are valueless is less obvious. For one thing, he is acknowledged by Achilles as "a privileg'd man" (2.3.57), a court fool. If we accept him as such, then if he is a liar he is also an anomaly among Shakespeare's acknowledged fools, who are notably truthful and incisive, if frequently disrespectful, characters. An even better reason for believing Thersites is that he so frequently echoes other characters' opinions or states what the spectator knows to be true. He sees no "matter" in Agamemnon (2.1.8–9); nor is an audience likely to. He tells Ajax that he is "bought and sold among those of any wit" and tells both Ajax and Achilles "There's Ulysses and old Nestor . . . yoke you like draught-oxen and make you plough up the wars" (2.1.46–47, 104–7), which we know from the previous scene is true. His contempt for Patroclus (2.1.114–15; 2.3.48–68; 5.1.14–36) is no greater than that of Ulysses and Nestor, albeit much more vividly expressed. His constant raillery against Ajax has parallels in the descriptions by Alexander, Nestor, and Ulysses (1.2.19–30; 1.3.188–92, 373–83). He says Helen is a whore (2.3.72); so does Diomedes. He says Menelaus is a cuckold (2.3.73; 5.1.53–66); so does everyone else. He says that Achilles and Patroclus may run mad "with too much blood and too little brain" (5.1.48–49), a statement similar to that of Ulysses that they "forestall prescience, and esteem no act / But that of hand" (1.3.199–200). What he says about Diomedes and Cressida (5.1.88–98; 5.2.10–11, 19, 24, 55–57, 65, 75, 113–14) is no more than accurate commentary.

Even when Thersites is particularly scurrilous, there is some truth to what he says. One example is a speech in which he manages to disparage half of the play's major characters in less than twenty lines:

> Now they are clapper-clawing one another; I'll go look on. That dissembling abominable varlet, Diomed, has got that same scurvy doting foolish [young] knave's sleeve of Troy there in his helm. I would fain see them meet, that that same young Troyan ass, that loves the whore there, might send that Greekish whoremasterly villain with the sleeve back to the dissembling luxurious drab, of a sleeveless arrant. A' th' t' other side, the policy of those crafty swearing rascals, that stale old mouse-eaten dry cheese, Nestor, and that same dog-fox, Ulysses, is not prov'd worth a blackberry. They set me up, in policy, that mongril cur, Ajax, against that dog of as bad a kind, Achilles; and now is the cur Ajax prouder than the cur Achilles, and will not arm today; whereupon the Grecians began to proclaim barbarism, and policy grows into an ill opinion. (5.4.1–17)

Not Thersites' most vehement detractor could deny the truth of much of this. Diomedes is dissembling, Troilus doting and foolish, Cressida faithless, Nestor old, and Ulysses cunning. Achilles and Ajax have repeatedly demonstrated their pride, and as for their being curs, Nestor has used the same term to describe them (1.3.389–90). Above all, it is interesting that Thersites here and elsewhere is aware of Ulysses and Nestor's plot; since he is not privy to their counsels, his knowledge can only be due to insight. Whether this insight can be seen in his more general commentaries on the war is, of course, debatable, but one final consideration is of interest. Although Thersites does not limit his raillery to the Greeks, he touches the Trojans—apart from Cressida—only lightly. Troilus is reviled as a fool and Paris is referred to as a "cuckold-maker" (5.7.9), but Hector is let off with only a casual curse for "fright-ing" Thersites (5.4.31–32). Thersites curses only Greeks—the villains of the piece—with any energy; the Trojan party remains essentially un-scathed.

But for many critics, I suspect, the question of whether what Thersites says is true is secondary. Acknowledging, however tacitly, that truth is the first casualty of war, the critical consensus seems to be that it is the political effect of satire, not its objective truth, that is important: "In the Greek plot there is definite condemnation of satire as practised by Pa-troclus and Thersites, which is harmful to the state and destructive of the specialty of rule" (Craig 1948, 240). This "condemnation" occurs in the speeches of the Greek "debate," and it is interesting to review what is actually said in this scene. Ulysses attributes the Greek failure to con-quer Troy to "neglection of degree" (1.3.127). Nestor agrees, and Aga-memnon asks what is to be done about it (1.3.138–41). Instead of answering that question, Ulysses says

> The great Achilles, whom opinion crowns
> The sinow and the forehand of our host,
> Having his ear full of his airy fame,
> Grows dainty of his worth, and in his tent
> Lies mocking our designs. With him Patroclus
> Upon a lazy bed the livelong day
> Breaks scurril jests,
> And with ridiculous and [awkward] action,
> Which, slanderer, he imitation calls,
> He pageants us.
>
> (1.3.142–51)

After a long and inexplicably detailed account of these mockeries, he is seconded by Nestor, who says that the bad example of Achilles and Patroclus has infected many others, specifically Ajax and Thersites (1.3.151–96). Ulysses then changes tack and says that these malcontents rail against the "policy" of the Grecian chiefs, preferring physical ex-ploits (1.3.197–210). At this point, Aeneas interrupts with Hector's chal-lenge. Following the Trojan's departure, Ulysses explains to Nestor a scheme to humble Achilles by setting up Ajax as the acknowledged champion of the Greeks; Nestor assents, and the scene ends (1.3.310–90).

Considered in light of the revenge theme, this is a fascinating scene. None of the Greek leaders expresses any interest in revenge on Troy.

Palmer maintains that "the Greeks, with right on their side, never ask whether [Helen] is worth the effort of recovery" (Introduction to the Arden edition, 1982, 45); in fact, there is no evidence in the play that the Greeks *do* have right on their side. An English play of this period may be assumed to have a Trojan bias, in the absence of other indications, and for the most part the Trojans are far more attractive characters than the Greeks. If the fact that the war is caused by Trojan vengeance is presumed to tip the balance, that fact should not be considered in isolation.[7] A more useful assessment might be made by measuring the most hotheaded of the Trojan revengers, Troilus, against the archetypal politic Greek, Ulysses, who cares nothing for Helen, heroics, or honor, but only that Troy be destroyed with the greatest possible dispatch.

This cannot be done, Ulysses says, until degree is restored to the Greek army, but he never really says explicitly how that can be done, although his final speech before Aeneas' arrival suggests that this crisis in morale may be caused by the Greek leaders' attempt to substitute policy for traditional heroics. Ulysses implies that reducing Achilles' pride—ironically, by inflating Ajax's—will restore order, but he never explains how this plan can be expected to work. Presumably, the point is to get Achilles back onto the battlefield. Accordingly, the Greek lords praise Ajax (2.3.144–266) and slight Achilles (3.3.38–190). And all of this has no effect whatever.

This statement undoubtedly requires some elaboration, cutting as it does against the grain of critical consensus. Knight, for example, maintains that "[Act 3, scene 3] exposes the weakness of individualism, its rational absurdity. Achilles is convinced. He decides to bestir himself, his folly exposed" ([1930] 1949, 57). Kaula states that "the final effect of [Ulysses'] strategy is to trigger Achilles' ferocious blood-lust for Hector" (1961, 281). These assertions, however, are simply not accurate. Ulysses is certainly right to call Achilles proud, and his plot wounds Achilles' pride (3.3.227–28), but pride is not the reason Achilles has been keeping to his tent, and Ulysses apparently knows this. The true reason is Achilles' love for Polyxena (3.3.190–215). That this is Achilles' predominant motive is proved by the fact that after he has threatened Hector and even promised to fight him the following day (4.5.242–46, 268–70), he relinquishes his purpose at a word from Polyxena:

My sweet Patroclus, I am thwarted quite
From my great purpose in to-morrow's battle.
Here is a letter from Queen Hecuba,
A token from her daughter, my fair love,
Both taxing me and gaging me to keep
An oath that I have sworn. I will not break it.

Fall Greeks, fail fame, honor or go or stay,
My major vow lies here; this I'll obey.

(5.1.37–44)

Inasmuch as Ulysses has told Achilles that

All the commerce that you have had with Troy
As perfectly is ours as yours, my lord

(3.3.205–6)

he must know that pride is not what is keeping Achilles from battle. Whether or not he knows, as the audience comes to, that Patroclus, far from distracting Achilles from the war, has been urging him to return to it (3.3.216–33), it is clear that Ulysses' scheme has little chance of success, since it is not pride, as he would have it, that is Achilles' besetting sin, but—as the despicable Thersites says of all his compatriots—lechery. Despite Ulysses' wonderful speech on degree, it would seem that he is actually trying, not to humble Achilles' pride, but to inflame it sufficiently to overcome Achilles' lechery.

The final irony is that what actually galvanizes both Achilles and Ajax into action is a motive beyond not only Ulysses' conspiring, but even his consideration. That motive is revenge, and it is appropriate that the politic Ulysses, all of whose means have produced no ends, is the character to announce the purely emotional cause that will produce the conclusion he desires:

O, courage, courage, princes! Great Achilles
Is arming, weeping, cursing, vowing vengeance.
Patroclus' wounds have rous'd his drowsy blood,
Together with his mangled Myrmidons,
That noseless, handless, hack'd and chipp'd, come to him,
Crying on Hector. Ajax hath lost a friend,
And foams at mouth, and he is arm'd and at it,
Roaring for Troilus. . . .

(5.5.30–37)

The brilliance of Ulysses' language seems to have blinded many critics to the fact that his plotting serves no purpose but to increase Ajax's pride (which is controlled, finally, by the influence of his illustrious cousin, Hector). Whatever Shakespeare is saying about revenge in this play, it is obvious that he is not making a case for policy. Ulysses, in fact, has many of the negative qualities of the Machiavellian stage revenger: he is cunning and politic, and revels in accomplices and conspiracy. He uses others to gain his own ends and conceals his true motives. In a play in which many characters are concerned with love and honor and loyalty, he is interested in trickery as a means and conquest as an end. Because he is clever and articulate, because he is surrounded by characters who are neither, and above all because he makes two great speeches in which commonplace ideas are memorably stated, he has been overvalued and seen as a mouthpiece for Shakespeare's sentiments. But just as Thersites' brilliant use of invective serves no purpose in the world of the play, so Ulysses' cleverness comes to nothing. Both characters use the means of revenge without having a legitimate reason for revenge. They are beneath revenge as Hector is above it.

Hector is above revenge and is the noblest and most admirable character in the play because of his adherence to a code of chivalry. In contrast to many of the other characters, he is driven not by a practical desire to destroy or save a city, possess a woman, or even, it seems, to surpass his colleagues, but simply by a wish to do the most honorable thing in any given set of circumstances. He seems a throwback to the knights of medieval romance who slay monsters and rescue maidens not out of personal animosity or desire, but because that is what their code of knighthood requires of them. Like these medieval heroes, he is not without frailties: he is capable of anger when struck down by an opponent (1.2.4–11, 33–36) and greed when he sees a beautiful suit of armor (5.6.27–31). Usually, however, he does the honorable thing because being what he is he cannot bear to do otherwise.

Hector presents two main arguments for relinquishing Helen. To begin with, he says, "she is not worth what she doth cost / The keeping" (2.2.51):

> Let Helen go.
> Since the first sword was drawn about this question,
> Every tithe soul, 'mongst many thousand dismes,
> Hath been as dear as Helen; I mean, of ours.
> If we have lost so many tenths of ours,
> To guard a thing not ours nor worth to us
> (Had it our name) the value of one ten,
> What merit's in that reason which denies
> The yielding of her up?
>
> (2.2.17–25)

The practical argument having had no effect on Troilus and Paris, Hector argues eloquently from a moral position:

> Nature craves
> All dues be rend'red to their owners: now,
> What nearer debt in all humanity

Than wife is to the husband? If this law
Of nature be corrupted through affection,
And that great minds, of partial indulgence
To their benumbed wills, resist the same,
There is a law in each well-order'd nation
To curb those raging appetites that are
Most disobedient and refractory.
If Helen then be wife to Sparta's king,
As it is known she is, these moral laws
Of nature and of nations speak aloud
To have her back return'd. Thus to persist
In doing wrong extenuates not wrong,
But makes it much more heavy.

(2.2.173–88)

Hector is the principal exponent of good sense among the Trojans, as Ulysses is among the Greeks. But just as Ulysses' intelligent pragmatism fails to effect his designs, so Hector's idealistic moralizing fails to dictate even his own actions:

                              Hector's opinion
Is this in way of truth; yet ne'er the less
My spritely brethren, I propend to you
In resolution to keep Helen still,
For 'tis a cause that hath no mean dependance
Upon our joint and several dignities.

(2.2.188–93)

Despite this abrupt reversal by Hector, commentators are much less critical of him than of his brother Troilus, whose words and actions are more consistent. This is not to say that Troilus is a perfectly steadfast character; at his first appearance, he has rejected the war altogether:

Peace, you ungracious clamors! peace, rude sounds!
Fools on both sides, Helen must needs be fair,
When with your blood you daily paint her thus.
I cannot fight upon this argument;
It is too starv'd a subject for my sword.

(1.1.89–93)

Furthermore, in the debate scene (as Palmer points out) Troilus shifts his ground during the course of the argument by using different concepts of honor as though they were the same (Introduction to the Arden edition, 1982, 46–47). But what really loses Troilus the sympathy of the critics is that he alludes to and defends the abduction of Helen as a revenge. This speech (and those of Paris) give Hector his opportunity to comment that

                              pleasure and revenge
    Have ears more deaf than adders to the voice
    Of any true decision.
                                                    (2.2.171–73)

As Oscar James Campbell sees it, "These wise words prove to be pro-
phetic. Troilus follows unreasonable pleasure and becomes the slave of
the wanton Cressida. He follows turbulent, irrational courses of revenge
and is left rushing wildly and futilely after his rival, whom he is doomed
never to overtake. . . . Troilus the warrior and Troilus the lover thus
represent different aspects of a life which has deliberately freed itself of
all rational control" (1943, 109–10).

It seems a little hard on Troilus to condemn him for what he says in
this scene. True, he denigrates "reasons," which he links with "fears"
(2.2.32, 36–50). True, he cites vengeance as a reason for keeping Helen
(2.2.72–96). But he points out that this vengeance—the "theft" of
Helen—was done "for an old aunt whom the Greeks held captive" and
"the Grecians keep our aunt" (2.2.77, 80). Furthermore, he continues,
the Trojans urged Paris on to the revenge and approved its outcome
(2.2.84–92). All of this may be wrong, but it is not without reason. Even if
it is wrong, however, it is not Troilus' primary argument, which is that
honor—whether construed as justice, justification, reputation, or
glory—demands that Helen be kept. Ultimately, both Hector and Troilus
separately reach the same conclusion, and Troilus explicitly names honor
as his primary motive while disparaging revenge, with Hector's approbation:

    Troilus: Were it not glory that we more affected
             Than the performance of our heaving spleens,
             I would not wish a drop of Troyan blood
             Spent more in her defense. But, worthy Hector,
             She is a theme of honor and renown,
             A spur to valiant and magnanimous deeds,
             Whose present courage may beat down our foes,
             And fame in time to come canonize us,
             For I presume brave Hector would not lose
             So rich advantage of a promis'd glory
             As smiles upon the forehead of this action
             For the wide world's revenue.
    Hector: I am yours,
             You valiant offspring of great Priamus.
                                                    (2.2.195–207)

This is not to say that Troilus is not a vengeful character, only that his
vengefulness is neither so pervasive nor so irrational as some critics

would have it. Troilus in the early part of the play seems to stand condemned simply for being the only character who takes note of what the war is supposed to be about. As he becomes increasingly overwhelmed with his own concerns, he becomes increasingly vengeful. He threatens Diomedes, vows to challenge him, and does so (4.4.126–29; 5.2.95–96; 5.4.19–23; 5.6.6–11). He is described as vengeful by Ulysses, and in light of the unquestioning condemnation of revenge in any context by many Shakespearean commentators, this speech is interesting:

> The youngest son of Priam, a true knight,
> Not yet mature, yet matchless, firm of word,
> Speaking [in] deeds, and deedless in his tongue,
> Not soon provok'd, nor being provok'd soon calm'd;
> His heart and hand both open and both free,
> For what he has he gives, what thinks he shows,
> Yet gives he not till judgment guide his bounty,
> Nor dignifies an impare thought with breath;
> Manly as Hector, but more dangerous,
> For Hector in his blaze of wrath subscribes
> To tender objects, but he in heat of action
> Is more vindicative than jealous love.
> They call him Troilus, and on him erect
> A second hope, as fairly built as Hector.
>
> (4.5.96–109)

The fascinating aspect of this speech is that it attributes vengefulness to Troilus as a positive trait, like honesty and generosity; vengefulness is not only accepted, it is considered (in a warrior like Troilus) a positive virtue, which makes him a more dangerous foe than even Hector. Surely this is a strange speech for Ulysses to make if Shakespeare's object is to condemn revenge. It is also a speech that should be kept in mind when Hector and Troilus have their final discussion, the subject of which is revenge:

> *Troilus:* Brother, you have a vice of mercy in you,
> Which better fits a lion than a man.
> *Hector:* What vice is that? Good Troilus, chide me for it.
> *Troilus:* When many times the captive Grecian falls,
> Even in the fan and wind of your fair sword,
> You bid them rise and live.
> *Hector:* O, 'tis fair play.
> *Troilus:* Fool's play, by heaven, Hector.
> *Hector:* How now, how now?
> *Troilus:* For th' love of all the gods,
> Let's leave the hermit pity with our mother,

And when we have our armors buckled on,
The venom'd vengeance ride upon our swords,
Spur them to ruthful work, rein them from ruth.
Hector: Fie, savage, fie!
Troilus: Hector, then 'tis wars.

                                                        (5.3.37–49)

Critics have tended to agree with Hector that the viewpoint Troilus expresses is savage. The consensus seems to be that Troilus takes the war too personally, his savagery inspired less by patriotism or a thirst for renown than by his personal losses, first of Cressida and later of Hector.[8] Troilus is condemned by critics both for what he says and what he does. But what he says in this speech—leaving aside for the moment his reference to vengeance—is simply logic and good sense. He says that it is foolish of Hector to spare his enemies, and that war is savage. This is not a gentle, moral, nice attitude; it is merely the truth. Of Hector's attitude it may be said, *"C'est magnifique, mais ce n'est pas la guerre."* However much we may admire this attitude, we should remember the reason for it; Hector is not a saint, but a sportsman who spares life not from compassion, but because " 'tis fair play." Furthermore, he is quite willing to kill a man for his armor (5.6.27–31; 5.8.1–2). To assert that his position is confirmed by the events of the last act is possible only by imposing preconceived ideas on what those events mean. The barest statement of the action is as follows: Troilus warns Hector against sparing his enemies; Hector spares Achilles; and Achilles treacherously slays Hector. To make this tell against Troilus, rather than Hector, it is necessary to equate Troilus with Achilles, and this is hardly justifiable. While it is true that both are inspired by vengeance, Troilus against Diomedes and Achilles against Hector, that is the extent of their similarity. Troilus proceeds against Diomedes only after his betrayal by Cressida, and in a spirit quite as chivalrous as even Hector could wish:

                              Proud Diomed, believe,
I come to lose my arm, or win my sleeve.

                                                        (5.3.95–96)

If this statement shows little patriotism, it is still not out of line with the tenor of the play, and certainly shows no less regard for Troy than Hector's mercy toward those who are trying to destroy his city. Furthermore, as the battle progresses, we learn that Troilus is not devoting himself to a purely personal revenge:

Ulysses: Ajax hath lost a friend,
          And foams at mouth, and he is arm'd and at it,

Roaring for Troilus, who hath done to-day
Mad and fantastic execution,
Engaging and redeeming of himself
With such a careless force, and forceless care,
As if that luck, in very spite of cunning,
Bade him win all.

(5.5.35–42)

Even this passage, a tribute to Troilus from the enemy, can be (and is) read as discreditable to him, provided he is seen as an exemplar of irrational revenge. Palmer, in his note to lines 41–42, maintains that "F's *luck* (Q *lust*) seems weak; it is Troilus' passion for revenge (as Ulysses had seen; and cf. V.ii), and not mere chance, which is wholly controlling him now" (the Arden edition, 1982, 292). But Ulysses here is not talking about Troilus' vengeful battle against Diomedes (which Troilus, far from winning all, has lost); he is talking about Troilus' general prowess and in particular his conquest of Ajax's unnamed friend, whose death we have no reason to attribute to revenge. If Troilus' great ability on this day is inspired by vengefulness, then he is turning his own loss to his country's benefit—no very ill activity. More significantly, reading "lust" for "luck," while it strengthens the interpretation of Troilus as madman, weakens the force of the passage. That Troilus engages and redeems himself with great force and no care and "in very spite of cunning" comes off victorious is surely attributable to "luck," the only force that could preserve him in his recklessness, and not to "lust."

That "lust" is not antithetical to "care" and "cunning" is demonstrated by Achilles' revenge on Hector. Achilles' lust for Hector's blood has been noted previously. Finding it impossible to defeat Hector by himself, Achilles carefully plots the assassination, instructing his Myrmidons to withhold themselves from other fighting (5.7.1–6), and cunningly attacking only after Hector has disarmed. Insofar as this attack is immediately inspired by Patroclus' death, it is revenge, and it is appalling. But it is a far cry from the vengeful behavior of Troilus, who, having twice fought Diomedes (once simultaneously with Ajax, while Hector cheered)—apparently without effecting any revenge—can be distracted from his personal concerns by the capture of Aeneas (5.6.11–12, 22–26).

The final bit of evidence frequently used to convict Troilus as an obsessive, irrational revenger is his antepenultimate line: "Hope of revenge shall hide our inward woe" (5.10.31). A more appropriate attitude, however, is difficult to imagine. Troilus' brother has just been treacherously slain. He foresees the "sure destructions" of his city and his people (5.10.6–9). His reaction may not be generous or charitable, but it is natural and human. If it does not bode well for the world of the play, that too is natural: "The ending of the tale is in accord with the facts of human experience; life often settles nothing, it leaves the innocent to suffer, and the guilty to prevail" (Lawrence 1960, 168). Nor can it be accurately said that Troilus learns nothing in the course of the play, for in his final lines he rejects Pandarus.

This rejection, coupled as it is with Pandarus' epilogue, in which he promises to bequeath his diseases to the audience, does not, of course, constitute a dramatically satisfying ending. But the ending is unsatisfying not because Troilus reaffirms his dedication to revenge, but because we have seen the better characters overcome by the worse. Troilus is betrayed by the faithless Cressida; Hector is slain by the treacherous Achilles; the noble Trojans are doomed to be destroyed by the pragmatic Greeks. And all of this has been caused by the quarrel of two foolish men over a worthless woman. Revenge plays a relatively small part in all of this, and the part it does play is not well-defined. Ulysses expresses no vengeful feelings, but it is questionable whether this ennobles him. He is politic—we never see him do anything heroic—and he is willing to use the vengeful feelings of others to gain his own ends. Hector likewise is virtually without a sense of vengeance, and his chivalry results in his death. No character is pure revenger; all have mixed motives. Achilles kills Hector because of pride and blood-lust, as well as the death of Patroclus. Troilus fights not only for revenge but for honor and the defense of Troy. Achilles' revenge is base, Troilus' is not. Nothing in *Troilus and Cressida* is clear cut or easy. The play is not a condemnation of love because Troilus is betrayed, nor a condemnation of honor because Hector is slain, but "love" and "honor" are profoundly questioned. Likewise, there is no evidence in the play that Shakespeare intended it as a condemnation of revenge. Revenge is subjected to more questions in this comedy than in any other, but no easy answers are reached.

All's Well That Ends Well is not a popular play. True, George Bernard Shaw defended it as an example of "those plays in which our William anticipated modern dramatic art by making serious attempts to hold the mirror up to nature" ([1897] 1961, 25); but a Shavian pronouncement is virtually guaranteed to contradict general opinion.[9] More nearly representative of the prevailing critical estimation of *All's Well* (though not necessarily of all of the last comedies) is Van Doren's statement: "The three comedies of Shakespeare which were written, if his chronology is rightly understood, between 'Hamlet' and 'Othello'—at the outset in other words of his great career in tragedy—may be said to indicate in their various ways that what he should have kept on writing at such a time was tragedy and nothing else. . . . [These] three comedies . . . are in any final view unsuccessful" (1939, 202). The feeling that *All's Well* is more than slightly tinged by tragedy, that if it is a comedy at all it is an exceedingly "dark" one, is apparent in a quotation from an anonymous leading article in the *Times Literary Supplement*, no. 1030 (31 October 1921, 650): "In *All's Well That Ends Well*—supremely cynical title—Shakespeare seems deliberately to take revenge on his own idealism of love. . . . The self-torturing mood of the play, the bitter mood of 'I'll show you a happy ending,' is only too apparent" (Lawrence 1960, 68). Even a critic who takes a less jaundiced view of the play recognizes that modern readers and audiences find it unsatisfying: "*All's Well* is not a dark comedy except to the refined taste of the modern world. To Shakespeare and his age the device by which Helena consummates her marriage with Bertram and thus fulfills the seemingly impossible conditions he has laid upon her was merely ingenious and rather cheerful" (Craig 1948, 222).

The principal modern objections to the play lie in the characters of Helena and Bertram. Helena is frequently perceived as a pushy, unfeminine, managing woman. Bertram is regarded as a cad. Thus the hero and heroine of the play can be seen to be in direct opposition, yet both of them wrong. In fact, it is only Helena's actions—never her words or the opinions of the other characters about her—that are open to question, while it is primarily Bertram's words, and the lack of action taken against him—the lack of revenge upon him—that make him a difficult character to accept. Since Helena's actions have more influence on Bertram than his words have on her, I will consider her first.

There seem to be two major reasons for disliking Helena: (1) she is in love with a man who is unworthy of her; and (2) she behaves unworthily to win him, whether she is viewed as degradingly passive or degradingly active.[10] The first objection is largely a matter of taste and is therefore difficult to dispute, but a few points may be made against it. To begin with, it is not unusual to find Shakespeare's comic heroines more strongminded and more attractive characters than his comic heroes, yet few critics worry whether Bassanio is worthy of Portia or Orlando of Rosalind, or wonder that the ladies love these gentlemen. Furthermore, no one in the play suggests that Helena should be blamed because the man she loves is behaving badly. Finally, if we cannot accept that even characters don't get to choose whom they fall in love with, at least it is obvious that Helena has been in love with Bertram for some time before he starts misbehaving. It is not, in fact, until she declares her love by choosing him as her husband that he does anything to lose our sympathy—and even at that point we may feel that he has a right to object to this somewhat unorthodox wooing. Once they are married, however, it is hard to see what else Helena could do but what she does, which leads to the second objection to her character.

Helena begins passively enough. Although desperately in love with Bertram, she declares

> I follow him not
> By any token of presumptuous suit,
> Nor would I have him till I do deserve him,
> Yet never know how that desert should be.

                                                                    (1.3.197–200)

She proposes to go to Paris to cure the king, although she honestly admits to the Countess

> My lord your son made me to think of this;
> Else Paris, and the medicine, and the King,
> Had from the conversation of my thoughts
> Happily been absent then.

                                                                    (1.3.232–35)

Finding the king reluctant to try her remedy, she risks her own life on its success (2.1.169–74, 179–86), and it is not until after the king accepts this offer that she asks for her reward, which is freely—and with no overt or implied reluctance or disapproval as in some of Shakespeare's sources— granted. The young lords who express themselves ready to marry her, the king who reiterates the service she has done and enumerates her virtues, and Lafew, who keeps up a running commentary on her worthiness, are all witnesses that Helena has deserved her reward (2.3.72– 144).

When the reward himself objects and flees to Florence, his own mother supports Helena (3.2.28–32, 66–68, 80–83, et al.), whose next action is to leave Rossillion so that Bertram will return to France rather than risk his life in the Italian war. In her letter to the Countess, Helena characterizes herself as Juno, the great mythological exemplar of the jealous and vengeful wife. When she arrives in Florence, incognito, she is still suffering guilt over her marriage, but hears her companions sympathize with the fate of Bertram's wife (3.5.59–67). Diana reflects well on Helena's nature with regard to Parolles (who has been reporting "coarsely" of Helena) when she says "Were I his lady, / I would poison that vile rascal" (3.5.57, 83–84), whereas Helena expresses no such vengeful sentiment.

In none of this is there anything discreditable to Helena. One may object, with Dr. Johnson, to the fact that a pilgrim leaving Rossillion for

Compostella should end up in Florence; but since none of the other characters seems to find it odd, and since "there's four or five, to Great Saint Jaques bound" already at the Saint Francis (3.5.95), it seems reasonable to infer that Helena's arrival at Bertram's place of residence is indeed providential. As to whether the bed trick planned by Helena and her fellow conspirators is a humiliating shift, there is no evidence that anyone in the play finds it so. While it contains elements of a revenge in the use of accomplices and in turning Bertram's evil intent on himself (4.2.73–76), and Helena refers to it as a "plot" (3.7.44), it is not done out of any desire for retribution. "This deceit so lawful" (3.7.38) allows Helena to reclaim her husband, provides Diana with a dowry, and saves Bertram from committing the sin of adultery. It is difficult to see how any of this reflects badly on Helena. Her actions certainly distinguish her from patient Griselda, and critics who find her an unsatisfactory heroine because she pursues Bertram fail to take into account the tradition in which women who pursue the men they love were likely to be panegyrized.[11]

Based simply on the outcome of Helena's actions (all's well that ends well), our judgment of her character must be positive; but there is a further reason for acknowledging her virtues: she is set in opposition to Bertram, surely—and understandably—the least-liked of Shakespeare's heroes. The classic summation of his character and the standard reaction to it are Johnson's: "I cannot reconcile my heart to *Bertram;* a man noble without generosity, and young without truth; who marries *Helen* as a coward, and leaves her as a profligate: when she is dead by his unkindness, sneaks home to a second marriage, is accused by a woman whom he has wronged, defends himself by falsehood, and is dismissed to happiness" ([1765] 1908, 103).[12]

Certainly it appears throughout the first three acts of the play that Bertram is a fitting object for at least comic revenge. Lafew makes it clear that in his estimation the young Count is not merely "an unseason'd courtier," as his mother describes him (1.1.71), but a fool: "I am sure thy father drunk wine—but if thou be'st not an ass, I am a youth of fourteen. I have known thee already" (2.3.99–101). When Bertram tries to refuse Helena, he is threatened with royal vengeance:

> Check thy contempt;
> Obey our will, which travails in thy good;
> Believe not thy disdain, but presently
> Do thine own fortunes that obedient right
> Which both thy duty owes and our power claims,
> Or I will throw thee from my care for ever
> Into the staggers and the careless lapse
> Of youth and ignorance; both my revenge and hate

Loosing upon thee, in the name of justice,
Without all terms of pity. Speak, thy answer.

(2.3.157–66)

Bertram's answer averts this vengeance, but after hearing of his flight to
Florence his mother anticipates the King's further "indignation" (3.2.28–
32). She herself disowns him (3.2.66–68) and after Helena's departure
envisions divine vengeance against him:

What angel shall
Bless this unworthy husband? He cannot thrive,
Unless her prayers, whom heaven delights to hear
And loves to grant, reprieve him from the wrath
Of greatest justice.

(3.4.25–29)

Bertram further strengthens his resemblance to Shakespeare's earlier
objects of comic revenge by giving his opponents the means to humble
him, as he gives away his ring.[13] Ultimately, however, it is Bertram's
language, rather than his foolishness, arrogance, or attempt at adultery
that disturbs an audience, no matter what excuses can be made for him,
including youth and the influence of Parolles.[14]

While Bertram, acknowledged as the hero of the piece, is generally
disliked, Parolles, a self-acknowledged villain, has received considerable
critical sympathy from some quarters:

Parolles has many of the lineaments of *Falstaff,* and seems to be the
character which *Shakespeare* delighted to draw, a fellow that had more
wit than virtue. Though justice required that he should be detected
and exposed, yet his *vices sit so fit in him* that he is not at last suffered to
starve. (Johnson [1765] 1908, 101)

At the end of *All's Well* we may feel more in sympathy with Parolles
than with any other character. (Leech [1965] 1968, 71–72)

It is hardly surprising that Parolles is not allowed to starve; the usual goal
of comic vengeance being to reveal erring characters' faults to themselves and—after reforming their behavior—welcome them back into the
society of the play, no character is ever allowed to suffer unduly. But it is
an extremely jaundiced view of the play that can find Parolles the most
sympathetic character in it. If he has "more wit than virtue," it is only
because he is completely devoid of the latter quality, for his wit is
sufficient only to fool the callow Bertram, and he is amusing only as the
butt of wittier characters.[15]

The embarrassment we feel on Parolles's behalf and our sense that "he acts as a scapegoat and takes at least some of the blame for Bertram's faults" (Hunter, Introduction to the Arden edition, 1959, xxviii) should not blind us to the fact that Parolles gets no more than he deserves—is, actually, let off with a good deal less. Every virtuous character in the play recognizes him as a threat to decent and orderly society:

Helena:	. . . I know him a notorious liar, Think him a great way fool, soly a coward.

(1.1.100–101)

Parolles:	My lord, you give me most egregious indignity.
Lafew:	Ay, with all my heart, and thou art worthy of it.
Parolles:	I have not, my lord, deserv'd it.
Lafew:	Yes, good faith, ev'ry dram of it, and I will not bate thee a scruple.

(2.3.216–22)

Clown:	. . . much fool may you find in you, even to the world's pleasure and the increase of laughter.

(2.4.35–37)

Countess:	A very tainted fellow, and full of wickedness.

(3.2.87)

First Lord:	. . . he's a most notable coward, an infinite and endless liar, an hourly promise-breaker, the owner of no one good quality worthy your lordship's entertainment.

(3.6.9–12)

In addition to all of the faults enumerated in these accusations, Parolles harbors vengeful feelings toward Lafew for seeing through him:

Well, thou hast a son shall take this disgrace off me, scurvy, old, filthy, scurvy lord! Well, I must be patient, there is no fettering of authority. I'll beat him, by my life, if I can meet him with any convenience, and he were double and double a lord. I'll have no more pity of his age than I would have of—I'll beat him, and if I could but meet him again. (2.3.235–41)

That Parolles is afraid to act on these thoughts—as proved when Lafew reappears to twit him again and depart unscathed—makes them no less ignoble. Lafew in this reappearance attempts to define Parolles's raison d'être:

By mine honor, if I were but two hours younger, I'd beat thee. Methink'st thou art a general offense, and every man should beat thee. I

think thou wast created for men to breathe themselves upon thee.
(2.3.252–56)

But there are more serious reasons for exposing Parolles: even if we
cannot credit the Countess's opinion of his bad influence on Bertram,
there is no reason to doubt Diana's statement that it is Parolles who leads
Bertram astray (3.5.82–83). Furthermore, as the Second Lord tells
Bertram,

> It were fit you knew him, lest reposing too far in his virtue, which he
> hath not, he might at some great and trusty business in a main danger
> fail you. (3.6.13–16)

And thus the plot against Parolles is constructed for the enlightenment
of Bertram and "the love of laughter" (3.6.34).

There is no evidence that the brothers Dumaine, who control the plot,
have any intention of reforming Parolles, although one of them, at least,
is clearly astonished to find that self-knowledge does not necessarily
lead to ethical behavior: "Is it possible he should know what he is, and
be that he is?" (4.1.44–45). In fact, Parolles's one redeeming feature—at
least for a modern audience—may be that he acknowledges himself a
rogue; it is this that gives him his only resemblance to Falstaff. In one
respect he is even more insightful than his great precursor, since he
recognizes that others besides Lafew are beginning to penetrate his
disguise: "They begin to smoke me, and disgraces have of late knock'd
too often at my door" (4.1.27–28). But confessed knavery remains knavery, and if such a statement as "under Lafeu's tender care, there may
even be hope for Parolles" (Prosser 1973, 76) means that we should
anticipate his reformation, it must simply be said that nothing in the play
gives evidence that Parolles will ever be anything but the thing he is,
which he admits to be a braggart and an ass (4.3.334–36).

But if the Dumaines have no hope of reforming Parolles, they do hope
to reform Bertram: "I would gladly have him see his company ana-
tomiz'd, that he might take a measure of his own judgments, wherein so
curiously he had set this counterfeit" (4.3.31–34). The judgments they
hope he will measure may extend farther than Parolles, since just before
this statement is made they deplore his seduction of Diana and both
before and after it his treatment of Helena (4.3.6–7, 14–27, 57–64). Since
Parolles has actually harmed no one involved in the plot against him, the
entire scene may be viewed in part as a revenge against Bertram for his
bad judgment, which, as the Dumaines see it, has "perverted" one
woman and killed another, as well as risking the safety of the army.
Parolles's verse and the Dumaines' comments remind Bertram that he,

too, is an object of this revenge; he receives this intelligence with curses and threats of his own vengeance (4.3.116, 222, 233–34, 237–38, 263–64, 275), in contrast to the first Dumaine, whose response to Parolles's derogatory comments about him are "I begin to love him for this" and "He hath out-villain'd villainy so far, that the rarity redeems him" (4.3.262, 273–74, although at 4.3.189 Dumaine seems to threaten violence in response to Parolles's slanders). Of course, Parolles must lie in order to malign the virtuous Dumaines, while the truth will suffice to blacken Bertram's reputation, though Bertram's faults are by this point as obvious as Parolles's.

As noted before, the humiliation of Parolles, despite its revenge format, cannot properly be said to be a dramatic revenge on him since he has harmed no one involved in it (except, perhaps, Bertram, and that only indirectly), and he is not reformed as a result of it. It looks more like a revenge against Bertram, who is at least shamed (although not into reformation) by it, though even that is open to question:

> The great influence given the three scenes which end in Parolles's unmasking is . . . a structural fault. If these built up to the exposure of one whose practices had directed the hero's relations with Helena—and if it were these very practices that they exposed—the emphasis they gain because of their length and position would be justified and their effect dramatically satisfying. If Bertram, on having his eyes opened to Parolles, rushed home to Rousillon, seeking Helena to make amends for wrongs done her, then they would certainly deserve their place. But these scenes teach Bertram only that Parolles is a generally worthless creature, and nothing about his own conduct: indeed, after the unmasking of Parolles he grows worse rather than better. The relations of Bertram and Helena remain exactly as before: it is still Helena's solitary task to bring her wayward husband into line. (Evans [1960] 1967, 160–61)

It is hard to understand how Parolles's humiliation could be expected to inspire Bertram to a reconciliation with Helena, since before this scene takes place he has been informed that she is dead (4.3.47–62, 87–91). It is easy, on the other hand, to see why Bertram does not apply the moral of Parolles's unmasking to his own case: "The discovery of 'seeming' at the end of *Measure for Measure* is given depth and reality because it coincides with the emergence of the true Angelo; Bertram has never really deceived anyone, and thus the central deceiver cannot be used to drive home this central interest of the play; the secondary character of Parolles has to bear the principal weight in this respect" (Hunter, Introduction to the Arden edition, 1959, xxiv). Bertram can neither save himself, nor can he be saved by Parolles's example. Only Helena can redeem him. Nevertheless, some critics have found that redemption unsatisfactory, because of Bertram's behavior, particularly in the final scene, and because he is let off so lightly.[16]

The major themes of the final scene—and, in fact, of the entire play—are set forth in the first exchange between the King, the Countess, and Lafew:

> *King:*   We lost a jewel of her, and our esteem
> Was made much poorer by it; but your son,
> As mad in folly, lack'd the sense to know
> Her estimation home.
> *Countess:*   'Tis past, my liege,
> And I beseech your Majesty to make it
> Natural rebellion, done i' th' blade of youth,
> When oil and fire, too strong for reason's force,
> O'erbears it, and burns on.
> *King:*   My honor'd lady,
> I have forgiven and forgotten all,
> Though my revenges were high bent upon him,
> And watch'd the time to shoot.
> *Lafew:*   This I must say—
> But first I beg my pardon—the young lord
> Did to his Majesty, his mother, and his lady
> Offense of mighty note; but to himself
> The greatest wrong of all.
>
>   (5.3.1–15)[17]

They agree that Helena was a jewel, and that Bertram has been mad, foolish, senseless, and unreasonable, but that his principal victim has been himself. Finally, the King forswears vengeance against Bertram, even insisting that Bertram should not ask for pardon—an order Bertram, characteristically, ignores (5.3.22, 36–37).

But no sooner has Bertram been forgiven and excused himself for his treatment of Helena than he gets into trouble again. Much has been made of Bertram's less-than-noble behavior in this scene, yet the truth gets him into such difficulties that perhaps his lies become more forgivable; almost, he might say "How all occasions do inform against me." For when he sends the ring he had from his supposed Diana to Maudlin, it is immediately recognized as being that which the King gave to Helena. Bertram repeatedly protests, in all honesty as far as he knows, that "the ring was never hers" (5.3.80, 89, 92. 112). The King, of course, does not believe him, and orders him held on suspicion of being Helena's murderer. No sooner is Bertram taken away than he is haled back again to answer the charge that he seduced and promised to marry Diana. By the time he returns, it appears that everyone is against him: Lafew disowns him as a potential son-in-law (5.3.147–48, 176–77), and the King openly declares his suspicions—significantly, to the Countess, whose reply is stern:

> *King:*   I am afeard the life of Helen, lady,
> Was foully snatch'd.
> *Countess:*   Now, justice on the doers!
>
> (5.3.153–54)

Standing already under a false accusation of murder, it is perhaps understandable that Bertram attempts to lie his way out of this additional charge. But his shabby attempts to disparage Diana lose him sympathy, and his lies deceive no one. When she produces his ring, which he has described as

> an honor 'longing to our house,
> Bequeathed down from many ancestors
>
> (4.2.42–43)

his own mother sees it as "a thousand proofs" against him (5.3.199). He has given away his honor, and it has returned to testify against him; in the best revenge tradition, his own actions are turned against him, following which his own words are turned against him, when Parolles is called to testify. Bertram himself stands revealed as what he accuses Parolles of being: one "that will speak any thing" (5.3.209).

But the King is less interested in lies and seduction than in the ring and the possibility of Helena's murder. When Diana teases him regarding the ring's provenance, he loses patience and becomes vengeful toward her:

> Unless thou tell'st me where thou hadst this ring,
> Thous diest within this hour.
>
> (5.3.83–84)

Diana proceeds to explain why she has accused Bertram, but her explanation is phrased as a series of riddles:

> Because he's guilty, and he is not guilty.
> He knows I am no maid, and he'll swear to't;
> I'll swear I am a maid, and he knows not.
> Great king, I am no strumpet, by my life;
> I am either maid, or else this old man's wife.
> .   .   .   .
>   But for this lord,
> Who has abus'd me, as he knows himself,

Though yet he never harm'd me, here I quit him.
He knows himself my bed he hath defil'd,
And at that time he got his wife with child.
Dead though she be, she feels her young one kick.
So there's my riddle: one that's dead is quick—
And now behold the meaning.

(5.3.289–93, 297–304)

But what is the meaning?[18] Why has Helena staged this elaborate charade? The answer may have to do with what Bullough has called the play's "considerable moral intensity" (1957, 2:380), which many people find out of place in a comedy. This moral intensity derives primarily from Helena; but objections to her character are generally phrased not in terms of why she does what she does (since on moral grounds she is unassailable), but in terms of *how* she does it: she is seen as "manipulative." Since the King, the Countess, and Lafew constantly refer to her virtue, and since she is seen in opposition to Bertram, it follows that Bertram must be bad. That so good a character as Helena uses all the tricks of the stage revenger is unsettling; that the object of her revenge is rewarded by forgiveness and marriage to this saint is practically unnerving. Where is the morality in all of this? The allegorical interpretation is to say that the "feelings" of the characters are irrelevant to Shakespeare's moral. The realistic interpretation is that saint and sinner are ill-matched, or in Charlton's words, that "for Bertram, there is the reformatory discipline of life with Helena" (1938, 218). But perhaps there is another explanation.

While it is true that the older characters emphasize Helena's virtue, that is not the limit of her character; we are told that she is good (necessarily, virtue being difficult to represent dramatically), but we see her being clever. If, correspondingly, we view Bertram not as a villain, but as a fool, it is easier to understand why he is let off lightly. And as a fool, he needs not a saint, but a teacher. If Helena is conceived of as a saint, then it is indeed difficult to reconcile her character to stratagems, deceits, and accomplices. But as a teacher, she naturally uses her intellect to help enlighten Bertram's. That this interpretation is not too far afield is indicated by the fact that the characters who praise Helena's virtue do not, on the whole, deplore Bertram's morals, but his lack of intelligence, as noted earlier. Granting, for a moment then, that Helena is a teacher, Bertram is her foolish and unwilling student, and her task is intellectual as much as moral, what is it she must teach him?

The answer "seems" obvious: Helena must teach Bertram the difference between seeming and reality. Bertram is taken in by Parolles because he looks and talks like a soldier. He repudiates Helena because he cannot distinguish apparent from true nobility. He makes mistakes that are obvious to every other character in the play, and when he gets into trouble he thinks he can get out of it by lying, because he expects other characters to be as ignorant of the difference between appearance and reality as he is. Helena reveals this lesson as her meaning when she reappears:

> *King:*   Is there no exorcist
> Beguiles the truer office of mine eyes?
> Is't real that I see?
> *Helena:*   No, my good lord,
> 'Tis but the shadow of a wife you see,
> The name, and not the thing.
>
> (5.3.304–8)

Bertram, in his final couplet, emphasizes the intellectual nature of his lesson:

> If she, my liege, can make me know this clearly,
> I'll love her dearly, ever, ever dearly.
>
> (5.3.315–16)

(It is interesting that this lesson occurs in the court, which Helena has earlier referred to as "a learning place" [1.1.91].) Helena reaffirms her confidence in her teaching by promising vengeance on herself—the destruction of all she's worked for—if everything is not what it seems:

> If it appear not plain and prove untrue,
> Deadly divorce step between me and you!
>
> (5.3.317–18)

Finally, the King confirms that what seems well is not to be trusted until the conclusion is known:

> All yet seems well, and if it end so meet,
> The bitter past, more welcome is the sweet.
>
> (5.3.333–34)

From the standpoint of revenge, *All's Well That Ends Well* has both similarities to and differences from the earlier comedies. Like most objects of Shakespeare's comic revenges, Bertram is more fool than villain; like most of his comic revengers, Helena cleverly uses plots and accomplices in turning her victim's own errors against him to teach him a lesson about social behavior. But unlike her vengeful predecessors, Helena shows little sense of grievance against her victim and expresses no desire to harm him even temporarily. And unlike those of Shylock,

Falstaff, Don John, and Malvolio, Bertram's reformation, we can anticipate, will change his mind and character, not merely his behavior. Despite its reputation as a "dark" comedy, therefore, *All's Well* is less characterized by the reputedly grim motive of revenge than many of the earlier, "brighter" comedies. If Helena had heeded the spirit of Parolles's advice to "get thee a good husband, and use him as he uses thee" (1.1.214–15), if she once expressed the idea that in deceiving Bertram as he attempts to deceive others she is giving him just what he deserves, if she showed a natural human desire for revenge, this play—ironically— might have seemed much lighter in tone. But for all her machinations, she never expresses any such sentiment. It is as though Shakespeare, in the writing of this play, had lost his concern for the theme of revenge in favor of the theme of forgiveness, but continued to find the apparatus of revenge useful.

None of Shakespeare's titles is more suggestive of revenge than *Measure for Measure*. Although the phrase itself may mean no more than strict justice, it recalls the Old Testament law often cited as vengeful:

> . . . thou shalt paye life for life,
> Eie for eie, tothe for tothe, hand for hand, fote for fote,
> Burning for burning, wonde for wonde, stripe for stripe.
> (Exod. 21:23–25)

This is the spirit in which the Duke uses the phrase:

> The very mercy of the law cries out
> Most audible, even from his proper tongue,
> "An Angelo for Claudio, death for death!"
> Haste still pays haste, and leisure answers leisure;
> Like doth quit like, and *Measure* still *for Measure*.
> (5.1.407–11)

Yet the phrase itself is from quite another context:

> Judge not, that ye be not judged.
> For with what judgement ye judge, ye shal be judged, and with
> what measure ye mette, it shal be measured to you againe.
> (Matt. 7:1–2; see also Luke 6:37–38)[19]

That the Duke in judging Angelo for judging Claudio should condemn him with a paraphrase of a biblical injunction condemning judging suggests a more complex irony than merely that "the ending of the play,

then, really contradicts the title" (Lawrence 1960, 116). Although a traditional objection to the play is that Angelo escapes any real revenge
(Stevenson 1966, 78), revenge is not absent from the play but is so
intertwined with justice and mercy that what are elsewhere separate and
even opposing qualities become, in *Measure for Measure*, almost indistin-
guishable.

The standard reading of the play, based on the Duke's explanation to
Friar Thomas (1.3.19–43), is that Vincentio intends Angelo to (re)enforce
the "strict statutes and most biting laws" of Vienna "to strike and gall"
the citizens. But this is not what the Duke says to Angelo; rather, he links
severity and leniency:

> Mortality and mercy in Vienna
> Live in thy tongue and heart.
>
> > (1.1.44–45)

> > Your scope is as mine own,
> So to enforce or qualify the laws
> As to your soul seems good.
>
> > (1.1.64–66)

Since the Duke does not tell Angelo to be severe, but tells Friar Thomas
that this severity is his aim in temporarily abdicating, if we take his
words at their face value we can only assume that his knowledge of
Angelo's character leads him to believe that Angelo will not err on the
side of mercy. Although he is certainly correct in that belief, it has been
asserted that the Duke fails to understand his deputy's character and is
thus responsible for Angelo's actions.[20] Not only does it seem rather
harsh to condemn the Duke for accepting Angelo's character as Angelo
presents it, but such a reading ignores another of Vincentio's purposes.
In deputizing Angelo, the Duke has made it clear that he has no respect
for a fugitive and cloistered virtue:

> Angelo:
> There is a kind of character in thy life,
> That to th' observer doth thy history
> Fully unfold. Thyself and thy belongings
> Are not thine own so proper as to waste
> Thyself upon thy virtues, they on thee.
> Heaven doth us as we with torches do,
> Not light them for themselves; for if our virtues
> Did not go forth of us, 'twere all alike
> As if we had them not.
>
> > (1.1.26–35)

Not only does the Duke wish to make use of Angelo's virtue for the good
of the state, he wishes to observe how Angelo's professed character is
affected by power:

> . . . Lord Angelo is precise;
> Stands at a guard with envy; scarce confesses
> That his blood flows; or that his appetite
> Is more to bread than stone: hence shall we see
> If power change purpose: what our seemers be.
>
> (1.3.50–54)

Angelo's trial begins with his judgment on Claudio, who enters not
merely arrested but exhibited publicly through the streets at Lord Angelo's "special charge." Claudio at first seems resigned to a just punishment for an admitted crime:

> *Claudio:* Thus can the demigod, Authority,
>   Make us pay down for our offense by weight
>   The words of heaven: on whom it will, it will;
>   On whom it will not, so; yet still 'tis just.
> *Lucio:* Why, how now, Claudio? whence comes this restraint?
> *Claudio:* From too much liberty, my Lucio, liberty:
>   As surfeit is the father of much fast,
>   So every scope by the immoderate use
>   Turns to restraint. Our natures do pursue,
>   Like rats that ravin down their proper bane,
>   A thirsty evil, and when we drink we die.
>
> (1.2.119–30)

But having explained the extenuating circumstances of his offense
(1.2.145–55), Claudio's tone changes. Although still admitting that he
broke the law, he expresses feelings of persecution:

> And the new deputy now for the Duke—
> Whether it be the fault and glimpse of newness,
> Or whether that the body public be
> A horse whereon the governor doth ride,
> Who, newly in the seat, that it may know
> He can command, lets it straight feel the spur;
> Whether the tyranny be in his place,
> Or in his eminence that fills it up,
> I stagger in—but this new governor
> Awakes me all the enrolled penalties
> Which have, like unscour'd armor, hung by th' wall
> So long that nineteen zodiacs have gone round
> And none of them been worn; and for a name

Now puts the drowsy and neglected act
Freshly on me—'tis surely for a name.

(1.2.157–71)

Our next glimpse of Angelo is likely to incline us to Claudio's latter view. Angelo's first argument in favor of executing Claudio is not that the punishment fits the crime but that the ultimate penalty is needed *pour encourager les autres*. When Escalus argues for mercy and suggests that in a similar situation Angelo himself might have acted similarly, Angelo rejects the argument (2.1.1–31). Not until later in the play does the irony of this rejection become clear: "Moreover—and it is one of the dramatist's most subtle and original uses of parallelism—Claudio's relation to Juliet had been almost of a piece with that of Angelo to Mariana. But where the one for worldly reasons left his already affianced bride in the lurch, the other with generous impetuosity had preferred disregard of an outward form to heartless desertion. Thus Claudio's transgression is in itself most venial, and Angelo is the last man justified in visiting it with condign penalties" (Boas 1896, 362). Whether or not Angelo would equate his situation with Claudio's, he calls down vengeance upon his own head if he ever commits Claudio's offense:

When I, that censure him, do so offend,
Let mine own judgment pattern out my death,
And nothing come in partial.

(2.1.29–31)

Our opinion of Angelo's severity is influenced by that of the other characters who enforce the laws in Vienna. Not only does Escalus plead for and pity Claudio, but the Justice remarks that "Lord Angelo is severe" (2.1.282) and the Provost risks Angelo's anger by questioning the order for execution (2.2.7–14) and comments to himself on Claudio's state:

Alas,
He hath but as offended in a dream!
All sects, all ages smack of this vice, and he
To die for't!

(2.2.3–6)

These characters serve to support the opinion that "Angelo (the name is patently ironical: he puns on it himself) is law or legalism, rather than justice. His hard, prim, precise ruling by the book is not felt to be just, because his rule makes all offences the same size; and to think of incontinence or fornication as if it were murder does violence to all normal human feelings" (Rossiter 1961, 121). In a minor key, however, Angelo's severity triumphs over his legalism when he expresses his hope for punishment in the case against Pompey and Froth, which he does not bother to hear:

> I'll take my leave,
> And leave you to the hearing of the cause,
> Hoping you'll find good cause to whip them all.

> (2.1.135–37)

Isabella, at first, seems to find it difficult to argue with Angelo. Admitting that Claudio's offense is

> a vice that most I do abhor,
> And most desire should meet the blow of justice

> (2.2.29–30)

she is easily swayed by Angelo's statement that his function is to punish criminals; declaring it a "just, but severe law" (2.2.41), she would abandon Claudio to his fate, if it were not for Lucio. Her succeeding (though unsuccessful) arguments are rather an odd mixture. She first suggests that Angelo might pardon Claudio "and neither heaven nor man grieve at the mercy" (2.2.50); to this, Angelo replies that he will not. She then argues that mercy is the greatest ornament of authority, and that if their positions were reversed Angelo would have sinned as did Claudio, but Claudio would not have condemned him for it; Angelo asks her to leave. She then pleads as a Christian:

> Why, all the souls that were were forfeit once,
> And He that might the vantage best have took
> Found out the remedy. How would you be
> If He, which is the top of judgment, should
> But judge you as you are? O, think on that,
> And mercy then will breathe within your lips,
> Like man new made.

> (2.2.73–79)

Angelo replies that "It is the law, not I, condemn your brother" (2.2.80), and Isabella again shifts her ground, first requesting a reprieve and then asking "Who is it that hath died for this offense?" (2.2.88). Angelo responds that the reawakened law, enforced, will prevent future evils. When Isabella asks him to "show some pity" (2.2.99), he equates that quality with justice:

> I show it most of all when I show justice;
> For then I pity those I do not know,

Which a dismiss'd offense would after gall,
And do him right that, answering one foul wrong,
Lives not to act another.

(2.2.100–104)

But Isabella replies to this with another equation, asserting that what Angelo calls justice is in fact tyranny (2.2.106–9, 110–23, 126–28, 130–31, 134–36), adding,

Go to your bosom,
Knock there, and ask your heart what it doth know
That's like my brother's fault. If it confess
A natural guiltiness such as is his,
Let it not sound a thought upon your tongue
Against my brother's life.

(2.2.136–41)

This argument now seems to affect Angelo, although he has already heard it from Escalus and rejected it (2.1.8–31). But we soon learn that it is not Isabella's varied pleas that justice be tempered with mercy that have affected Angelo's professed conviction that harsh justice for Claudio is mercy for Vienna. Angelo's final speech in this scene reveals how her arguments have touched him: "Isabella has insisted that there is a natural, sexual man hidden below Angelo's exterior of virtue. And at her bidding the sexual man steps forth with a ve[n]geance" (Stevenson 1966, 42). Realizing this, Angelo (in soliloquy) completely reverses his previous argument:

O, let her brother live!
Thieves for their robbery have authority
When judges steal themselves.

(2.2.174–76)

Finally, he sounds the first note of vengeance in the play with his invocation of the tempter who seeks to avenge his fall on mankind:

O cunning enemy, that to catch a saint,
With saints dost bait thy hook!

(2.2.179–80)

With these lines Angelo, the villain of the piece, reveals that he feels himself a victim of diabolical revenge. But since he attributes the revenge to his righteousness, it is difficult to feel much sympathy for him even before he begins plotting his crimes.

At their second meeting, Angelo and Isabella continue to debate justice and mercy even though the subject of the argument has widened to include Isabella's chastity as well as Claudio's life. Isabella, however, is concerned now with divine justice, rather than the divine mercy she invoked in their previous argument, while Angelo concentrates on earthly concerns:

> *Angelo:* Which had you rather, that the most just law
> Now took your brother's life, [or,] to redeem him,
> Give up your body to such sweet uncleanness
> As she that he hath stain'd?
> *Isabella:*   Sir, believe this,
> I had rather give my body than my soul.
> *Angelo:* I talk not of your soul. . . .
>
>   (2.4.52–57)

Angelo insists that divine justice is earthly cruelty, that there might be "a charity in sin" (2.4.63), but Isabella insists on maintaining distinctions:

> *Isabella:* Better it were a brother died at once,
> Than that a sister, by redeeming him,
> Should die for ever.
> *Angelo:* Were not you then as cruel as the sentence
> That you have slander'd so?
> *Isabella:* Ignomy in ransom and free pardon
> Are of two houses; lawful mercy
> Is nothing kin to foul redemption.
>
>   (2.4.106–13)

Ultimately, their debate results in threats of revenge:

> *Isabella:* Ha? little honor to be much believ'd,
> And most pernicious purpose! Seeming, seeming!
> I will proclaim thee, Angelo, look for't!
> Sign me a present pardon for my brother,
> Or with an outstretch'd throat I'll tell the world aloud
> What man thou art.
>
>   (2.4.149–54)

> *Angelo:*   Redeem thy brother
> By yielding up thy body to my will,
> Or else he must not only die the death,
> But thy unkindness shall his death draw out
> To ling'ring sufferance.
>
>   (2.4.163–67)

While Angelo's righteousness crumbles, we see the disguised Duke combining justice and mercy by trying Juliet's repentance (2.3.21–36) and counseling Claudio to be absolute for a death that the Duke's presence insures he will not suffer (3.1.5–41).[21] Moreover, this presence, and in particular the Duke's eavesdropping on Claudio and Isabella, may direct our opinion of her passionate outburst against her brother's plea that she yield to Angelo.

Various critics have found repugnant Isabella's conviction that "more than our brother is our chastity" (2.4.185).[22] But the Duke, our principal standard of ethics in the play, expresses no such repugnance; on the contrary, he describes Isabella as "having the truth of honor in her" and tells her "the hand that hath made you fair hath made you good" (3.1.164, 180–81). As for the possibility that she is affected by "her recoil from her rage at Claudio" (Stevenson 1966, 46), there is no evidence of it; not only has she previously threatened to expose Angelo, but before the Duke proposes his plot and assuming that Claudio will already have been executed, she tells Vincentio "But O, how much is the good Duke deceiv'd in Angelo! If ever he return, and I can speak to him, I will open my lips in vain, or discover his government" (3.1.191–94). If Isabella suffers any loss of innocence, it is due to the discovery of evil in Angelo and cowardice in Claudio; both discoveries make her justifiably angry, but they do not affect her virtue, which, as the Duke says, is bold (3.1.208). As for the "duplicity" of the plot, the Duke has answered the question before it was asked: "the doubleness of the benefit defends the deceit from reproof" (3.1.257–58).

The deceit is particularly interesting for the multiplicity of purposes it serves, as the Duke suggests more than once (3.1.199–204, 251–55). It allows the Duke to provide justice for Mariana and Angelo, mercy for Claudio, and pleasure for himself, in addition to allowing Isabella revenge on Angelo by turning his own scheme against him. The rightness of the plot is reinforced by the various episodes in the remainder of act 3, in which we see the Duke act justly toward various transgressors. After attempting in vain to persuade Pompey of the error of his ways, he concludes

> Correction and instruction must both work
> Ere this rude beast will profit.
>
> (3.2.32–33)

Similarly, he tries to dissuade Lucio from slandering the Duke and, failing that, challenges him to stand by his slanders when the Duke returns (3.2.116–57). Finally, he comments on Angelo and on his own plans:

> If his own life answer the straitness of his proceeding, it shall become him well; wherein if he chance to fail, he hath sentenc'd himself. (3.2.255–57)

Craft against vice I must apply.
With Angelo to-night shall lie
His old betrothed (but despised);
So disguise shall by th' disguised
Pay with falsehood false exacting,
And perform an old contracting.

(3.2.277–82)

The Duke's use of craft is further justified when Angelo compounds his tyranny with treachery, refusing to pardon Claudio after all (4.2.120–26). Driven to further shifts to save Claudio, the Duke also tries to deal both justly and mercifully with "the magnificent and horrible Barnardine" (Rossiter 1961, 166), seeking to advise, comfort, and pray with him before his deserved execution (4.3.50–52). But being unwilling to damn Barnardine's soul, he is compelled to spare him.[23]

But though Barnardine is spared, Isabella is not, for the Duke tells her that Claudio has been executed. His excuse for this cruel lie—

But I will keep her ignorant of her good,
To make her heavenly comforts of despair,
When it is least expected

(4.3.109–11)

—is hardly convincing. A more likely explanation for such behavior from a character who throughout the play tests and interrogates others is that he is preparing to test Isabella. The actual test, however, will not take place until the last act. Although Isabella's reaction to the news of her brother's death—"O, I will to him [Angelo], and pluck out his eyes!" (4.3.119)—is that of a stage revenger rather than a novice nun, it meets, in tenor if not in immediate action, with the Duke's full approbation:

                              If you can pace your wisdom
In that good path that I would wish it go,
And you shall have your bosom on this wretch,
Grace of the Duke, revenges to your heart,
And general honor.

(4.3.132–36)

Revenge is likewise on Angelo's mind. Apprised of the Duke's return and of his proclamation that citizens craving redress of injustice may petition him upon his arrival, he is forced to consider, although he rejects, the possibility that Isabella may avail herself of this opportunity. Further, he explains his reason for proceeding (as he thinks) with Claudio's execution:

                              He should have liv'd,
Save that his riotous youth with dangerous sense

Might in the times to come have ta'en revenge,
By so receiving a dishonor'd life
With ransom of such shame.

(4.4.28–32)

Just as the Duke administers to Isabella

a physic
That's bitter to sweet end

(4.6.7–8)

so to Angelo he administers praise that will make the blame to come
more bitter (5.1.4–8, 9–16). After Isabella has made her accusation, he
twists the knife further, pretending to disbelieve what he knows—in
intent, at least—to be true and expressing an opinion of Angelo's
character that—though popularly thought true—he knows to be false:

By heaven, fond wretch, thou know'st not what thou speak'st,
Or else thou art suborn'd against his honor
In hateful practice. First, his integrity
Stands without blemish; next, it imports no reason
That with such vehemency he should pursue
Faults proper to himself. If he had so offended,
He would have weigh'd thy brother by himself,
And not have cut him off.

(5.1.105–12)

The Duke's behavior toward Angelo is compounded of justice, mercy,
and revenge. It is just to make him suffer the mental anguish that he has
inflicted on Claudio, Isabella, and Mariana. Like the criminals the Duke
advised in his role as a friar, Angelo can receive mercy only after he has
been made to feel true remorse. Finally, the entire plot against Angelo,
with its disguises, accomplices, and presentation to him first of Isabella's
false charge (which he believes to be true) and Mariana's true charge
(which he believes to be false), is a classic revenge. Angelo is hoist with
his own petard—caught doing what he condemned Claudio for doing,
although he thought he was doing something much worse.

Although the Duke is entrapping Angelo, and allowing Lucio to
entrap himself, we can feel little sympathy for them because of their
shameless persistence in their evil ways. Angelo, still believing he can
bluff his way out of the case against him, calls down the law's vengeance
on his own head, even though he is perceptive enough to see that his
secret is out and that several people are plotting against him:

I did but smile till now.
Now, good my lord, give me the scope of justice,

My patience here is touch'd. I do perceive
These poor informal women are no more
But instruments of some more mightier member
That sets them on. Let me have way, my lord,
To find this practice out.

(5.1.233–39)

Similarly, Lucio attempts to cover his own guilt by slandering an innocent friar (and thereby, although he doesn't know it, again slandering
his prince). It is therefore appropriate that, urged on by Angelo, "when
Lucio plucks off the Friar's hood and discovers the Duke, the impudent
buffoon also accomplishes his own exposure" (Oscar James Campbell
1943, 130)—and Angelo's.

Although both Angelo and Lucio recognize that they are caught, they
react very differently to the knowledge. Lucio merely remarks "This may
prove worse than hanging" (5.1.360), while Angelo begs to be punished:

> O my dread lord,
> I should be guiltier than my guiltiness,
> To think I can be undiscernible,
> When I perceive your Grace, like pow'r divine,
> Hath look'd upon my passes. Then, good Prince,
> No longer session hold upon my shame,
> But let my trial be mine own confession.
> Immediate sentence then, and sequent death,
> Is all the grace I beg.

(5.1.366–74)

The Duke, having given Mariana justice by marrying her to Angelo,
seems willing to grant Angelo's request for immediate execution, but he
phrases the sentence in such a way as to reassure the audience that death
will not be allowed to mar the ending of this comedy. "An Angelo for
Claudio, death for death!" (5.1.409) would be strict justice; but in fact no
death has occurred, and it would therefore be unjust to execute Angelo.
As Isabella says, in another context:

> His act did not o'ertake his bad intent,
> And must be buried but as an intent
> That perish'd by the way. Thoughts are no subjects,
> Intents but merely thoughts.

(5.1.451–54)

But at this point in the play, neither Angelo nor Isabella knows that
Claudio is still alive. In addition to drawing out Angelo's punishment,
the Duke seems to be testing Isabella's reaction to her brother's "murderer," although he is subtle about it. When Mariana asks Isabella to join
her in pleading for Angelo's life, the Duke maintains that for her to do so

would be so unnatural as to call down (or, in this case, up) supernatural vengeance:

> Against all sense you do importune her.
> Should she kneel down in mercy of this fact,
> Her brother's ghost his paved bed would break,
> And take her hence in horror.
>
> (5.1.433–36)

Isabella nevertheless does join Mariana in her pleading, but her charity changes nothing, since the Duke continues to uphold Angelo's death sentence and Angelo himself professes to prefer death to mercy (5.1.455, 474–77).[24] It is not until Claudio is revealed to be alive that the Duke pardons Angelo, and the "quickening" in the latter's eye indicates, presumably, that he has resigned himself to life (5.1.494–95).

Yet even as he forgives Angelo, Claudio, and Barnardine, the Duke declares

> I find an apt remission in myself;
> And yet here's one in place I cannot pardon.
>
> (5.1.498–99)

Since Lucio's crime seems to us far less serious (and far more amusing) than Angelo's, this statement and the Duke's later speeches concerning Lucio have been taken by some critics as indications that Vincentio is vengeful rather than just in this case.[25] In fact, however, the Duke behaves toward Lucio very much as he has toward Angelo, allowing him to suffer the apprehension of justice for his crimes and then extending mercy. Even the punishment that Lucio suffers is merely justice to the woman he has wronged.

If the Duke is more vindictive in his threats to Lucio than in those to Angelo, it may be excused on a number of counts. Angelo has, up to the point of his "temptation" by Isabella (and excluding his treatment of Mariana), been reputed a righteous man; even his condemnation of Claudio, although harsh, is within the law. It is difficult to imagine Lucio being able to plead a previous good character, and his victim, the Duke, is apparently entirely innocent of the accusations Lucio makes against him. Angelo's wicked designs remain merely "intents"; Lucio, on the other hand, actually commits the crime of "slandering a prince." Finally, Angelo professes remorse and craves punishment; Lucio makes excuses and seeks to avoid punishment. At the end of the play, there is hope that Angelo may truly reform; Lucio, like Barnardine, is forgiven because of the virtue of the Duke, not because he has deserved forgiveness or because we can even imagine him deserving it.

The play as a whole, and particularly the ending, have provoked a variety of critical responses. Oscar James Campbell, who sees the play as a satire on hypocrisy—as embodied by Angelo—and libertinism—as embodied by Lucio—finds the ending false: "the play does not end as a satire should. Angelo is exposed but not ejected from the play with a final burst of derision. . . . Angelo deserves not a wife, but scornful ridicule" (1943, 125). If we assume that the "darker" aspects of the play do, in fact, indicate a satirical intention, this may be a valid criticism, but not every critic is willing to make such an assumption: "however much incidental gloom or bitterness may be there, the themes of mercy and forgiveness are sincerely and not ironically presented" (Tillyard 1950, 139). Knight takes an entirely different angle, viewing Angelo and Lucio as neither satiric figures nor objects of mercy but, in some degree, the heroes of the piece: "The punishment of both is this only: to know, and to be, themselves. This is both their punishment and at the same time their highest reward for their sufferings: self-knowledge being the supreme, perhaps the only, good" ([1930] 1949, 94–95). Finally, Chakravorty sees the play as a statement that mercy is superior to justice: "Punishment is the function of justice and belongs to the State which is an impersonal machinery; mercy or forgiveness, on the other hand, is the function of a superior ethic and belongs only to the individual" (1969, 259).

None of these positions seems to me to be completely accurate. *Measure for Measure* does not appear to be any kind of sustained satire. Angelo is not, at least at the beginning, entirely without merit, and even Lucio behaves well in trying to help his friend Claudio and urging Isabella on against Angelo. Although there are elements of the puritan in Angelo and of the swaggerer in Lucio, neither character is merely a conventional type; they are too individual to be the straw men of satire. On the other hand, there is no direct evidence that either character attains self-knowledge, except insofar as Angelo learns that he is not proof against temptation; Lucio merely attains self-pity. Although mercy is certainly a theme in the play, it is not presented in isolation or in opposition to justice or revenge. Rather, what the Duke achieves at the end of the play is a balanced combination of these three qualities, in which malefactors are lured by the devices of the stage revenger into betraying themselves, threatened with the force of justice, and finally pardoned. Angelo and Lucio do not get off without suffering or without making at least some restitution; Isabella does not declare that she loves Angelo, nor the Duke that he loves Lucio. The Duke alone is able to extend mercy (though others can ask for it), but he does not do so by nullifying justice. Rather, by applying "craft against vice," he takes revenge against wrongdoers, establishes justice for everyone, and at last extends a limited forgiveness to Angelo and Lucio not because they deserve it, but because his power, wisdom, and magnanimity allow him to be generous.

5

Conclusion

The sun by day shines hotly for revenge.
The moon by night eclipseth for revenge.
The stars are turned to comets for revenge.
The planets change their courses for revenge.
The birds sing not, but sorrow for revenge.
The silly lamb sits bleating for revenge.
The shrieking raven sits croaking for revenge.
Whole herds of beasts come bellowing for revenge.
And all, yea all the world I think,
Cries for revenge, and nothing but revenge.
                              —*The True Tragedy of Richard III*

The danger in concentrating on one theme in a body of work as rich as
Shakespeare's comedies is that one may begin to see it everywhere and
magnify its importance wherever it is seen. It seems probable that some,
perhaps many, readers of this work may feel that I have not avoided this
danger. To such I can only reply that while their judgments may differ
from mine in particular instances, I would hope that the overall emphasis of this book will serve as a corrective to what seems to me the usual—
but (again, to me) inexplicable—neglect of the theme of revenge in the
comedies. Although I would hesitate to argue that revenge is the main
theme in any of the comedies, I do maintain that it is a major concern in
many and at least a minor one in most of them. Furthermore, in those
comedies, such as *Two Gentlemen of Verona* and *As You Like It*, in which
vengeance is hardly touched upon, I think its absence raises interesting
questions.

Shakespeare uses comic revenge to restore justice by foiling fools and
knaves, who are sometimes themselves revengers. His comic revengers
are generally admirable characters, often the most admirable in their
plays, and invariably more likeable than the victims of their plots. These
victims are either villains or potentially good people who need to be
taught a lesson. Shakespeare's comic revengers practice limited revenge;
they do not inflict as much injury as they could or as they might be

169

justified in inflicting; they mix mercy, as well as justice, with revenge. Furthermore, they frequently express an interest in reforming their victims. Finally, they often articulate a social as well as a personal purpose, and they are invariably successful in restoring harmony to their worlds, although their victims may exclude themselves from this harmony.

Perhaps it is worth reemphasizing that, in my view, revenge as Shakespeare used it in the comedies is not antithetical either to justice or to mercy. It may be difficult for us, conditioned as we are to regard the legal system as the only proper and civilized mechanism for attempting to secure justice, to accept that revenge can have any relation to equity. Yet even "in a world of law, the absence of just revenge poses as great a threat to both liberty and order as revenge gone wild" (Jacoby 1983, 149). Although we do not want to see comic heroes or heroines behave cruelly, neither do we want them to appear as cold, rational dispensers of justice; nor do we want to see fools and knaves who have caused or intended harm to more virtuous characters simply pardoned. In fact, it is harder to associate justice and mercy through the legal system than to associate either quality with revenge, since to pardon a guilty offender provides mercy at the expense of strict justice. This conflict between justice and mercy, both of which are necessary if the ending of a comedy is to be both happy and satisfying, may be the reason why most of the victims of Shakespeare's comic revengers commit actions that are not crimes.[1] Shakespeare's comic revengers are generally not judges who may condemn or pardon under the law, but private individuals who use extra-legal means to punish and, having done so, offer forgiveness.[2] Revenge provides a means whereby Shakespeare can gratify our desire to see fools and knaves punished while humanizing and thereby allowing us to identify with the characters who provide justice and, finally, mercy— all while inviting us to laugh. It is difficult to imagine how justice and mercy and the requirements of comedy could be better served.

A recent study of justice in Shakespeare's comedies finds that "while Middleton and Jonson often deal out some type of justice to their characters, Shakespeare always distributes an excess of mercy" (Makaryk 1980, 381).[3] Although a philosophy of "use every man after his desert, and who shall scape whipping?" certainly pervades the comedies, I am not convinced that these charitable endings result from "a combination of deserved happiness (due to a character's repentance, reform or transformation) and luck" (Makaryk 1980, xvi). Although we may accept that Proteus, Ford, Bertram, and Angelo learn from their experiences, we are given no reason to believe that Shylock, Falstaff, Don John, or Malvolio will change or be changed in any significant fashion; these characters are simply prevented from committing the harm they intend. This prevention is due not to luck, but to the active plotting of more virtuous characters who explicitly take on the task of revenge but generally limit that revenge and end it with forgiveness.

"Revenge" remains a concept with such negative overtones that it seems impossible for many commentators even to consider the possibility that it may have positive uses. But revenge is a concept of as immediate an interest to us as it was to the Elizabethans; our conceptions of love, friendship, and religion may have changed over the last four hundred years, but our desire to get even with a villain or show up a fool remains unchanged. Although fools and knaves may ultimately be forgiven, our sense of justice is unlikely to be satisfied unless forgiveness is preceded by exposure or punishment or both. Comic justice, like Miss Prism's definition of Fiction, means that the good end happily and the bad unhappily (although not *too* unhappily). Shakespeare insures this outcome in many of his comedies by making social offenders victims of revenge plots by those they have injured, who are often acting—consciously or not—on behalf of society. Revenge devices become the means of establishing justice in the comedies: plots and accomplices bring together the virtuous or at least relatively harmless characters in opposition to the villainous or misbehaving ones. Simultaneously, revenge itself becomes a kind of wild justice, since it is through revenge that social transgressors are exposed, thwarted, and punished. Revenge in Shakespeare's comedies becomes a positive force, providing entertainment while restoring social harmony.

Notes

Chapter 1. INTRODUCTION

1. All definitions in this chapter are taken from the *Oxford English Dictionary*, 1971 compact ed., s.v. "revenge."

2. Jacoby (1983, 278) quotes Justice Potter Stewart's statement in his concurring opinion in *Furman v. Georgia*, " 'The instinct for retribution is part of the nature of man . . .' "; she points out, however, that this statement "emphasized his disagreement with those justices who regarded retribution as an impermissible ingredient of the criminal-justice system."

3. Civil actions can sometimes be brought by victims, but these are separate from criminal proceedings.

4. "Revenge, like love and the acquisition of worldly goods, is one of the grand themes of western literature, a fountainhead of epic and drama. It appears in every guise known to man and woman: as comedy and tragedy; as a sickness of the soul and as emotional liberation; as disgrace and as honor; as an enemy of social order and a restorer of cosmic order; as mortal sin and saving grace; as destructive self-indulgence and as justice" (Jacoby 1983, 14).

5. Jacoby points out that this verse, "usually cited as an injunction against revenge, is as much a pledge of divine action as a prohibition of human retribution" (1983, 5).

All biblical quotations are taken from *The Geneva Bible: A Facsimile of the 1560 Edition* (Madison: Univ. of Wisconsin, 1969).

6. All quotations from Bacon are taken from "Of Revenge" in *The Essays of Lord Bacon* (London: Frederick Warne, 1889).

7. Auden expands on this idea in "The Joker in the Pack": "Finally, one who desires personal revenge desires to reveal himself. The revenger's greatest satisfaction is to be able to tell his victim to his face—'You thought you were all-powerful and untouchable and could injure me with impunity. Now you see that you were wrong. Perhaps you have forgotten what you did; let me have the pleasure of reminding you' " (249–50).

8. Lily B. Campbell maintains that "to the prince or magistrate, therefore, was intrusted by God the execution of justice which in discussions of revenge was called public revenge" (1931, 289).

9. For another view, see Ornstein, who maintains that "there is not one great tragedy of the [Elizabethan] period in which the ethical attitude towards blood revenge is a central moral issue" (1960, 23).

10. Villain-revenger plays include *The Turk, Women Beware Women,* and *The Duchess of Malfi;* antirevenge plays include *A Fair Quarrel, The Unnatural Combat,* and *The Changeling;* and "decadent" revenge plays include *Osmund the Great Turk* and *Aglaura.* See Bowers (1940) 1959.

11. For condemnations of revenge by James I and Chief Justice Coke and indications that "the Elizabethans were conscious of the earlier periods of lawlessness when revenge was a right," see Bowers (1940) 1959, 10–11.

Gardner sensibly summarizes one problem with much contemporary evidence: "I have read more than one book in which the author establishes by detailed, indeed relentless, accumulation of statements by preachers and moralists that the Elizabethans thought murder unethical and private revenge sinful. What else should we expect preachers and moralists to say?" She goes on to give a brief description of the Bond of Association of 1584, the signers of which—"thousands" of "law-abiding and God-fearing men"—bound themselves " 'to take the uttermost revenge' " on anyone who attempted or profited from an attack on Queen Elizabeth (*The Business of Criticism*, 36–37).

12. I am aware that the preceding discussion treads dangerously near to the "critical convention . . . which states that revenge was rejected by Christian teaching, but instinctively approved of by the fiery Elizabethan gentleman" (Camoin 1972, 124), although I would prefer to summarize my view by saying that revenge is likely to be condemned by the official, established institutions of any society (unless revenge is incorporated as part of those institutions), but that this condemnation is unlikely to eradicate either the desire for or practice of revenge.

13. For the multitude of references to *Hamlet*, see McGinn 1938.

14. More interestingly, though perhaps no more to the point, is the use some playwrights made of the stage as a vehicle for their own revenges: *Histriomastix*, *Every Man Out of His Humour*, and especially *Satiromastix* and *The Poetaster* are revenge comedies in the sense that they were written at least in part as instruments of revenge.

15. ". . . plot complications, like three-syllable rhymes, are inherently funny. They are, however, much funnier when they are incidental . . ." (Frye [1965] 1967, 23).

16. Bowers (1940) 1959, 10.

17. "In comic revenge . . . proportionality, in both its private and public meanings, comes to the fore" (Jacoby 1983, 45). Although it may be doubted if even comic revengers commonly maintain proportionality in revenge in the world outside the theater, this is neither an anomaly nor a reflection on the dramatic ideal: "If the tragic poet subjects man's desire to the limitations of reality, the comic poet changes experience in accordance with the demands of desire. . . . The poet may twist the given facts of experience to suit himself, his unconscious characters, and the desire of his audience" (Jagendorf 1984, 13–14).

18. Although I recognize that some readers may object that I am here describing these characters as though they have human personalities and motivations, I think it is reasonable in discussing them as revengers to take a stance similar to that frequently taken in discussing tragic revengers. Their role as revengers is the subject of much of what follows, but not to the exclusion of what Salingar calls their "quality of an inner life" (1974, 222). For a recent consideration of comic characterization, see Newman 1985.

19. "The Elizabethan disapproval of revenge was directed less toward the impulse itself than toward the social consequences of its violent expression; in comedy, getting even and getting hurt (in any permanent way) are far from synonymous. The comic notion of revenge is truly sweet, because punishment—while it may be exquisitely appropriate—is never allowed to magnify the importance of a trivial offense. A man who behaves like an ass is treated like an ass, and that is the end of the matter" (Jacoby 1983, 45–46).

20. "Another great theme of revenge tragedy is the connection between the thirst for vengeance and the thirst for justice. Revenge and justice were not seen as antipodes but as regions of the same moral territory: one might all too easily move from the permitted to the prohibitive zone. This proximity is responsible both for the force of the religious injunction against vengeance and increasing awareness of the need for social institutions to dispense just retribution. In the sixteenth century, these institutions were thought of in relatively narrow terms—mainly as instruments of social order and criminal justice" (Jacoby 1983, 48).

21. For a discussion of "moral revenge" in *Titus Andronicus, Hamlet,* and the histories, see Chakravorty 1969, who also deals with three other tragedies and, briefly, six of the comedies.

22. For a discussion of Elizabethan legal opinion concerning malice and revenge, see Bowers (1940) 1959, 8–11.

Chapter 2. EARLY COMEDIES

1. The obvious exception to this statement is *A Midsummer Night's Dream*, in which Puck, directed by Oberon, causes Demetrius's change of heart. But Oberon is not interested in punishing Demetrius; he simply takes a friendly interest in Helena, with whose plight he sympathizes (2.1.245–46) as does Puck, although he mistakes Hermia for her (2.2.70–81). Oberon does, of course, express a desire to punish Titania.

2. As Hamilton points out, "Shakespeare shapes his entire comedy most obviously through the device of Egeon's tragic story, which serves as both the point of departure and the resolution of the comedy of errors" (1967, 92).

All quotations from Shakespeare are taken from *The Riverside Shakespeare*, textual editor G. Blakemore Evans et al. (Boston: Houghton Mifflin, 1974).

3. Brooks suggests that Shakespeare chose Ephesus as a setting because of these very associations (1961, 65).

4. Although critics have noted the distinct differences in the experiences of the Antipholi (see, for example, Hamilton 1967, 95–99, and Ann Barton's Introduction to the play in *The Riverside Shakespeare*, 80), less attention has been paid to the Dromios. Craig maintains that "the more staid and responsible traveler is given the more jocular and impudent Dromio, a sort of all-licensed fool, who apparently is flogged and expects to be flogged rather frequently" (1948, 24). "Flogging," however, seems a rather extreme description for the punishment we see meted out to the Dromios, and, in fact, S. Dromio—like S. Antipholus—fares far better than his brother. Not only does he get away with his threat to beat E. Antipholus, but he is beaten only once in the course of the play (2.2.22–25), and even then his master gives him an explanation (if not an apology) and advice on how to avoid beatings in the future. (See Tillyard 1965, 55–56).

5. Charlton maintains that Shakespeare dispensed with Peniculus because a parasite "would have been an utter foreigner in Elizabethan England" (1938, 66). Apparently, however, Gascoigne had no hesitation about including the parasite in his version of *I Suppositi;* one suspects that few cultures in any era would be unfamiliar with parasites.

6. For an enumeration of the differences between the situations of E. Antipholus and Menaechmus the citizen and an explanation of our differing reactions to them see Brooks 1961, 62.

7. *Oxford English Dictionary,* 1971 compact ed., s.v. "pinch": "pressure, stress (usually of want, misfortune, or the like); difficulty, hardship. . . . Said of the painful action of cold, hunger, exhaustion, or wasting disease: including the physical effects (to contract, make thin or shrunken), the painful physical sensations, and often the mental affliction or social injury." Also, "the pain or pang caused by the grip of death, or of remorse, shame, etc. . . . A case, occasion, or time of special stress or need; a critical juncture; a strait, exigency, extremity. . . . Said of actions causing a painful bodily sensation: To hurt, pain, torture, torment. . . . To press upon, straiten, reduce to straits or distress; to bring into difficulties or trouble; to afflict, harass."

8. Craig finds Plautus's scene between the doctor and his "patient" superior to Shakespeare's (1948, 22, 28).

9. Brooks maintains that the vengeance on Pinch owes "a debt to the dramatization of Edward's sufferings" in Marlowe's *Edward II* (1968, 78).

10. "Dynamic progress is strongly felt in the mounting violence, from the first mere thwack to the drawing of swords, thrashing with a rope's end, overpowering of 'madmen', and elaborate (narrated) vengeance upon Pinch" (Brooks 1961, 70).

11. Of Egeon, Ann Barton notes: "Egeon allowed Shakespeare to open the play under the shadow of death and to keep this threat alive in the background, like a sword that has been drawn and not sheathed, until it flashes into prominence again in Act V, only to dissolve before the discoveries and accords of the final scene" (*The Riverside Shakespeare,* 80).

12. "At the general recognition at the end of the play [Egeon] finds a willing surety in his son, and the joy of the reunited family so turns poverty to wealth that, as soon as surety is offered, the Duke spares both his life and fine, a deed which he had previously declared to be impossible" (Brown 1962, 56).

13. All of this would seem to contradict Parrott's assertion that Petruchio's "explosions of violence are wordy rather than physical" (1949, 152).

14. "*The Taming of the Shrew* . . . is not a drama of the emotions at all. It is a comedy, or more strictly a farce, in the true sense. It approaches its theme, the eternal theme of the duel of sex, neither from the ethical standpoint of the Elizabethan pulpiter [*sic*] nor from that of the Pioneer Club. It does not approach it from an ethical standpoint at all, but merely from that of humorous and dispassionate observation, which is at least one of the permitted attitudes of Thalia towards all the facts of human life. The humour of strange

bedfellows; that is its burden. . . . That the point is not a sociological one is shown by the fact that it would be in no way lost if the positions were inverted, and the dominating will give to the wife instead of the husband; as indeed was done by John Fletcher, whose *The Tamer Tamed* presents Petruchio *en secondes noces*, the butt of a verier shrew than either Katherina or himself" (Chambers 1925, 44).

15. Johnson (1765) 1908, 80; similarly, Johnson's comment on Isabella may be taken as an explanation of Sylvia's silence in the face of Valentine's offer of her to Proteus: "I am afraid our Varlet Poet intended to inculcate, that women think ill of nothing that raises the credit of their beauty, and are ready, however virtuous, to pardon any act which they think incited by their own charms" (idem., 80).

16. The vengeful Launce also uses the curse "a vengeance on't" while working out the symbols representing his family (2.3.19).

17. Though Valentine later adds

Come, Proteus, 'tis your penance but to hear
The story of your loves discovered

(5.4.170–71)

this seems intended more for the enlightenment of the other characters than as punishment.

18. See Bradbrook 1951, 151, and Robert Grams Hunter 1965, 86–87.

19. Craig 1948, 30. The other main feature is "the pursuit of a wayward lover by a maiden disguised as a page." (Hamilton, on the other hand, maintains that "if plot alone were its soul, this play would be a tragedy" [1967, 111].)

20. In fact, Valentine may be more Christ-like than Jesus, who, after all, was not without a temper; see Mark 11:12–14, 20 (Matt. 21:18–19) and Mark 11:15–17 (Matt. 21:12–13, Luke 19:45–46).

21. For another view, see Parrott: "As a matter of fact, there is not the slightest possible resemblance between the mathematicians, geographers, and misogynists of Raleigh's group and the 'well-accomplished,' merry, and amourous King of Navarre and his lords" (1949, 121).

22. Similarly, if less grimly: "What Shakespeare aimed at in *Love's Labour's Lost* was something deeper and more permanent than a contemporary 'school of night'; it was the whole body of pedantry, affectation, and formal control of life, which flew in the face of nature. . . . *Love's Labour's Lost* is in essence a laughing philippic against both pedantry and affectation" (Parrott 1949, 121).

23. Charlton neatly summarizes the plot: "Four men take an oath to segregate themselves from the society of woman for a term of years: circumstance at once compels them to a formal interview with four women: they break their oath. That is the whole story. Complications are avoided. For instance, the tale of four pairs of lovers runs its course without the slightest hint of possible rivalries and jealousies: a theme of such sort would have added intrigue to the story, but would have detracted from the interest in manners" (1938, 270–71).

24. Even this punishment may have been lessened, since Dull tells Armado that Costard "must fast three days a week" (1.2.129–30). But Dull rarely gets anything right.

25. Subsequently (1.2.131), Dull says "she is allow'd for the dey-woman," but we do not know whether she had that employment before her encounter with Costard.

26. Despite the devastating side-effects of Oberon and Titania's quarrel on the human world, one must agree with Barber's assessment that Shakespeare's fairies are "less malicious, dangerous, and terrifying than the fairies of 'popular belief' " ([1959] 1963, 144).

27. Parrott sees a parallel between Puck and another dramatic type, maintaining that Puck's "function is that of the Vice in the Morals" (1949, 129).

28. On the Brownies' reputation for "exposing [servants'] misdeeds, or punishing them," see Briggs 1976, 47 and 337.

29. "He is a merry-making, mischievous wanderer of the night, and his aim is not to profit either himself or anyone else but to 'jest to Oberon, and make him smile'. . . . He has thus the characteristics of both the intriguing slave of Latin comedy and the Eliz-

abethan clown, but as he is not a human mortal his activities have a lightness and grace and a degree of irresponsibility which creatures of the earth cannot command" (Sen Gupta 1950, 118).

30. On the reasons for the royal fairies' misbehavior and its grounding in traditional fairy lore, see Charlton 1938, 116–117.

31. Bottom is, however, in his transformation, a reminder of similar revenges. Kermode notes that "in the first place, the plot of Oberon is like that of the Cupid and Psyche episode [in Apuleius], for Venus then employs Cupid to avenge her by making Psyche (to whom she has lost some followers) fall in love with some base thing" (1961, 218). Bullough recalls other parallels: "The setting of an ass's head on Bottom recalls Circe's charms. It is a piece of poetic justice like the well-known story of Phoebus's revenge on King Midas. . . . Note that Bottom too pretends to 'have a reasonable good ear in music' with a preference for 'the tongs and the bones' (IV.i.30). Midas has only his ears changed. Bottom's assification is more like that of the amorous Apuleius [*sic*] in *The Golden Asse* . . . but nearer still to Shakespeare is a version of this story of witches' spells found in Scot [VII], who disbelieves it, but also refers to Pope Benedict IX, condemned after death to walk the earth in a bear skin and an ass's head '*in such sort as he lived*' " (1957, 1:372–73). (See also Wilson 1962, 215.) Finally, although the parallel may be only coincidental, another classical revenge story is alluded to by the fairies who call on "philomel" (the nightingale) to sing Titania's lullaby; for Philomel's story is in part that of a wife who revenges herself for her husband's conduct with another woman by means of their little boy.

32. As Hamilton points out, this reversal has a special relevance in Theseus's case, since earlier "At one moment he makes ready to 'Turn melancholy forth to funerals' (l. 14); at the next he invokes a law to condemn the lovers for an action—the stealing of love—through which he has gained his own happiness" (1967, 221). Although Theseus's reactions to particular events are invariably reasonable, they are not always self-consistent.

33. For speculations on the objects of Shakespeare's mockery in this episode, see Bullough 1957, 1:374; Chakravorty 1969, 1–2; Chambers 1925, 86–87; Johnson (1765) 1908, 70; Levin 1949, 297–302; and Parrott 1949, 132.

34. See Barber (1959) 1963, 159–62; Pettet 1949, 112; and Rose 1972, 17–19.

35. Hippolyta undergoes a different shift of viewpoint, beginning with a standard critical perception (she does not wish to see a bad play badly performed) through "This is the silliest stuff that ever I heard" and "Beshrew my heart, but I pity the man" to, finally, "I hope she will be brief" (5.1.85–86, 210, 290, 317).

Chapter 3. ROMANTIC COMEDIES

1. The exception to this statement and much of what follows in the introduction to this chapter is *As You Like It*, from which revenge is almost totally absent, except in one subplot.

2. *The Merry Wives of Windsor* should, perhaps, receive the dubious distinction of being the Shakespearean comedy most associated with revenge, but most critics apparently consider it something between an embarrassment and a disgrace, and would prefer not to consider it at all.

3. Nicholas Rowe, "Life" in *W[or]ks of Shakespeare* (1709), quoted in Brown's Introduction to the Arden edition, xxxiv.

4. On the nature of the comparisons in this speech, see Barber (1959) 1963, 182.

5. It is wrong to see Shylock as an exemplar of the *lex talionis* ("And you shall give eye for eye, tooth for tooth . . . life for life") as does Bradbrook (1951, 172), since this is a law limiting the extent of justifiable revenge; according to this standard, Shylock would be perfectly justified in spitting on, kicking, and otherwise insulting and degrading Antonio, but not in seeking to kill him.

6. On Shylock's decision, "to feed upon the prodigal Christian," see the Arden edition, 50 n. 14–15, and Barber (1959) 1963, 169 n. 1.3.47–48.

7. Auden disagrees: "When we learn that Jessica has spent fourscore ducats of her father's money in an evening and bought a monkey with her mother's ring, we cannot take this as a comic punishment for Shylock's sin of avarice; her behavior seems rather an example of the opposite sin of conspicuous waste" ("Brothers and Others," 234). But the

Elizabethans were far more forgiving of prodigality than of its opposite (as, for example, Bassanio); and why should one sin not be the proper punishment for its opposite? Certainly Shylock feels Jessica's conduct to be a(n undeserved) punishment.

8. A similar instance of Shylock's sowing the seeds of his own destruction is suggested by Burckhardt 1962, 260: "When [Portia] asks Shylock to provide a surgeon to staunch the blood, does she know yet that it is on this point she will presently hang him? Or is it not rather Shylock himself who leads her to the saving inspiration?"

See Brown for a description of how Shylock inspires other characters to respond to him with uncharacteristically cruel reactions that are nevertheless suitable because evoked by his own actions (1962, 74).

For a summary of critical views on whether Shylock's conversion is a punishment or a blessing, see Makaryk 1980, 119–21.

9. Wilson 1962, 106; a brief summary of both views may be found in idem., 105–9.

10. On Shylock's dependence on legal formalities, see Barber (1959) 1963, 184.

11. "Starting high and moving by degrees downward, [Portia] extends three generous invitations to Shylock to prove his affinity with humankind—and he rejects each" (Evans [1960] 1967, 64).

Tillyard describes this rejection as indicative of Shylock's "spiritual stupidity" (1965, 192; see also 193–94).

12. Earlier at Belmont we have heard of an odd little incident within Portia's satirical comments on her suitors:

Nerissa: What think you of the Scottish lord, his neighbor?
Portia: That he hath a neighborly charity in him, for he borrow'd a box of the ear of the Englishman, and swore he would pay him again when he was able. I think the Frenchman became his surety and seal'd under for another.

(1.2.77–83)

Since this incident has no apparent relationship to anything else in the play, it appears to be the author's patriotic jab at the troublesome Scots and meddling French. For a fuller explication of the contemporary relevance of these lines, see the notes on them in the Arden edition, 18–19.

13. Rossiter ignores the play in *Angel with Horns and Other Shakespeare Lectures*: "As you know, Shakespeare never staged his own times: his settings are historic, exotic, fairy-tale; he never touched the 'realistic' modern-life, satirical-comedy field worked by Jonson, Chapman, Marston and Middleton" (1961, 150).

14. "It is even more consistently light-hearted than the gay *Love's Labour's Lost*, since it contains no messenger of Death to convert hilarity into sobriety at the close of the play" (Wilson 1962, 91).

"Gravely to discuss the theme of a play put together in this way is to risk breaking the butterfly upon the wheel" (Oliver, Introduction to the Arden edition, lxvii).

15. Dowden 1881, 328–29. Dowden concludes this tirade by quoting Hartley Coleridge (*Essays and Marginalia*, 2:133–34) to the effect "that Queen Bess should have desired to see Falstaff making love proves her to have been, as she was, a gross-minded old baggage" (330). On the other hand, see Gordon: "*The Merry Wives*, we are told, was written at Queen Elizabeth's command, and I can well believe it. It was the most feminist proceeding of her reign" (1944, 33–34).

16. "The real Falstaff of Eastcheap would have seen through Ford's plot in a minute, and he would no more have believed in the fairies than he did in the men in buckram" (Crofts 1937, 112).

17. "That Falstaff should come off second best in any encounter is, in the eyes of some critics, the height of Shakespeare's offending. . . . [But] the Falstaff of *Henry IV* is likewise often discomfited" (Oliver, Introduction to the Arden edition, lxvii).

18. Opinions as to the extent of such possible satire range from the cautionary to the absolute; see Oliver, Introduction to the Arden edition, l–lii; Hotson 1931, 85–89, 130–31.

19. Oliver, the Arden edition, 2 n. 9, citing C. J. Sisson, *Essays and Studies* 13 (1960): 10–11. Oliver gives little credence to either suggestion. Oscar James Campbell, however, sees

"the ridicule of Dr. Caius" as an attack on the inflated reputation of "foreign physicians, particularly Frenchmen" (1943, 80).

20. Oliver, the Arden edition, 3 n. 13; also see Wilson: "Nym is probably deliberately introduced as a skit either on Jonson himself or on his mannerism" and "may perhaps be the 'purge' which Shakespeare was reported to have administered to Ben Jonson himself" (1962, 92 and n.).

21. See Bowers 1937.

22. The Brooke/Broome question has inspired much critical ingenuity. For speculations regarding possible satirical intent, see Crofts 1937, 103–5; Green 1962, 107–20; Hotson 1931, 15; and Oliver, Introduction to the Arden edition, lvi–lviii.

23. In his generally vengeful mood, Caius also adds to Mistress Quickly: "By gar, if I have not Anne Page, I shall turn your head out of my door"; to which she replies: "You shall have Anne—fool's-head of your own" (1.4.123–25, 126–27).

24. For reference to an illicit post-warrant issued by Lords Thomas Howard and Montjoy, see Crofts 1937, 32–35; for reference to Frederick, Duke of Württemberg and Teck, Count Mompelgard, see Green 1962, 121–50.

25. It seems to have gone unnoticed in earlier commentary that there is no inherent reason why Caius and Evans themselves could not have made two of the "Germans." They appear after Bardolph, who has had time to return on foot, and there is no more probability of the Host's recognizing them in such disguises than of Falstaff's recognizing Evans as a fairy.

26. For possible reference in this scene to the vengeful hero of Marlowe's *Dr. Faustus*, see Oliver, the Arden edition, 125 n. 65.

27. The horse-stealing episode may be considered in some respects similar to the Gadshill robbery in *1 Henry IV*, which does not seriously discredit Prince Hal.

28. Even if the scene is assumed to be perfect (in transmission, if not otherwise), this does not rule out the possibility that Shakespeare intended the Caius-Evans and cozen-German plots to be synonymous, for the time scheme of the play is hopelessly muddled elsewhere. As Crofts points out: "Mrs. Quickly hurries to the Garter Inn, only to arrive there next morning; Mrs. Ford's urgent message of apology does not arrive until the day after her offence; and, worst of all, Falstaff enters obviously fresh from his ducking a whole day and night after his ducking had occurred" (1937, 88).

29. Note should also be made of the mythological stories of vengeance referred to throughout the play. Mistress Page refers to the vengeance exacted by the gods on the insolent Titans who tried to climb to heaven at 2.1.79–80. The Host (1.3.6) refers to Falstaff as "Hercules," in one sense a suitable reference for a hero who was not only plagued by a goddess, but who in one episode of his life was forced to dress in women's clothing and serve a woman (Omphale). But the most important mythological reference in the play (2.1.118; 3.2.43) is to Actaeon, as Bullough notes (1957, 2:18): "That Shakespeare had Ovid in mind when Falstaff assumed the disguise [of Herne] is proved by the latter's allusions at V.5.2–17 to the amorous metamorphoses of Jove; but the position of Falstaff is comically different. Mistress Page and Mistress Ford are very unlike the nymphs who on seeing a man smote their breasts with sudden shriekings, and he is punished for evil intent; but his chaste goddess certainly pursues him with vengeance. When he dons the horns which he would have placed on Ford's brows he suffers the poetic justice of a failed Don Juan."

30. It is interesting that the wives hit on a monetary punishment for Falstaff, since they give no indication of realizing that it is their money, and not themselves, that attracts him. It is also a neat twist that when it comes to pass that Falstaff's horses are arrested, it is at the instigation of Ford/Brooke, whose wife he has tried to seduce and whose money he has taken.

31. Although the play's final scene is clearly one of comic revenge, Bertrand Evans perceives the presentation of Mistress Quickly as the fairy queen as a literary revenge: a deliberate insult by Shakespeare to Queen Elizabeth for making him write this play ([1960] 1967, 116–17).

For the stage directions that are the authority for Mistress Quickly playing the fairy queen, see Oliver's note to 5.5.37 in the Arden edition, 138. Oliver sensibly concludes that "she has replaced Anne, as part of the counter-scheming."

32. As in *A Midsummer Night's Dream,* it is hard to say how much fairy lore Shakespeare borrowed and how much he invented. Mrs. Page, in her description of the plot (4.4.57–61), seems to consider pinching a standard fairy revenge against mortals. But one wonders whether it was a common belief that fairies (even Welsh ones) were apt to turn a man into a piece of cheese (5.5.81–82).

33. It should be noted that by helping Fenton steal away his bride, the Host, in effect, revenges himself on both Caius and Evans (who had supported Slender's suit).

34. Oliver compares and contrasts Caius's final threat with that of Malvolio (Introduction to the Arden edition, lxxii–lxxiii).

35. Shaw expands on this theme in "A Dressing Room Secret" (1910) 1961, 243–49.

36. Poison, the classic weapon of the stage revenger, is something of a minor theme in the play, although verbal, rather than physical, poison is emphasized. Borachio refers to their plot as poison (2.2.21) and Hero, ironically, remarks that

> One doth not know
> How much an ill word may empoison liking
>
> (3.1.85–86).

Finally, following Borachio's confession, Don Pedro asks Claudio "Runs not this speech like iron through your blood?" and Claudio replies "I have drunk poison whiles he utter'd it" (5.1.245–46).

37. It is, of course, possible that Don John's statement is made for Claudio's benefit, but this seems unlikely. It is not apparent that Don John recognizes the disguised Claudio when he makes this remark; his comment on the bystander is merely that "one visor remains" (2.1.157–58). Certainly Borachio does not think that Don John recognizes the gentleman, since he immediately informs his master of Claudio's identity. Of course, it is conceivable that Don John may have intended his comment to be overheard and reported to Claudio, but it seems more likely that Don John's gullibility here is a function of (1) his inability to believe in a disinterested action on the part of anyone; (2) the susceptibility of most of the play's characters to fall for any plot—however obvious—with which they are confronted; or (3) the tendency of the play's characters to trust their senses of sight and hearing rather than their own knowledge, most obviously exemplified by the gullibility of Don Pedro and Claudio when they "see" Hero at the window.

38. It is not, however, quite correct to say (as Smith does, Introduction to the Arden edition, xvii) that "Unlike Richard [III], [Don John] cannot dissemble." True, he says he cannot; but he is, after all, a liar, and his hypocrisy at 3.2.95–97 is much like Shylock's at 1.3.137–41 of his play. To be sure, it's not very good dissembling, but certainly it is an attempt.

39. For commentary on Don John's revenge motives, see Smith, Introduction to the Arden edition, xvii; on the public accusation of Hero, see Phialas 1966, 177–78.

40. On Claudio's youth as a mitigating factor in our judgment of him, see Smith, Introduction to the Arden edition, xxi.

41. Fergusson ([1954] 1966, 19–20) describes Claudio's behavior as the sort of foolishness with which the audience sympathizes while smiling.

It should be noted that, public as Claudio's vengeance is, it is another revenge "plot." No character in this play is capable of independent action; everyone must have a confidante with whom to scheme and carry out a plan.

42. One seeks in vain, however, for evidence that Claudio ever strives against his uncertainty; he seems to yield to it at every opportunity.

43. "It is a major part of the play's delight that the audience always knows more than the actors: hints are dropped throughout; a Sophoclean comic irony pervades every incident" (Storey [1959] 1966, 40).

44. Certainly it is true that Dogberry, in particular, is self-important to a degree, and preens himself inordinately at having made an arrest. But the watch is centrally important to the plot of the play. It is not so much that they feel themselves to be more important than they are, but rather that they feel themselves to be important for the wrong reasons, having no suspicion of the value of their actions to the other characters in the play.

45. Don John, of course, having been given a correct report of the truth by Borachio, mistrusts it; see n. 37, above.

46. Presumably, it is Borachio who is being spoken of here, though it is rather difficult to be sure. Certainly, both Borachio and Conrade have been brought in; Conrade does not speak, although he is specifically referred to by Dogberry (5.1.304–6), unless the good Constable has confused the two plotters. For some reason, however, Leonato tells Dogberry that he discharges him of his "prisoner" [sic], and Dogberry responds "I leave an arrant knave with your Worship" (5.1.319–21). At any rate, Leonato is using the plural again by line 330.

47. Frye notes that the watch reminds us "of the scriptural passage about God using the foolish things of the world to confound the wise" ([1965] 1967, 126).

48. For Kyd as the source of "the savage bull" quotation, see Smith, the Arden edition, 82 n. 234. For Ovid as the source of Kyd's line, see Thomson 1952, 108. As Smith comments on Kyd, the creator of the most popular of the early Elizabethan revenge plays, *The Spanish Tragedy:* "None of his contemporaries amused Shakespeare so much as Kyd, and few influenced him more." Benedick has previously suggested the yoked bull as the symbol of the husband at 1.1.200–201 and he alludes to "bullocks" again at 2.1.194–95.

49. "It is in this way that intellectuals pay the penalty for an excess of intellect. When, therefore, a plot is laid which discerns their pride and makes an appeal as much to their pity as to their love, they fall easy victims, and the defeat of their intellect is the triumph of what we may call the Life-Force" (Sen Gupta 1950, 147).

50. It is interesting that Don Pedro describes his plot as "one of Hercules' labors" (2.1.364–67), since those labors are part of Hera's revenge for Zeus's infidelity. Earlier, Benedick too has referred to Hercules in order to describe Beatrice as a particularly shrewish Omphale (2.1.253–54).

51. Curiously, after their reference to Hero, their next two references are to revenge stories. Claudio's "moreover, God saw him when he was hid in the garden" (5.1.179–80) refers to Adam's inability to escape God's wrath for his sin, and Don Pedro's "But when shall we set the savage bull's horns on the sensible Benedick's head?" (5.1.181–82) is a reference, as previously noted, to a play in which the hero takes revenge against royalty for the murder of his child. What Claudio and Don Pedro fail to realize, of course, is that Benedick has become a "savage bull" in a different sense (though due to a woman) and sees himself as an instrument of divine justice.

52. "No one laughs as Claudio scores points off a victim who is not playing the game" (Jagendorf 1984, 141).

53. Benedick repeats this repudiation of his challenge to Claudio at 5.4.109–11, and Claudio replies in a mock-vengeful vein.

54. Some critics have seen the play as a kind of literary revenge, although the force and direction of the attack are in dispute. See Oscar James Campbell 1943, 55; Phialas 1966, 221; Van Doren 1939, 151; Wilson 1962, 153-54; for a summary of "Jaques and contemporary satirists," see Latham's Introduction to the Arden edition, xlvi–li).

55. Jaques is generally described as a satirist, but critics also see him as the object of satire and "the mouthpiece of Shakespeare's own satiric comment" (Bradbrook 1951, 226; Oscar James Campbell 1943, 51). Phialas asserts that "Jaques satirizes real life" (1966, 234), whereas Barber maintains that "neither Jaques, the amateur fool, nor Touchstone, the professional, ever really gets around to doing the satirist's work of ridiculing life as it is" ([1959] 1963, 229). Gardner sees Jaques as a cynic, whereas Phialas sees him as "the most vulnerable pseudo-idealist in the play" ("As You Like It," 64; 1966, 234). Finally, Oscar James Campbell sees him as a "wretched malcontent," whose "melancholy is artificial and [whose] disgust with everything at home is a pose," while Latham maintains that Jaques "is entirely free of the malcontent's sense of personal injury," describing him as a true melancholy man, whose contemplation honors "one of the great pastoral values" (1943, 55, 49; Introduction to the Arden edition, xlviii).

Touchstone is the subject of similar critical disagreement. He is described as "the ironic satirist of both idealized pastoralism and romantic love," "the sound critic of folly," and "the parodist" who is "life's master" (Phialas 1966, 230; Oscar James Campbell 1943, 56; Gardner, "As You Like It," 63); on the other hand, Barber (as quoted above) denies him the role of the true satirist, and Latham finds little sense in him (Introduction to the Arden edition, lii).

56. All quotations from *Rosalynde* are taken from Bullough, vol. 2.

57. John Shaw, Jr., suggests that "by not clarifying the basis for the conflict between Oliver and Orlando and between Frederick and Rosalind, which he might easily have done, Shakespeare has actually emphasized the Nature-Fortune motif" (1955, 49). This does not, however, explain why the victims of the evil characters so seldom consider revenge.

58. For a similar exchange of revenges between brothers, see the synopsis of *The Tale of Gamelyn* in Bullough 1957, 2:143–45.

59. For an identification of Orsino with Actaeon, see Johnson (1765) 1908, 91.

60. "Outraged nature has its full and comic revenge when Olivia falls passionately in love with a male exterior and acts with an aggressiveness which makes Orsino seem almost feminine" (Summers [1955] 1966, 113).

61. Van Doren notes parallels between *Twelfth Night* and *The Merchant of Venice* (1939, 161).

62. For sympathetic views of Malvolio, see Barber (1959) 1963, 256; Hazlitt 1818, 248–49; and Lamb (1822) 1949, 528–29.

63. For the possibility that Malvolio is a caricature of a contemporary figure, see Bullough 1957, 2:284, and Hotson 1954, 98–118; for an opposing view, see Lothian and Craik, Introduction to the Arden edition, xxix n. 2). On Malvolio as a portrait of a Puritan, see Barber (1959) 1963, 256.

64. For Malvolio as an "upstart" and "an enemy to the time-honored English hospitality and liberality," see Oscar James Campbell 1943, 86–87.

If indeed Malvolio is to be seen as a representative of the new man of the approaching era, he may in some sense be said to have made good his final threat: "seen in the perspective of literary and social history, there is a curious appropriateness in Malvolio's presence, as a kind of foreign body to be expelled by laughter, in Shakespeare's last free-and-easy festive comedy. He is a man of business, and, it is passingly suggested, a hard one; he is or would like to be a rising man, and to rise he *uses* sobriety and morality. One could moralize the spectacle by observing that, in the long run, in the 1640's, Malvolio *was* revenged on the whole pack of them!" (Barber [1959] 1963, 257).

65. Crane finds that "the baiting of Malvolio is unrelieved in its comic heartlessness, and is not even superficially moral in its purpose" (1955, 5). For opposing views, see Barber (1959) 1963, 255; Evans (1960) 1967, 134; and Williams (1961) 1968, 36–37.

66. Malvolio's final appearance inspires varied reactions. Barnet finds Malvolio "potentially tragic" but ultimately unsympathetic (1954, 181–82). Chakravorty believes that "Malvolio is at last cured of his 'self-love' " (1969, 258), whereas Oscar James Campbell seems to feel that he is only temporarily purged (1943, 86). Hotson maintains that Malvolio's "furious threats of revenge in the end are laughed out of court" (1954, 118). Summers, although asserting that Malvolio "is justly punished," adds that "as a result of his humiliation he has also earned some sort of redress. Yet he is ridiculous in his arrogance to the end, and his threatened revenge, now that he is powerless to effect it, sustains the comedy and the characterization and prevents the obtrusion of destructive pathos" ([1955] 1966, 117).

67. If any doubt remains that Shakespeare took trouble to present Malvolio in a negative light, and in opposition to nearly every sympathetic character in the play, recall that even the unnamed but virtuous sea captain who befriends Viola lands "in durance, at Malvolio's suit" (5.1.276), a fact that is mentioned even though (since Feste has already appeared with Malvolio's letter, which could easily be used to bring Malvolio back on stage) it is not necessary to advance the plot.

68. Although some critics have made much of "Let some of my people have a special care of him. I would not have him miscarry for the half of my dowry" (3.4.62–63), it seems reasonable to consider this as a combination of charity, *noblesse oblige*, and hyperbole, and not—in light of Olivia's other comments on Malvolio—as evidence of any particularly high regard for his qualities.

69. Barber finds that "[Maria's] part in the housekeeping and its pleasures is a homely

but valued kind of 'courtiership'" ([1959] 1963, 252, and Chakravorty feels that "Maria's 'revenge' is, of course, good-hearted—nothing more than a desire to teach [Malvolio] a lesson" (1969, 257). Goddard, however, sees Maria as "ambitious and envious" and concludes that "there is a cruel streak in her as there generally is in practical jokers. She is in that third degree of fun where what might originally have been a sense of humor becomes perverted and commits suicide" (1951, 1:298).

70. For the significance of the fool's song at 4.2.72 ff. as a minor revenge, see the Arden edition, 125 n. 75.

71. Hollander presents various justifications for this revenge, including the assumption that Malvolio "is only treated as he would himself treat anyone whom he believed to be mad" ([1959] 1966, 125).

72. "Feste is ridiculed by Malvolio as a stale clown, and in revenge forces Malvolio into a clown role. When Olivia says to Malvolio 'Alas, poor fool, how have they baffled thee!' the application of the word 'fool' to Malvolio is a signal for Feste to mark the completion of the action by his reference to the whirligig of time" (Frye [1965] 1967, 95).

73. "The happiness of the lovers would seem to have been bought at a price which excludes Malvolio, and we may feel that this circumscribes and diminishes the final effect of their happiness" (G. K. Hunter [1962] 1966, 96).

"Illyria, like the France and Italy of *All's Well*, cannot exist without a strain of cruelty, of persecution" (Leech [1965] 1968, 71).

"The impotent misery and fury of the humiliated Malvolio's last words, 'I'll be reveng'd on the whole pack of you,' call in question the whole comic scheme by which, through misunderstandings and mistakes, people come to terms with themselves and their fellows" (Gardner, "As You Like It," 64–65).

74. "In earlier comedies, the characters who rejected the ordered conclusions have left the stage without the lovers sparing much thought for them. . . . But in *Twelfth Night*, Malvolio is considered. . . . There is no communal feast, music, or dance to close this play—that must wait until 'golden time convents' (l. 391); but as the lovers leave the stage together we know that their generosity and desire for harmony can, after the realization of their own follies and disorders, reach to one who has 'had but justice', and that but a kind of wild justice" (Brown 1962, 181).

Chapter 4. PROBLEM COMEDIES

1. Jacoby has stated this position for one of these plays: "*Measure for Measure* is a perennially disturbing and unsatisfying play precisely because no real retribution is exacted for acts that are—by the standards of our own day as well as Shakespeare's—truly evil" (1983, 46).

2. Craig maintains that "the editors of the First Folio seem to have decided that *Troilus and Cressida* was a tragedy," adding that "they might have thought of it as a history, certainly never as a comedy" (1948, 222). Sen Gupta, on the other hand, concludes that "we have . . . no alternative to calling it a comedy, recognizing, however, that it has certain peculiarities distinguishing it from the norm of its class" (1950, 186).

3. Oscar James Campbell maintains that the play should be "regarded as Shakespeare's conscious imitation of the comical satires of Jonson and Marston" (1943, 98); Tillyard disputes this reading (1950, 46–48), as does Pettet (1949, 140 n. 3). Frye sees the play as "pure irony" ([1965] 1967, 119), while George Bernard Shaw, in "Shakespear and Romantic Acting," maintains that "Shakespear made exactly one attempt, in Troilus and Cressida, to hold the mirror up to nature; and he probably nearly ruined himself by it. At all events, he never did it again" ([1896] 1961, 261).

A dissenting view is expressed by Craig, who maintains that "Shakespeare has merely put on the stage the medieval Troy story, and has elevated rather than debased the tale in so doing. The point is that the tale was ready-made. Shakespeare had no choice, no latitude for manipulation" (1948, 239).

4. Pettet sees the play as "the extreme of Shakespeare's recoil from romance—his most deliberate, sustained and scarifying satire on the whole romantic code of love and honour"

(1949, 140). Kaula offers the opinion that "in the contrast between the chivalric Trojans and the realpolitical Greeks it is tempting to see a suggestion of the political situation in England during the late 1500's and early 1600's" (1961, 271). Various critics have seen references in the play to the "War of the Theatres," or at least to participants in that war: see Craig, 1948, 237; Frye (1965) 1967, 35; and Rossiter 1961, 149–50.

Some critics see the play as an attack on Chapman's Homer, although they disagree on whether it is the work or the author that is under attack: see Boas 1896, 378, and Thomson 1952, 213–14.

George Bernard Shaw, in a report of a paper he presented to the New Shakespeare Society in 1884, maintains that the play was not only a satire on Chapman's *Iliad*, but a revenge by Shakespeare against himself: "Chapman's 'Homer' appeared and [Shakespeare] saw it was only his Henry V; and it was to expose and avenge his mistake and failure in writing Henry V that he wrote Troilus and Cressida" (1961, 194).

Still another suggestion is that the play, at least in part, is Shakespeare's private revenge against actors: "Some sense of personal rancour, freed perhaps by the fact that the play may not have been designed for the public stage, seems to inform his picture of the

> strutting player whose conceit
> Lies in his hamstring, and doth think it rich
> To hear the wooden dialogue and sound
> 'Twixt his stretch'd footing and the scaffoldage—
> Such to-be-pitied and o'er-wrested seeming
> He acts thy greatness in. . . .

> (*Troilus and Cressida*, I, iii, 153–158)"
> (Righter 1962, 182–83)

Finally, there is the suggestion that the play represents Shakespeare's revenge against life or art or both: " 'Troilus and Cressida' is either Shakespeare's revenge upon mankind for losing its power to delight him or his revenge upon the theme for refusing to tell him how it should be treated" (Van Doren 1939, 203).

5. Shakespeare seems to be reminding us of the reason for the Trojans' vengeful abduction of Helen by alluding to Ajax as the son of the kidnapped Trojan princess Hesione (4.5.120–21). Although Ajax's father, Telamon, was married to Hesione, the classical authors cited by Lemprière state that Ajax's mother was Periboea (or Eriboea) and that Hesione was the mother of Ajax's half-brother Teucer ([1788] 1978, s.v. "Ajax," "Teucer").

6. Pettet finds that "Thersites' voice may . . . be one of several voices of choric commentary, but what Thersites says about the Grecian knights is, beneath its extravagant scurrility, the truth of the play" (1949, 155). Oscar James Campbell, however, insists that "Thersites is neither a chorus nor a clown. . . . The spectators as well as all the characters in the play realize that his opinions are worthless, that his sentiments are as odious as the man himself" (1943, 105).

7. The Trojan revenge should be considered in the light of the original injury by the Greeks (the abduction of Hesione) and the ultimate Greek revenge of the war.

8. Prosser finds that "throughout the play, revenge is the nurse of barbarism and irrational frenzy," and associates Troilus with the "bestial savagery" of Achilles (1973, 82). But Achilles has shown a savage nature well before Patroclus' death, when entreating the heavens to tell him how he will destroy Hector (4.5.242–46). For further condemnation of Troilus as a revenger, see Oscar James Campbell 1943, 116; Kaula 1961, 278; and Sen Gupta 1950, 194.

9. Furthermore, Shaw seems to be rather cavalier and inconsistent in his views on Shakespeare. As noted earlier (n. 3, above), he elsewhere states that Shakespeare "made exactly one attempt, in Troilus and Cressida, to hold the mirror up to nature" ([1896] 1961, 261).

10. Rossiter maintains that "if you analyse [Helena], you find that her only *noble* qualities are courage and the Stoical reserve which can take a blow with dignity and few

words" (1961, 99–100). Pettet, on the other hand, asserts that "what is admirable in Helena is, as we guess from a few odd glimpses, and the opinion of such characters as the Countess, her normal essential self; for most of the play, a dupe to her emotions, she is blindly and stupidly in love with a worthless young fellow, prepared to stoop to any shift and humiliation to win him. In other words, she too [like Bertram] is degraded, but, with her, degradation springs from the irrationality of love" (1949, 138). Bradbrook simply finds Helena generally "unsatisfactory" (1951, 169).

One of Helena's few defenders is George Bernard Shaw, who sees her as "an early Ibsenite heroine" [n.d.] 1961, 250). One suspects, however, that he likes her largely because he sees her as similar to his own female characters, since he praises her by denigrating the more popular Rosalind and the audience that prefers her ([1905] 1961, 4).

11. See Bullough for the praise lavished on the heroines of the parallel stories in *Gl'Ingannati* (1957, 2:335) and *Riche his Farewell to Militarie Profession* (1957, 2:362). As Bullough summarizes, "no Elizabethan audience would feel great repugnance at Helena's means of getting herself married or of getting her marriage consummated: The idea was too old and well-known to cause lifting of eyebrows; moreover, in real life the marriage ceremony carried with it certain rights which a wife had every justification for pursuing" (1957, 2:379).

12. For a similarly harsh but more detailed view of Bertram, see Bradbrook 1951, 163.

13. On the relationship between Bertram's family pride, his ring, and the conditions he imposes on Helena, see Boas 1896, 354.

14. On Bertram's lies and on "Parolles, or Words" as the cause of "Bertram's fall," see Bradbrook 1951, 163–64, and Halio 1964, 40. Rossiter, however, feels that "Parolles offers no temptations whatever. . . . Bertram is fallen, and needs little 'inducement' " (1961, 95–96).

15. Pettet describes Parolles as a caricature "composed of broad humours" and compounded of "several sources: he is partly the classical parasite, partly the *miles gloriosus*, and partly the contemporary real-life 'Captain' who did so much to vitalise this second type" (1949, 139).

16. On Bertram's behavior in the trial scene, see Johnson (1765) 1908, 102, and Rossiter 1961, 90–91.

17. As G. K. Hunter points out, "the Countess, Lafew, and the King—whose part is much expanded by Shakespeare—are used to define a norm of propriety against which the tale of Bertram and Helena is seen in added moral perspective, no longer the brisk contest of wits that Boccaccio devised" (Introduction to the Arden edition, xxviii).

Brown maintains a position similar to that of Lafew in stating that "as Parolles had been a traitor to his true self, so had Bertram; the one should have been a fool, the other truly noble" (1962, 191).

18. Evans provides one explanation: "Helena's subtly designed torture inexorably compels him to indulge in an orgy, a last wild spree of falsehood, so violent that it must purge his system of vileness for ever. When this spree is over, he lapses into a silence broken only by his cry at sight of his personal nemesis and saviour: 'O, pardon!' " ([1960] 1967, 166).

Another meaning is proposed by Bradbrook: "Bertram's conversion must be reckoned among Hellen's miracles. It is notable that on the fulfillment of the bargain she turns to seek, not her husband, but the King. What is achieved is public recognition of her right, which he concedes her. She has been acknowledged by her lord; that her personal happiness is simply irrelevant, and the ending neither hypocritical nor cynical, can be granted only if the play is seen as a moral debate on the subject: Wherein consists true honour and nobility?" (1951, 168).

19. This chapter of *Matthew* contains many verses that mirror themes of *Measure for Measure*, including 3–5, 12, 15, and 18–21.

20. "Angelo is not a conscious hypocrite: rather a man whose chief faults are self-deception and pride in his own righteousness—an unused and delicate instrument quite useless under the test of active trial. This he half-recognizes, and would first refuse the proffered honour. The Duke insists: Angelo's fall is thus entirely the Duke's responsibility" (Knight [1930] 1949, 85).

21. As Parrott points out, "Even to an auditor unfamiliar with the story, this secret presence of the all-powerful ruler would give a sense of security; Isabella could not lose her honor nor Claudio his life while the Duke was still in Vienna to protect them" (1949, 361).

22. Knight feels that it represents a satire upon sexual inhibition and smallness of soul ([1930] 1949, 92–93), while Stevenson maintains that "at the end of her reviling of Claudio's wish to live at the expense of her chastity, Isabella has lost some of the fierce bloom of innocence. We sense that her recoil from her rage at Claudio has made her capable of enjoying the more warmly human notion of revenge on Angelo, has made her capable of the duplicity of guiding him to an assignation with Mariana" (1966, 46–47). For an opposing view, see Craig 1948, 222.

23. Although this episode may be viewed as a foreshadowing of later mercy by the Duke, at least one critic sees it rather as a triumph of mercy over justice within the play's author: "For after Shakespeare had given himself so much trouble to find a head the cutting off of which would offend no one's humanity, he himself had not the heart to cut the head off. The old reprobate, brought into being to be executed, so used these last few moments of his life that he blustered his way into Shakespeare's sympathy, and was reprieved. To reprieve him, Shakespeare the dramatist did not mind committing the heinous crime of sheer coincidence. . . . The whole episode is a manifest revelation of Shakespeare's sense of human life; his first scruples only to destroy what manifestly deserves destruction, and then his sudden discovery that the apparently worthless human being still has his humanity with which to excite sympathy in a fellow-mortal" (Charlton 1938, 217).

24. When Isabella does kneel to plead for Angelo's life, her reasoning and attitude are much more complex and interesting than might be expected, as Bullough explains: "Isabella responds to Mariana's desperate prayer, but the terms she herself uses are rational and earthly. She pardons; she says Angelo was probably sincere until he met her; she admits that Claudio was justly condemned; she distinguishes between the act and the intention; but this is not full Christian forgiveness. She does not love her enemy; nor should we wish it. That made the end of Cinthio's novella monstrous.

"Shakespeare here shows himself rather the *anima naturaliter Christiana* than the exponent of particular Christian doctrines, though it is wrong to limit his religious ideas to wellings up from an unconscious heritage, in view of the treatment of Barnardine and pervasive references to Christian teaching. Rather the Christian heritage is blended in a wide pattern of humane ethics which allows of inconsistencies, touches of pagan feeling, bawdiness, delight in crooked ways. Like most believers Shakespeare is the incomplete Christian, and the Duke is not Christ but a good Duke" (1957, 2:416–17).

25. ". . . the Duke's treatment of *Lucio* is harsh and not far from spiteful" (Rossiter 1961, 165).

"After the pardon of two murderers *Lucio* might be treated by the good *Duke* with less harshness; but perhaps the Poet intended to show, what is too often seen, *that men easily forgive wrongs which are not committed against themselves.*" (Johnson [1765] 1908, 80).

Knight, on the other hand, sees Lucio's punishment as deserved, although he sees Lucio as a somewhat attractive character and the Duke as possessing a rather strange set of priorities: "Lucio's treatment at the close is eminently, and fittingly, undignified. He is threatened thus: first he is to marry the mother of his child, about whose wrong he formerly boasted; then to be whipped and hanged. Lucio deserves some credit, however: he preserves his nature and answers with his characteristic wit. He cannot be serious. The Duke, his sense of humour touched, retracts the sentence. . . . Idleness, triviality, thoughtlessness receive the Duke's strongest condemnation" ([1930] 1949, 90–91).

Chapter 5. CONCLUSION

1. It is interesting that in plays where the legal system is used as part of the machinery of justice, such as *The Merchant of Venice* and *Measure for Measure*, there is frequently much critical controversy over whether justice is really served.

2. "Legal mercy involves considerations of motive, mitigating circumstances, and de-

grees of responsibility—not religious absolution or the forgiveness men and women may accord one another in their private lives. Those who administer the law have the right to punish or to determine that no punishment is required; they have neither the right nor the duty to forgive" (Jacoby 1983, 116).

3. "This excess of happiness, which is out of all proportion to the characters' deserts, may be viewed as a type of dramatic grace: we are rewarded even more than we deserve to be" (Makaryk 1980, xvi).

Works Cited

Auden, W. H. 1968. "Brothers and Others." In *The Dyer's Hand and Other Essays,* 218–38. New York: Vintage.

———. 1968. "The Joker in the Pack." In *The Dyer's Hand and Other Essays,* 246–72. New York: Vintage.

Bacon, Francis. [1597] 1889. "Of Revenge." In *The Essays of Lord Bacon,* 7–8. London: Frederick Warne.

Barber, C. L. 1959. *Shakespeare's Festive Comedy: A Study of Dramatic Form and Its Relation to Social Custom.* Princeton University Press. Reprint. Cleveland: World Publishing, 1963.

Barnet, S. 1954. "Charles Lamb and The Tragic Malvolio." *Philological Quarterly* 33:178–88.

Bevan, Elinor. 1967. "Revenge, Forgiveness, and the Gentleman." *Review of English Literature* 8, no. 3:55–69.

Boas, Frederick S. 1896. *Shakspere and His Predecessors.* New York: Charles Scribner.

Bowers, Fredson Thayer. 1937. "The Audience and the Poisoner of Elizabethan Tragedy." *Journal of English and Germanic Philology* 36:491–504.

———. 1934. "The Audience and the Revenger of Elizabethan Tragedy." *Studies in Philology* 31:160–75.

———. 1940. *Elizabethan Revenge Tragedy, 1587–1642.* Princeton University Press. Reprint. Gloucester, Mass.: Peter Smith, 1959.

Bradbrook, M. C. 1936. *The School of Night: A Study in the Literary Relationships of Sir Walter Raleigh.* Cambridge: Cambridge University Press.

———. 1951. *Shakespeare and Elizabethan Poetry: A Study of His Earlier Work in Relation to the Poetry of the Time.* London: Chatto and Windus.

Briggs, Katharine. 1976. *An Encyclopedia of Fairies: Hobgoblins, Brownies, Bogies, and Other Supernatural Creatures.* New York: Pantheon.

Brooks, Harold F. 1968. "Marlowe and Early Shakespeare." In *Christopher Marlowe,* edited by Brian Morris, 65–94. London: Ernest Denn.

———. 1961. "Themes and Structure in *The Comedy of Errors.*" In *Early Shakespeare,* edited by John Russell Brown and Bernard Harris, 55–71. Stratford-upon-Avon Studies, no. 3. New York: St. Martin's.

Broude, Ronald. 1975. "Revenge and Revenge Tragedy in Renaissance England." *Renaissance Quarterly* 28:38–58.

Brown, John Russell. 1962. *Shakespeare and His Comedies.* 2d ed. London: Methuen.

Bullough, Geoffrey. 1957. *Narrative and Dramatic Sources of Shakespeare.* 8 vols. London: Routledge and Kegan Paul.

Burckhardt, Sigurd. 1962. "*The Merchant of Venice:* The Gentle Bond." *ELH* 29:239–62.

Camoin, François André. 1972. *The Revenge Convention in Tourneur, Webster, and Middleton.* Salzburg: Institut für Englische Sprache und Literatur.

Campbell, Lily B. 1931. "Theories of Revenge in Renaissance England." *Modern Philology* 28:281–96.

Campbell, Oscar James. 1943. *Shakespeare's Satire.* New York: Oxford University Press.

Chakravorty, Jagannath. 1969. *The Idea of Revenge in Shakespeare*. Calcutta: Jadavpur University.

Chambers, E. K. 1925. *Shakespeare: A Survey*. London: Sidgwick & Jackson.

Charlton, H. B. 1938. *Shakespearian Comedy*. London: Methuen.

Craig, Hardin. 1948. *An Interpretation of Shakespeare*. Columbia, Miss.: Lucas Brothers.

Crane, Milton. 1955. "*Twelfth Night* and Shakespearian Comedy." *Shakespeare Quarterly* 6:1–8.

Crofts, John. 1937. *Shakespeare and the Post Horses: A New Study of "The Merry Wives of Windsor."* Bristol: University of Bristol.

Dowden, Edward. 1881. *Shakspere: A Critical Study of His Mind and Art*. 3d ed. New York: Harper Brothers.

Evans, Bertrand. 1960. *Shakespeare's Comedies*. Oxford: Oxford University Press, Clarendon Press. Reprint. Oxford: Oxford University Press paperback, 1967.

Fergusson, Francis. 1954. "Two Comedies." *The Sewanee Review* 62:24–37. Reprint. In *Discussions of Shakespeare's Romantic Comedy*, edited by Herbert Weil, Jr., 15–24. Boston: D. C. Heath, 1966.

Frye, Northrop. 1965. *A Natural Perspective: The Development of Shakespearean Comedy and Romance*. New York: Columbia University Press. Reprint. New York: Harcourt, Brace & World, Harbinger Books, 1967.

Gardner, Helen. 1959. "As You Like It." In *More Talking of Shakespeare*, edited by John Garrett. New York: Theatre Arts Books. Reprint. In *Discussions of Shakespeare's Romantic Comedy*, edited by Herbert Weil, Jr., 52–66. Boston: D. C. Heath, 1966.

———. 1959. *The Business of Criticism*. Oxford: Oxford University Press, Clarendon Press.

Gilbert, Allan. 1959. *The Principles and Practice of Criticism: "Othello," "The Merry Wives," "Hamlet."* Detroit: Wayne State University Press.

Goddard, Harold C. 1951. *The Meaning of Shakespeare*. 2 vols. Chicago: University of Chicago Press.

Gordon, George. 1944. *Shakespearian Comedy and Other Studies*. London: Oxford University Press.

Green, William. 1962. *Shakespeare's "Merry Wives of Windsor."* Princeton: Princeton University Press.

Halio, Jay. 1964. "All's Well That Ends Well." *Shakespeare Quarterly* 15:33–43.

Hallett, Charles A., and Elaine S. Hallett. 1980. *The Revenger's Madness: A Study of Revenge Tragedy Motifs*. Lincoln: University of Nebraska Press.

Hamilton, A. C. 1967. *The Early Shakespeare*. San Marino, Calif.: Huntington Library.

Harbage, Alfred. 1947. *As They Liked It: A Study of Shakespeare's Moral Artistry*. New York: Macmillan. Reprint. New York: Harper Torchbooks, 1961.

———. 1962. "Intrigue in Elizabethan Tragedy." In *Essays on Shakespeare and Elizabethan Drama in Honor of Hardin Craig*, edited by Richard Hosley, 37–44. Columbia: University of Missouri Press.

Hazlitt, William. 1818. *Characters of Shakespeare's Plays*. Boston: Wells and Lilly.

Hollander, John. 1959. "*Twelfth Night* and the Morality of Indulgence." *The Sewanee Review* 67:220–38. Reprint. In *Discussions of Shakespeare's Romantic Comedy*, edited by Herbert Weil, Jr., 119–31. Boston: D. C. Heath, 1966.

Holloway, John. 1961. *The Story of the Night: Studies in Shakespeare's Major Tragedies*. Lincoln: University of Nebraska Press.

Hotson, Leslie. 1954. *The First Night of "Twelfth Night."* London: Rupert Hart-Davis.

———. 1931. *Shakespeare versus Shallow*. Boston: Little, Brown.

Hunter, G. K. 1962. "Twelfth Night." In *Shakespeare: The Late Comedies*. London: Longmans, Green. Reprint. In *Discussions of Shakespeare's Romantic Comedy*, edited by Herbert Weil, Jr., 92–101. Boston: D. C. Heath, 1966.

Hunter, Robert Grams. 1965. *Shakespeare and the Comedy of Forgiveness*. New York: Columbia University Press.

Jacoby, Susan. 1983. *Wild Justice: The Evolution of Revenge*. New York: Harper & Row.

Jagendorf, Zvi. 1984. *The Happy End of Comedy: Jonson, Molière, and Shakespeare*. Newark: University of Delaware Press.

Johnson, Samuel. 1908. *Johnson on Shakespeare: Essays and Notes Set Forth with an Introduction*. Edited by Walter Raleigh. London: Oxford University Press.

Kaula, David. 1961. "Will and Reason in *Troilus and Cressida*." *Shakespeare Quarterly* 12:271–83.

Kermode, Frank. 1961. "The Mature Comedies." In *Early Shakespeare*, edited by John Russell Brown and Bernard Harris, 211–27. Stratford-upon-Avon Studies, no. 3. New York: St. Martin's.

Knight, G. Wilson. [1932] 1953. *The Shakespearian Tempest: With a Chart of Shakespeare's Dramatic Universe*. 3d ed. London: Methuen.

———. 1930. *The Wheel of Fire: Interpretations of Shakespearian Tragedy with Three New Essays*. London: Oxford University Press. Reprint. London: Methuen, 1949.

Knowland, A. S. 1959. "*Troilus and Cressida*." *Shakespeare Quarterly* 10:353–65.

Lamb, Charles. [1822] 1949. "On Some of the Old Actors." In *The Portable Charles Lamb*, edited by John Mason Brown, 525–39. New York: Viking.

Lawrence, W. W. 1960. *Shakespeare's Problem Comedies*. 2d ed. New York: Frederick Ungar.

Leech, Clifford. 1965. "*Twelfth Night*, or What Delights You." From chap. 2 of "*Twelfth Night*" *and Shakespearian Comedy*, 29–55. Toronto: University of Toronto Press. Reprint. In *Twentieth Century Interpretations of "Twelfth Night": A Collection of Critical Essays*, edited by Walter N. King, 70–74. Englewood Cliffs, N.J.: Prentice-Hall, 1968.

Lemprière, J. [1788] 1978. *Lemprière's Classical Dictionary of Proper Names Mentioned in Ancient Authors*. Revised by F. A. Wright. London: Routledge & Kegan Paul.

Levin, Harry. 1949. "An Echo from *The Spanish Tragedy*." *Modern Language Notes* 64:297–302.

McGinn, Donald Joseph. 1938. *Shakespeare's Influence on the Drama of His Age Studied in "Hamlet."* New Brunswick, N.J.: Rutgers University Press. Reprint. New York: Octagon Books, 1965.

Makaryk, Irene Rima. 1980. *Comic Justice in Shakespeare's Comedies*. Salzburg: Institut für Anglistik und Amerikanistik.

Newman, Karen. 1985. *Shakespeare's Rhetoric of Comic Character: Dramatic Convention in Classical and Renaissance Comedy*. New York: Methuen.

Ornstein, Robert. 1960. *The Moral Vision of Jacobean Tragedy*. Madison: University of Wisconsin Press.

Parrott, Thomas Marc. 1949. *Shakespearean Comedy*. New York: Russell & Russell.

Pettet, E. C. 1949. *Shakespeare and the Romantic Tradition*. London: Staples.

Phialas, Peter G. 1966. *Shakespeare's Romantic Comedies: The Development of Their Form and Meaning*. Chapel Hill: University of North Carolina Press.

Prosser, Eleanor. 1973. *Hamlet and Revenge*. Stanford: Stanford University Press.

Quiller-Couch, Sir Arthur. 1918. *Shakespeare's Workmanship*. London: Ernest Benn.

Righter, Anne. 1962. *Shakespeare and the Idea of the Play*. London: Chatto and Windus.

Rose, Mark. 1972. *Shakespearean Design*. Cambridge: Harvard University Press, Belknap Press.

Rossiter, A. P. 1961. *Angel with Horns and Other Shakespeare Lectures*. Edited by Graham Storey. London: Longmans, Green.

Salingar, Leo. 1974. *Shakespeare and the Traditions of Comedy*. Cambridge: Cambridge University Press.

Sen Gupta, S. C. 1950. *Shakespearian Comedy*. London: Oxford University Press.

Shakespeare, William. *All's Well That Ends Well*. The Arden Shakespeare. Edited by G. K. Hunter. London: Methuen, 1959.

———. *As You Like It*. The Arden Shakespeare. Edited by Agnes Latham. London: Methuen, 1975.

———. *The Merchant of Venice*. The Arden Shakespeare. Edited by John Russell Brown. London: Methuen, 1955.

———. *The Merry Wives of Windsor*. The Arden Shakespeare. Edited by H. J. Oliver. London: Methuen, 1971.

———. *Much Ado About Nothing*. The Arden Shakespeare. Edited by J. C. Smith. Boston: D. C. Heath, n.d.

———. *The Riverside Shakespeare*. Boston: Houghton Mifflin, 1974.

———. *Troilus and Cressida*. The Arden Shakespeare. Edited by Kenneth Palmer. London: Methuen, 1982.

———. *Twelfth Night*. The Arden Shakespeare. Edited by J. M. Lothian and T. W. Craik. London: Methuen, 1975.

Shaw, George Bernard. 1961. *Shaw on Shakespeare: An Anthology of Bernard Shaw's Writings on the Plays and Production of Shakespeare*. Edited by Edwin Wilson. New York: Dutton.

Shaw, John, Jr. 1955. "Fortune and Nature in *As You Like It*." *Shakespeare Quarterly* 6:45–50.

Stevenson, David Lloyd. 1966. *The Achievement of Shakespeare's "Measure for Measure."* Ithaca: Cornell University Press.

Stoll, Elmer Edgar. [1927] 1942. *Shakespeare Studies: Historical and Comparative in Method*. 2d ed. New York: Frederick Ungar.

Storey, Graham. 1959. "The Success of *Much Ado About Nothing*." In *More Talking about Shakespeare*, edited by John Garrett. London: Longmans, Green. Reprint. In *Discussions of Shakespeare's Romantic Comedy*, edited by Herbert Weil, Jr., 37–51. Boston: D. C. Heath, 1966.

Summers, Joseph. 1955. "The Masks of *Twelfth Night*." *The University of Kansas City Review* 22:25–32. Reprint. In *Discussions of Shakespeare's Romantic Comedy*, edited by Herbert Weil, Jr., 111–18. Boston: D. C. Heath, 1966.

Thomson, J. A. 1952. *Shakespeare and the Classics*. London: George Allen & Unwin.

Tillyard, E. M. W. 1965. *Shakespeare's Early Comedies*. London: Chatto and Windus.

———. 1950. *Shakespeare's Problem Plays*. London: University of Toronto Press.

Trewin, J. C. 1978. *Going to Shakespeare*. London: George Allen & Unwin.

Van Doren, Mark. 1939. *Shakespeare*. New York: Henry Holt.

Williams, Porter, Jr. 1961. "Mistakes in *Twelfth Night* and Their Resolution: A Study in Some Relationships of Plot and Theme." *PMLA* 76:193–99. Reprint. In *Twentieth Century Interpretations of "Twelfth Night": A Collection of Critical Essays*, edited by Walter N. King, 31–44. Englewood Cliffs, N.J.: Prentice-Hall, 1968.

Wilson, John Dover. 1962. *Shakespeare's Happy Comedies*. London: Faber and Faber.

Index